Social Banking

Promise, Performance and Potential

Dr Deepali Pant Joshi

FOUNDATION® BOOKS

BANGALORE • CHENNAI • DELHI • HYDERABAD • KOLKATA • MUMBAI

Published by
Foundation Books Pvt. Ltd.
CAMBRIDGE HOUSE
4381/4, Ansari Road, Daryaganj
New Delhi - 110002

C-22, C-Block, Brigade M.M., K.R. Road, Jayanagar, **Bangalore** 560 070
Plot No. 80, Service Industries, Shirvane, Sector-1, Nerul, **Navi Mumbai** 400 706
60, Dr. Sundari Mohan Avenue, 1st Floor, **Kolkata** 700 014
21/1 (New No. 49), 1st Floor, Model School Road, Thousand Lights, **Chennai** 600 006
House No. 3-5-874/6/4, (Near Apollo Hospital), Hyderguda, **Hyderabad** 500 029

First published 2006

ISBN 81-7596-281-X

Typeset by Techastra Solutions Pvt. Ltd., Hyderabad

Published by Manas Saikia for Foundation Books Pvt. Ltd.
Printed & bound at Raj Press, R-3 Inderpuri, New Delhi -110 012.

For my father

Shri Jagdish Mohan Pant

(former Administrator General and Official Trustee of the State of Uttar Pradesh)

whose blessings make all things possible

Contents

Foreword

At the beginning of the twenty-first century, India emerged as one of the fastest growing economies in the world. There is a widely shared view that by 2025 India will be the third largest economy in the world (after the United States and China). At the same time, despite its high growth potential, India also continues to have the largest number of persons below the poverty line in the world. As many as 350 million Indians do not earn enough to ensure the minimum intake of food and nutrition. The conditions prevailing in a few of India's urban slums and rural areas are among the worst in the world.

Among the developing countries, India was a pioneer in development planning with the proclaimed objective of removing poverty within a reasonable period after its independence from colonial rule in 1947. India was also among the early proponents of Social Banking as a vital instrument for increasing agricultural productivity and generating employment opportunities. With this specific purpose in view, all large commercial banks were nationalised in 1969 and brought under direct government ownership and control. And yet, the results on the ground have not lived up to the early expectations of the country's planners and decision-makers.

The dichotomy between a 'shining' fast-growing India and its persistent poverty is a puzzle which has baffled economists and policy makers. In her new book on Social Banking, Dr Deepali Pant Joshi has attempted to find some answers to this puzzle and outline a programme for the future. According to her, the development challenges for India now lie in four priority areas: high economic growth, social justice, human development, and a cross-cutting theme of reform and governance. Her book, in her own words, is an attempt to "view these themes holistically with their theoretical underpinnings, conceptual nuances and operational details rather than confining them to a mechanistic frame".

The book provides a rich historical perspective of developments in different areas of Social Banking and poverty alleviation strategies, including the working of cooperative credit banks, regional rural banks, microfinance institutions, and self-help groups. It also tries to draw lessons from the working of similar, but more successful banking institutions in other countries, particularly Indonesia and Bangladesh.

There are two interesting case studies of successful Social Banking models in India, namely Swayam Krishi Sangam (SKS) of Andhra Pradesh and Prathama Bank of Uttar Pradesh.

A survey of the past experience in India and abroad brings out some important lessons for the future. Thus, while formulating policies for higher growth in the agricultural sector, it is important to remember that private investment or better credit availability should not be considered as substitutes for higher public investments. Dr Joshi rightly observes that agricultural performance in India in the 1990s was adversely affected by a decline in public investment even though private investment had shown an increase. Similarly, delivery of credit alone cannot alleviate poverty in developing countries. It is necessary to supplement low-cost credit with other vital services for the poor, including land reform. In recent years, microfinance has emerged as an important instrument for delivery of credit to the small-scale sector. While micro-finance institutions and self-help groups deserve to be fully supported, past experience also highlights the need to move away from the model of microfinance delivered exclusively through government-sponsored programmes. There is need to develop a market-based institutional capacity with transparency of operations and due accountability.

In her book, Dr Joshi has highlighted several other issues of importance, which in her opinion, are essential for generating agricultural dynamism along with higher growth and social justice. While there can be differences of views on the specific suggestions for the future, there is no doubt that this book is an important contribution to the existing literature on banking and financial reforms in India.

Bimal Jalan
former Governor of the Reserve Bank of India
17 August 2005

Preface

Economic growth is a necessary but not a sufficient condition for the alleviation of poverty. Inclusive paradigms of growth are a necessity. The composition of growth is as relevant as the rate of growth. Growth in the primary sector serves to ratchet economic growth. For increasing opportunities for employment and for ensuring food security, it is necessary to focus on agricultural productivity. Economic growth with equity or distributive justice is not an either-or choice but is mutually reinforcing. High growth is necessarily linked to agricultural dynamism. Agriculture is the major employer as 65% of our people are still engaged either in direct agriculture or in activities related to agriculture. We cannot afford jobless economic growth. The poor are more vulnerable to inflation. Hence, it is necessary to ensure inflation control. To promote ready access of the poor to institutional sources of credit, financial deepening was promoted through the nationalisation of banks. Banks have been engaged in Social Banking since 1969. There is a policy space to pursue pro-poor growth. This book recognises the importance of institutional microfinance, i.e., microfinance extended by Self-help groups (SHGs) linked to banks. The SHGs generate employment opportunities; they enable the banks to locate and focus on rural or backward areas and pay attention to the endowments of the poor, i.e., labour. Economic policy must focus on provision of basic goods and services. Social capital of groups can be utilised by banks to channelise credit to the poorest of the poor. An 'inclusive' paradigm of development is realised in this way. A society which does not cater to the needs of all its members cannot be considered a healthy society. Hence, banks have an important role to play in ensuring the flow of credit to the poor to make them part of the economy both as producers and consumers of goods and services. This is also a necessary condition for a sustainable economic growth paradigm.

This book is based on the premise that the nationalisation of banks in 1969 represented a watershed in India's economic development strategy and policies since independence. The tasks which were set for the banking system at the time, the reasons for nationalisation, the need for increasing the credit flow to agriculture to ensure pro-poor growth and poverty alleviation still remain valid for the banks to engage in Social Banking through an overall interventionist framework of policy. As long as we have to contend with these realities as Jawaharlal Nehru expressed in the *Discovery of India* "the need to ensure an adequate standard of living for the masses; in other words to get rid of the appalling poverty of the people" it will be necessary for the banking institutions to contribute to the process of ensuring growth with equity as part of India's development strategy. We need to reconcile economic efficiency with social equity to achieve growth which will have a tangible impact on the alleviation of poverty.

Development as a process must lead to the augmentation of the value of three sets of assets – human and social capital, physical and financial capital and environmental capital. Our overarching concern has rightly been with the distributive and equity aspects of growth. Policy makers have striven to leverage the banking sector for achieving these goals of socio-economic development. How has the banking services sector responded to the growing challenge of shareholder and stakeholder expectations on performance in poverty reduction? This book argues that both risk and opportunity have become established elements in pro-poor banking. The banking sector is part of the process to advance the pro-poor growth agenda of economic development. This book testifies to the increasing response of the financial services sector to this call and provides an overview of achievements in recent years.

Chapter one 'Institutional Credit Delivery System: Policy Intervention' initiates the discussion of the roots of post-Independence economic Planning and the thinking which preceded the nationalisation of banks in 1969. Chapter two 'Indian Agriculture Perspectives' discusses the central focus and the continuing need of finance for agriculture. Chapter three 'Commercial Banks: Strategic Opportunites' elaborates the objectives and the policy framework of post-Nationalisation banking and details the economic performance of the banks stressing the need for partnership with civil society. Chapter four 'The Regional Rural Banks' discusses the achievements, shortcomings and continuing relevance of the Regional Rural Banks. Chapter five describes the acute crisis in the cooperative banking sector due to which it was not able to meet the burgeoning needs of the agricultural sector. The financial crisis of the cooperative banks precipitated the nationalisation of commercial banks. Chapter six 'Institutional Microfinance' discusses the remaining tasks and focuses on the micro-finance sector which has emerged as a sector which offers possibilities of partnership between banking institutions and civil society organisations such as the NGOs and the SHGs. Chapter seven 'Microfinance Initiatives for Equitable and Sustainable Development' concludes with some thought on the prospects for the future.

The Government of India has paid considerable attention to the development challenge in India and has identified four priority themes to take this forward: high economic growth, equitable growth and social justice, human development and the crosscutting theme of reform and governance. In this work an attempt has been made to view these themes not merely confining them to a mechanistic frame but holistically with their theoretical underpinnings, conceptual nuances and operational details. The views expressed are personal and not the views of the institution I am associated with. This book addresses itself to questions of Social Banking and concludes that banks still have a very crucial role to play in the process of economic development. The assumptions and conclusions reached would be relevant to policy makers, administrators, social scientists, professionals, students of the Indian economy, central bankers and practitioners in the field, bureaucrats and bankers who implement and operationlise policies. This book addresses this vast target audience.

Acknowledgements

This book would not have been possible without the blessings of my father, elders, and munificence and grace of the good God Hanuman who blesses all my endeavours.

Thanks are due for inspiration (without implication) to Governor Dr Y. V. Reddy who has always encouraged academic activity within the RBI, Dr C. Rangarajan, Dr Bimal Jalan, Prof Hanumanth Rao and Prof S. Mahendra Dev of Cess. For consistent affection and support I would like to thank my mother Prof Chandra Pant, my husband Rajeev Joshi, my sons Paritosh and Kunal and my brothers Pankaj and Andleeb. For guidance I thank my uncles Shri B. B. Pande, Shri I. D. Pande, Shri Kamal Pande and Smt Namita Gokhale. Sincere thanks to Foundation Books for making the book possible. Finally, anticipatory thanks to the prospective readers, reviewers and all those who will take the trouble of going through the book.

Dr Deepali Pant Joshi

ONE

Institutional Credit Delivery System: Policy Intervention

Planning: A Historical Perspective

The early 1950s marked the inception of Planning in India, with the objective of translating the aspirations of a newly-independent nation into achievements. The foundation of post-Independence economic planning was laid in the pre-Independence era, predominantly by the National Planning Committee of the Indian National Congress, and also by other individuals and groups. The first attempt at formulating a plan for India's development was made by Sir M. Visveswaraya in 1934. He identified the lack of industrialization in India as the cause of India's under-development, and proposed doubling the national income in 10 years. The National Planning Committee constituted in 1938 under the chairmanship of Pandit Jawaharlal Nehru laid down the overarching objective of planning, which was "to ensure an adequate standard of living for the masses, in other words, to get rid of the appalling poverty of the people". The Committee laid down the principles governing land and credit stating that "We, or some of us at any rate, hoped to evolve a specialized system of credit. If banks, insurances etcetera were not to be nationalized they should at least be under the control of the State, thus leading to a state regulation of capital and credit."

The People's Plan of the Indian Federation of Labour (1944) identified "the central problem of the Indian economy as the problem of poverty". It also stated that "In order that the plan may be successfully implemented and may attain its objectives, it will also be necessary for the state to exercise an effective control over banking and other financial institutions in the country." A group of businessmen put together the so-called 'Bombay Plan' with the objective of doubling per capita income within a period of 15 years. Thus there was widespread agreement across the political spectrum, from labour unions on the left to businessmen on the right, on the overarching objectives of articulating a National Development Plan and implementing it. These plan models were clearly influenced by the perception of Soviet Planning and its success. In the 1950s and 1960s, the dominant view in the literature on development economies was that the government had an important role to play and that it should undertake activities that would compensate for 'market failure'.

Soon after Independence, as India embarked upon planned economic growth, the need for a strong and efficient financial system that could fulfill the multifarious needs of credit and development was felt. To achieve this objective, a mixed pattern of economic development was adopted, and a financial system to support such development was devised. The success it achieved, particularly in taking banking to the masses and making the banking system a potent vehicle for furthering public policy, has few parallels in the world.

Economic and/or social policy is shaped in the light of historical circumstances. In the early 1950s and 1960s, development thought tended to view 'credit' as the missing piece which would lead to economic growth and the resurgence of the economy. The Five Year Plans were influenced by Soviet Planning and its success. The First Plan document brought out the economic and social aspects of Planning in terms of propelling the economy to a faster growth trajectory through sustained efforts to mobilize resources and invest them effectively.

The Central Objective of Planning

The central objective of Planning in India was designated thus in the First Plan document: "to initiate a process of development which would raise living standards and open out to the people new opportunities for a richer and more varied life". The problem of development of an underdeveloped economy was perceived as one of utilizing more effectively the potential resources available to the community; this involves economic planning. The economic condition of a country at any given time is a product of the broader social environment, and economic planning has to be viewed as "an integral part of a wider process aiming not merely at the development of resources in a narrow technical sense, but at the development of human faculties and the building up of an institutional framework adequate to the needs and aspirations of the people".

The First Plan made clear that

> in defining the objectives, priorities and techniques of planning in India, it is necessary to bear in mind the scale and dimensions of the problem as well as the basic values which must find expression in the economic and social pattern to be evolved. It is no longer possible to think of development as a process merely of increasing the available supplies of material goods; it is necessary to ensure that simultaneously a steady advance is made towards the realization of wider objectives such as full employment and the removal of economic inequalities. Maximum production, full employment, the attainment of economic equality and social justice which constitute the accepted objectives of planning under present-day conditions are not really so many different ideas but a series of related aims which the country must work for. None of these objectives can be pursued to the exclusion of others; a plan of development must place balanced emphasis on all of these. For instance, even the limited objective of increased production cannot be attained unless the wider objectives of social policy are constantly kept in mind and steadily pursued. On the other hand, equality and social justice will have little content unless the production potential of the community is substantially raised. Development, thus conceived, is a process which calls for effort and sacrifice on the part of the entire body of citizens. For such effort and sacrifice to come forth, psychological conditions have to be created which provide an incentive for all to give of their best.

Early Years of Hope and Expectation

The First Plan document further states that

> it follows from all this that the problem is not merely one of making the existing economic institutions work more efficiently, or making small adjustments in them. What is needed is a transformation of the system so as to secure greater efficiency as well as equity and justice. The central objective of planning is to create conditions in which living standards are reasonably high and all citizens, men and women, have full and equal opportunity for growth and service. There is need not only to build up a big productive machine – though this is no doubt a necessary condition of development – we have at the same time to improve health, sanitation and education and create social conditions for vigorous cultural advance. Planning must mean coordinated development in all these fields.

> In this task of securing simultaneous advance along several fronts, it would be unrealistic to hold out the hope that rapid and spectacular progress can be made in the initial period of planning. Within a limited period, there is always a measure of conflict between one objective and another and, in the formulation of a Plan for a given period, it is necessary to proceed in terms of priorities as between these objectives themselves, laying more stress on some and less on others. This problem of balancing competing objectives is implicit in all planning, and the quality of a plan depends upon the soundness of its judgments regarding the relative emphasis on the various objectives. Only to the extent that the Plan succeeds in striking a right balance can consistent policies be formulated and pursued. There is, to begin with, the problem of choosing, on the one hand, between a moderate increase in the standard of life in the near future with relatively small additions to capital equipment and, on the other, a substantially higher standard of life perhaps for the next generation at the cost of continued austerity and privation to the present generation in the interests of rapid capital formation.

The major task before the planners in India was to remove the constraint of the deficiency of capital by increasing the savings rate and by transforming such savings into productive investment.

As the Second Five Year Plan made clear, "the task is not merely one of reaching any fixed or static point such as doubling of living standards but of generating a dynamism in the economy which will lift it to continually higher levels of material well-being and of intellectual and cultural achievement". Thus, the Second Five Year Plan outlined a strategy of sustainable long-term growth and the role of the State in implementing this strategy. The framework, developed by Prof. Mahalanabois aimed at:

- a sizeable increase in national income so as to raise the standard of living in the country
- rapid industrialization with particular emphasis on the development of basic and heavy industries
- expansion of employment opportunities
- a reduction of inequalities in income and wealth and a more even distribution of economic power.

Unlike the Harrod Domar model, which stressed on shortage of savings, the Mahalanabois model focused on the bottleneck that could be created by the shortage of capital goods. The model stressed the allocation of a higher proportion of the total investment to capital goods, as opposed to consumer goods.

The programme of development incorporated in the Plans was calculated to strengthen the economy at the base and initiate institutional changes that would facilitate more rapid advancement in the future. The Second Five Year Plan aimed to carry forward the process initiated in the First Plan period. It had to provide for a larger increase in production, investment and employment. Simultaneously, it had to accelerate the institutional changes needed to make the economy more dynamic and more progressive, in terms of social as well as economic ends.

In the Second Five Year Plan, it was made clear that an effective reduction in the trend of incomes and spending power accruing to a few can be brought about only through institutional changes that place an increasing proportion of the community's surpluses directly in the hands of public authorities. The reduction in inequalities has to proceed from both ends. On the one hand, measures have to be taken to reduce excessive concentration of wealth and incomes at higher levels, and on the other hand, incomes in general, and particularly at the lower levels, have to be raised. The promotion of co-operative forms of production, the elimination of functionless rent receivers, the substitution of private credit by institutional credit, the control of private monopoly and the enlargement of the public sector in strategic lines of production and trade are of far reaching significance in this context.

The Counterfactual Argument

As a counterfactual argument to the conventional theories of Planning, the Wage Goods Model was advocated by P.R. Brahmananda and C.N. Vakil in 1956. C.N. Vakil, in an early critique of Planning, had pointed out that the adoption of the Heavy Industries Model with inflationary finance resulted in unfortunate consequences for the country – increase in poverty and unemployment as well as a continuous state of inflation which added to the misery of the poor. For rural development to be autonomous and permanent, and at the same time cheaper and effective, he laid stress on the human factor. He put forth a tentative scheme involving the rural people in the effort. His view was that any progress in rural areas imposed from above or done by others is not likely to have any lasting effect. The people themselves should have the urge and the willingness to change and work for it; and simultaneously, they should be provided with facilities and training for such a conscious transformation.

This analysis leads us to the conclusion that, initially, our planners placed absolute reliance on economic growth. The Mahalanabois model, adopted in the early years of Planning in India, relied on growth to 'Trickle Down' to the lower deciles of the population. The 'Trickle Down' did not work and became synonymous with benign neglect. The Second Plan (1955–60) had laid strong emphasis on the heavy industries and capital goods sectors. It was primarily a strategy to forge forward and backward links. However, though the Second Plan was an industrialization plan, it also laid emphasis on co-operative farming, land reform, and agrarian reconstruction, on which there was a separate chapter. While the First Five Year Plan set the overall interventionist framework of policy, the Second Plan authored by Prof. P.C. Mahalanabois provided the analytical foundation for the development strategy that was pursued for the next 35 years. It emphasized the development of heavy industries, import substitution across the board and the vast expansion of the public sector. The massive investment (relative to resources available for its financing) proposed in the Second Plan precipitated a balance of payments crisis. In response, an elaborate system of controls (which was expanded in subsequent decades) was put in place to enforce the plans and their underlying development strategy. The Third Plan accorded due primacy to agriculture.

Exogenous Shocks: Shift in Thinking

Indian Planning faced an exogenous shock due to the wars with China in 1962 and Pakistan in 1965 and harvest failures and drought in 1965 and 1967. The crisis on the food front was met with PL 480 wheat imports from the US. It brought into sharp focus the need to build food self-sufficiency. Between 1966 and 1969, due to successive shocks, Five Year Plans were abandoned.

With the Fourth Plan, planning for agricultural and rural development came into sharp focus. This was the basis for roping in commercial banks to extend finance to agriculture. The Fifth, Sixth and Seventh Plans laid emphasis on eradication of poverty, on providing employment opportunities, human resources and infrastructure development and removal of inequality. They expanded the system of food security and stressed increase in productivity in agriculture and industries. Agricultural and rural development were identified as the priority areas demanding attention. Thus, the growing needs of agriculture and the realization of its importance in development prompted the thinking that positive policy intervention was possible through the institutional credit delivery system. There were two broad strands of policy thinking, which were translated into two basic approaches: one which relied on economic growth to 'Trickle Down' to the lowest deciles – the economic growth approach, and the second, which relied on a direct frontal attack on poverty – the economic development approach.

Greater Realism

The primary distinction between the two approaches is between creating income (and hence consumption) and providing consumption (in kind or through doles). The latter necessarily involves redistribution between different groups unless the financing comes from external sources, while the former need have no such component – though complementary policies to bias the creation of income towards the poor often involve redistributive elements. In the indirect growth-oriented route, policy bias towards the poor can be inbuilt through, inter alia, policies that facilitate borrowing and investment by the poor. The direct route is self-explicit, and is targeted at the needs of the poor through state transfers and subsidies. The optimal policy design should generally involve a mix of these two approaches. If we have recourse solely to the indirect route and growth concentrates incomes entirely in the hands of the non–poor there is no social mobility, and growth can then be shown to be immiserizing to the poor, i.e., growth tends to marginalize or impoverish significant sections of the population. In this situation the relative rate of return on the adoption of the indirect route to poverty eradication would be negative. In such an eventuality, the case for exclusive reliance on the direct route would become overwhelming. The two critical and compelling caveats for this being, first that it should be demonstrable that the factors, both economic and political, that constrain the effectiveness of the growth process, in indirectly reducing poverty do not simultaneously and equally afflict the direct route and prevent it from effectively providing benefits to the poor. Second, the neglect of the growth process, which leads to negligible increases in income, is harmful, as it reduces the impact on poverty. This may impair the ability of the State to sustain the expenditures required to finance the more productive direct route in the long run, especially in an economy with a growing population.

Both approaches have been experimented with in economic thinking and in economic policy. Thus the 1950s and 1960s were decades dominated by the growth route, the indirect route to poverty eradication. By the 1970s this ideology had fallen into disfavour and the direct route in the form of a Basic Needs package was adopted as a mantra for development. By the 1990s the indirect route was in favour again, and in the current decade the pendulum has swung back towards a direct frontal attack on poverty.

Need for Rapid Growth: Pragmatic Policy Shift

We have to appreciate the centrality of growth. There does not appear to be an alternative path. The strategy of rapid growth has therefore been decided upon as a way of making a sustained impact on poverty. It seems necessary to effectively combine both policies to encourage growth and develop human resources and physical infrastructure. Investment in infrastructure and human resources will make a greater impact on poverty than mere resource transfers/subsidies. The last few decades have demonstrated the rates of growth that we could achieve through the adoption of new economic policies.

If we had not introduced economic reforms in July 1991, the economic crisis of 1991 would have led to a crisis with falling production and employment opportunities, high inflation rates and worsening balance of payments situation. In such a condition, the poor would have been hit the hardest. The impact of the increase in prices of fertilizers, diesel etcetera would have severely affected supply and directly impacted agricultural production, industrial growth and transportation. The new economic policies have helped us to better integrate and mesh with the world economy.

The poor stand to gain from acceleration in growth, which widens opportunities, provides the resources needed to invest in human development, and creates the foundation that would increase the returns for human capital. The new approach which views growth and inflation control as the best anti-poverty programme is conceived to lift people out of poverty as opposed to the earlier 'Trickle Down' approach.

An interventionist role, not laissez-faire considerations, is assigned to the State in both approaches. The government has to be critically involved in raising internal and external savings; in guiding, if not allocating, investment. By ensuring faster growth we can bring gainful employment and increase the income of more people. Institutional mechanisms such as mandated directed lending through banks and special credit facilities for the poor have been developed and sustained to ensure a policy-induced pro-poor bias.

Social Banking: Rationale and Relevance

Social Banking was a grand idea. Banks were not there to cater to the needs of the few, but to enable the realization of the entrepreneurial needs of all, and to generate economic growth with sustainable development. Social Banking was envisaged as 'mass' banking as opposed to 'class' banking. It was not perceived as antithetical to commercial banking, rather one was to be a subset of the other.

Thirty-five years after the nationalisation of banks, it is necessary for us to evaluate the gains and attribute reasons for the losses. Has Social Banking, the way it has been practised in our country, lived up to the high expectations we had – and continue to have – of it? What is the distance between what we set out to achieve and what we have achieved?

Role of Banks in Economic Growth and Development

The Indian rural credit system, as it has emerged, is a product of both evolution and intervention. Till the late 1960s, following the recommendations of the All India Rural Credit Survey Committee (1954), policy interventions in the area of rural credit were mostly confined to the Cooperatives. Cooperatives were considered the primary and most suitable purveyors of rural finance. The report of the All India Rural Credit Review Committee (1966) marked a turning point in the policy's perception of the rural sector. The Committee pointed out that despite the support extended, Cooperatives had begun to exhibit several weaknesses – in the form of overdues and organizational ineffectiveness. They were not geared for meeting the growing needs of the agricultural sector that was emerging as a result of the Green Revolution. The application of modern technology and innovations in production, processing and marketing, tractors, fertilizers, better equipment, machinery and seeds required larger amount of credit. The Committee therefore recommended a significantly enlarged role for commercial banks in both current production and long-term investment. With the nationalisation of major commercial banks in 1969, branch banking in the rural areas acquired a new momentum and the outreach of the commercial banking system was considerably enlarged within a relatively short period. The strategy devised in the post-nationalisation era to develop and enlarge financial services in the rural areas comprised geographical and spatial expansion of the institutional structure, directed lending and concessional credit. It is accepted that the strategies adopted resulted in real gains. There was a broadening of the rural infrastructure for credit delivery, an increase in outreach and a weakening of the stronghold of the informal agencies as evidenced by increase in the relative share of institutional sources in the cash debts of rural households and substantially stepped up credit flows for agriculture and allied activities.

Role of State Intervention

The design of public policy to generate employment and consequently eliminate poverty has been at the centre of policy for more than five decades since Independence. It has been at the core of Planning efforts. These values or basic objectives have been summed up in the phrase 'Socialist pattern of society'. Essentially this means that the basic criterion for determining the lines of advance must not be private profit but social gain. The pattern of development and the structure of socio-economic relations should be so planned that they result not only in appreciable increases in national income and employment, but also in greater equality in incomes and wealth. Major decisions regarding production, distribution, consumption and investment, and in fact all significant socio-economic relationships, must be made by agencies informed by social purpose. The benefits of economic development must accrue more and more to the relatively less privileged classes of society and there should be a progressive reduction of the concentration of income, wealth and economic power in the hands of a few.

There is no immediate solution to the immense problem of poverty. The issue is not whether resources can be moved further towards the margin from the indirect growth-based route to the direct minimum-needs route. The important lesson seems to be that within each route we can and must get significantly more returns, than we have to date. Our growth rate has reduced the poverty ratio; however, absolute numbers of the poor are still at a level of over 300 million.

Role of Civil Society Organisations

Civil society voluntary agencies and social action groups have an overarching role in furthering the processes of growth and development. The micro-finance approach has clearly illustrated that private-public action and civil society have an increasingly critical partnership. Growth-mediated efforts had been operationalised through the State, and the institutional credit delivery system had been pressed into service with banks being critical partners in the effort to raise agricultural productivity. The objectives of this policy were to institutionalize credit, to enlarge its coverage, and to ensure the provision of timely and adequate finance at reasonable rates to as large a segment of the population as possible, to achieve anticipated growth rates in agricultural production and employment. This policy design negatively impacted the health of institutional credit agencies purveying credit and led to an alternative policy design with emphasis on growth and the sustainability of financial institutions.

Theories of Economic Growth

Prior to the 1970s, the control of financial markets was followed and favoured in capital-scarce countries. Usury could be better prevented, the money supply better controlled and higher investment–savings targets met this way, than if the financial markets were left free. In the early 1970s Ronald McKinnon and Edward Shaw (1973) published their seminal work on 'Financial Repression' a term used to describe a system in economies in transition (developing economies) in which the government determined who got and gave credit and at what terms. The government administered this system through the ownership of banks, and controlled other financial intermediaries and international financial movements. The McKinnon–Shaw hypothesis was that such controls maximize welfare. Stiglitz has (1984/1994) supported this thesis by showing that financial repression can encourage the flow of capital to designated sectors with beneficial technological spillovers.

The supply-led development theory, which held sway in the 1950s and 1960s, was predicated on the assumption of the need to make direct resources of credit readily available to the farmer and the poor agriculturalist. The drought of the early 1960s made food security a necessary objective. In India, nationalization of banks and the initiatives on the part of the State which preceded and succeeded this between 1969 and 1990 were in keeping with this thinking.

Development thinking in the 1990s moved from restricting itself to supply-led initiatives to meeting demand-side challenges. This view posed the problem of the outreach of the banking system versus its sustainability. It questioned whether interventions through the institutional credit delivery system had made any effective difference to the condition of the poorer sections, or whether the banking system had merely overextended itself in the process and thereby weakened itself.

Large-scale formal credit interventions by the State through priority-sector lending began to be rapidly perceived as ineffective in targeting those really in need of assistance. Widespread loan default by the poor suggested that such interventions were not fulfilling the roles of even subsidy or credit amnesty schemes. They had created a sophisticated rentier system and the rents inherent in the social banking process implied the capture of the system by the rural elite. This promoted financial repression and worsened lending terms for the poor in the informal markets.

The rationale of the Indian Social Banking experiment of the early 1950s and 1960s was simple. It sought to displace the 'evil' moneylender and reduce credit rationing in the rural areas. The strategy rested firstly on encouraging the establishment of branches of banks in rural locations in hitherto un-banked locations. Secondly, it aimed at increasing bank lending towards rural households, especially in agriculture and small-scale industry, via the mandatory prescription of priority-sector requirements. Thirdly, it planned to keep the costs of credit low by fixing interest rates through the administered interest rate regime.

Crisis of the 1990s and the Paradigm Shift it Generated

The 1990s were eventful for India. The acceptance of the recommendations of the Narasimhan Committee on Financial Sector Reform introduced some significant changes in the financial sector. The reform policies impacted the financial sector in the following three areas. The first broad set of issues related to the overall monetary policies adopted including the maintenance of reserve requirements, interest rates, refinance facilities and the activation of internal debt management instruments. The second set of issues relate to the strengthening of banks and institutions by way of prescription of prudential norms, asset classification, cleaning up balance sheets, capital adequacy and the recapitalization of banks. The third set of issues relate to the overall competitiveness of the financial structure – restructuring banks and financial institutions to reap economies of scale, permitting mergers/ amalgamations, and allowing the entry of new banks in the private sector.

New Institutional Approaches: Rural Financial Architecture

New institutional approaches to developing financial systems for the rural poor – ranging from microfinance, revamped regional rural banks and restructured agricultural development banks to cooperative banks and commercial banks – offer a choice of financial instruments: savings, credit and lately, insurance services.

If financial intermediation is to be treated as central to development efforts, suitable policy changes would need to be introduced. Decentralization and finance are relevant to the poor but a much wider transformation of the institutional framework is required to lead to a fairer distribution of the opportunities and benefits of economic growth. Even today, access to conventional formal financial institutions is inversely related to income. The poorer a person is, the greater the difficulty of access.

Self-help groups (SHGs) succeed in providing access where formal financial institutions fail, as their loans are not linked to the provision of credit. Microfinance for the poor/women has received extensive recognition as a strategy for poverty alleviation, employment and economic empowerment. How does microfinance help the poor? Typical microfinance clients are low-income borrowers. Microfinance helps the poor to increase income, build viable businesses and reduce their vulnerability to external shocks. It is also an instrument of self-empowerment and enables women, who bear the double burden of being poor and being women, to become economic agents of change.

Poverty is multi-dimensional; income generation through addition to household income has attendant benefits – food security, education for children, the ability to weather shocks. It enables women to step out of the inner courtyard and carry out transactions in the public space, thereby increasing their self-confidence and helping them lead better lives and have a voice in essentially discriminatory and patriarchal societies.

Is microcredit a panacea? Is it the Holy Grail for development practitioners? Does it successfully provide a safety net for the poor – even the asset-less and the destitute – in all situations? Does it help combat economic uncertainties, loss of livelihood, seasonal unemployment or natural disasters? Can it effect distributive justice and ensure growth with equity which will enable the poor to access development resources and use them to their best advantage?

Intrinsic Strengths of the Poor

The poor ultimately work their own way out of poverty. They have the knowledge of their own environment, which imbues them with the survival skills necessary to cope with the world. Institutional credit and specially subsidized credit do little for them. They prompt a culture of dependence instead of encouraging independence. The poor, especially women, have repeatedly displayed the will and the capacity to grasp opportunities to better their lives and make themselves and their families less vulnerable. Most of India, and especially rural India, is poverty-stricken, with subsistence agriculture and low levels of alternative economic activity. Local employment options are meagre. Poverty is both seasonal and stochastic. Those looking for security migrate in search of wage labour. Small investments in agriculture do not go very far beyond farming and allied activities; there is little economic growth in much of rural India. There are few exploitable opportunities in the manufacturing trade or services sector that the poor have access to. Choices of starting enterprises, if ever exercised, range from opening small provision shops in the village to starting a dairy unit – which is linked precariously to fodder, water and assured market linkages.

Higher returns from farming in these conditions need much more in place. New levels of sustainable economic activity require adequate backward and forward links to technology, infrastructure and markets. Credit is not the sole input, but one of the inputs for development. Even for agriculture to be viable we need more roads and electricity, investments in irrigation, input supply, extension of infrastructure for storage, handling and processing, and functioning, favourable commodity markets. These create positive externalities and are in the domain of the State. State spending on infrastructure and the social sectors needs to be increased. SHGs are useful models of development – they are able to provide timely credit and are creating new social opportunities for the lowest deciles of the population, who still need to be uplifted and integrated with the mainstream of society.

Policy Choices

India has a differentiated financial structure – having diverse strategies and sound policies – and with a conducive policy and regulatory environment, different types of financial institutions can be sustained and form the building blocks of an effective rural financial system. With appropriate strategies and the adoption of an institutionalized-bank-led approach to microfinance, institutional sustainability and outreach can be made compatible and mutually reinforcing. There may, however be short-term trade-offs among them which may require special State/policy intervention. There is a consensus on the importance of ensuring both outreach and financial sustainability. Only sustainable financial institutions can reliably provide adequate financial services and continually increase their outreach to the poor. The strength of financial institutions lies in their ability to reduce transaction costs, make their resources grow dynamically, allocate scarce resources efficiently and manage risks. The underlying challenge of rural poverty and unemployment cannot be met without core economic investments, technology and employment generation among the poor in rural areas. Several challenges remain to be addressed. As at the commencement of the post-Nationalization era, so also now there is much that the formal financial sector has to contribute to these processes of growth and development.

Evaluation

Over the last five decades credit growth has shown an increase. The emphasis on achieving quantitative targets has had certain consequences; inadequate attention has been paid to the qualitative aspects of lending, resulting in erosion of repayment ethics. The consequential result has been an accretion in loan defaults. Lax contract enforcement has negatively impacted the profitability of rural financial institutions such as Cooperatives and Regional Rural Banks (RRBs) threatened the sustainability of the social banking experiment. The cost-effectiveness and penetration of the rural financial system has been a cause of growing concern.

Finance can facilitate economic growth by easing liquidity constraints in production – by providing capital to start new production or adapt new technology and help producers assume production risk. In recent years, finance has also been used as an anti-poverty tool. It helps the unemployed become employed, thereby increasing income and consumption and reducing poverty.

A variety of problems including imperfect information and imperfect enforcement, covariate risks of agricultural production and political interference have created difficulties in building sustainable rural financial institutions. Sustainable rural financial institutions are possible if the following conditions are met:

- The government does not see financial institutions as public transfer mechanisms or interfere with them in any way except to provide prudent regulation and supervision.
- Financial institutions are allowed to set interest rates that reflect market forces and adjust with inflation rates.
- Loan contracts are enforced through social and economic incentives or other means such as group pressure.
- Programme design and periodic programme evaluation exercises are taken up to assess the progress made.
- Interventions are carefully targeted.

Existing Strengths

Through the adoption of a broad-based institutional capacity we now have in place a financial infrastructure which can make possible efficacious and efficient credit delivery to the agricultural and rural sector. Issues, which have assumed increasing importance, are increasing the flow of credit to the agriculture sector. They include ensuring the viability of rural lending, strengthening the rural financial institutions, improving the recovery climate and appreciating the role of voluntary agencies and the non-governmental organisations (NGOs) in financial intermediation. A systematic reform of rural credit is essential. The existing financial infrastructure of the multi-agency system needs to be streamlined and strengthened to enable these institutions to become efficient purveyors of rural credit. Given the need for securing an efficient agricultural base, it is essential that the flow of rural credit is maintained at an appropriate level to support productive activity.

Inherent Weaknesses

Despite considerable attention paid to it, both in terms of institutional development and expansion of the resource base, the rural credit delivery system has several endemic weaknesses inherent in it. Cumbersome lending procedures, inadequate supervision and the apathy of bank staff have resulted in delayed and untimely credit, and are responsible for diversion of credit and credit default. The major factors that have constrained the capacity of the poor to borrow from organized credit institutions have been lack of skills, unawareness of economic opportunities and of markets and their inability to overcome the intricate procedural requirements.

The share of supply of credit to rural areas through institutional sources has increased substantially since 1971. The All India Debt and Investment Survey (AIDIS), 1991 shows that out of the total credit supplied to the rural households nearly 64% were met by institutional sources as against approximately 30% in 1971. Despite the fact that over the years there has been an increase in overall outreach and absolute disbursement of credit from institutional sources, from 1990 there has been deceleration in the growth of bank credit in rural areas. The share of rural credit in the total credit disbursed by scheduled commercial banks was 3.5% in 1971 which steadily increased to 15% over the two decades.

Table 1.1 Advances to the Priority Sector by Public Sector Banks
(as on the last reporting Friday)

	No. of Accounts (in lakhs)					Amount outstanding (Rupees in Crores)				
Sector	June 1969	March 2001	March 2002*	March 2003*	March 2004*	June 1969	March 2001	March 2002*	March 2003*	March 2004*
1	2	3	4	5	6	7	8	9	10	11
1. Agriculture	1.7	188	161	168	177	162	53,571	63,082	73,507	86,187
						(5.4)	(15.7)	(15.9)	(15.4)	(15.4)
(i) Director	1.6	185	157	164	174	40	38,137	44,908	51,799	61,957
						(1.3)	(11.2)	(11.3)	(10.8)	(11.1)
(ii) Indirect						122	15,434	18,174	21,708	24,230
						(4.0)	(4.5)	(4.6)	(4.5)	(4.3)
2. Small-scale industries						257	48,400	49,743	52,988	58,278
						(8.7)	(14.2)	(12.5)	(11.1)	(10.4)
3. Other priority sector advances						22	40,791	53,712	71,448	94,959
						(0.7)	(12.0)	(13.5)	(15.0)	(17.0)
4. Total priority sector advances †						441	1,49,116	1,71,185	2,03,095	2,45,672
						(14.6)	(43.7)	(43.1)	(42.5)	(44.0)
5. Net Bank credit						3,016	3,41,291	3,96,954	4,77,899	5,58,849

* Data is provisional.
† Inclusive of advances to setting up industrial estates, funds provided to RRBs by sponsor banks, loans to software industries, food and agro processing sector, SHGs and venture capital.
Note: Figures in brackets represent percentages to net bank credit.
(Source: Report on Trend and Progress of Banking in India, 2003–04, RBI.)

After 1990 there was a decline in the off take of rural credit. Inadequate investment in agricultural and rural development has led to underdeveloped physical infrastructure and weak support services for market business development and extensions, which in turn hamper the creation of credit absorption capabilities. This contributes to the increase of risk and poor credit offtake. An inadequate financial infrastructure, including the lack of an enabling legal framework, inadequate information systems, weak accounting and audit systems, and the lack of appropriate follow-up of loans by banks are only some of the problems that plague the system.

New Hope

Microfinance is the extension of microcredit. This can be delivered through institutional credit delivery agencies such as the RRBs, Cooperatives and commercial banks, and non-institutional agencies such as SHGs with NGOs acting as facilitators. Microfinance is emerging as the new mantra. Taking cognizance of the need to further accelerate the availability of banking services in rural areas and leverage the existing socially active organizations in the process, two significant statements were included in the Union Budget 2005–6. They are as follows:

> Paragraph 48: Government intends to continue with its effort to turn the focus of commercial banks, regional rural banks (RRBs) and cooperative banks towards providing credit, especially production credit, to rural households and farm households. Particularly in agricultural credit, innovations are possible. Propose to request the Reserve Bank of India (RBI) to examine the issue of allowing banks to adopt the 'agency model', by using the infrastructure of civil society organizations, rural kiosks and village knowledge centers, to provide credit support to rural and farm sectors.
>
> Paragraph 53: At present, micro finance institutions (MFIs) obtain finance from banks according to guidelines issued by RBI. MFIs seek to provide small scale credit and other financial services to low income households and small informal businesses. Government intends to promote MFIs in a big way. The way forward, I believe, is to identify MFIs, classify and rate such institutions, and empower them to intermediate between the lending banks and the beneficiaries. Commercial banks may appoint MFIs as 'banking correspondents' to provide transaction services on their behalf. Since MFIs require infusion of new capital, I propose to re-designate the existing Rs.100 crore Micro Finance Development Fund as the 'Micro Finance Development and Equity Fund', and increase the corpus to Rs.200 crore. The fund will be managed by a Board consisting of representatives of NABARD, commercial banks and professionals with domain knowledge. The Board will be asked to suggest suitable legislation and I expect to introduce a draft Bill in the next fiscal year.

While not denying the need of these pro-poor interventions, it is also necessary to strike a note of caution. Microfinance alone cannot overcome poverty. Microfinance is not a panacea for poverty but is a significant tool for helping the poor to harness economic opportunities. Fundamentally it is broad-based economic growth that reduces poverty.

An effort is being made to deepen the reach of the formal financial system through the synergy of the formal and the informal systems. Developing a financial institution for the poor requires that an additional financial condition be met: the poor need to be targeted with financial services. Providing credit to the poor is often considered risky because the poor have no collateral-land or other physical assets to offer for bank loans. Moreover, since the poor may not be able to bear the risk of self-employment as they lack entrepreneurial skills, financial institutions serving only the poor may face high default rates. Sustained poverty reduction requires an enabling environment, actions and policies designed to improve and increase the productive and human capital of the poor. Programme design is critical.

Policy interventions need to be correctly targeted if benefits are to reach the poor. Sustained poverty reduction requires actions and policies that help improve both, the capital of production and human capital. In the ultimate analysis, markets and policies have to be integrated into a plan that incorporates social priorities. The needs of agriculture remain important, as agriculture remains the most critical sector for growth, employment and poverty alleviation. The banking system requires to be geared to meet the emerging challenges.

References

Alagh, Y. K. 1995. *India's Development Planning and Policy: A Revaluation.* Vikas.

Brahmananda, P. R., D. M. Nanjudappa and B. K. Narayanan. 1979. *Indian Economic Development and Policy: Essays in Honour of Progress.* Vikas.

Byres, Terence J., ed. 1998. *The Indian Economy: Major Debates since Independence.* Oxford University Press.

Das, D. K. 1998. *Indian Economy after fifty years of Independence: Experiences and Challenges.* Deep & Deep Publications.

Government of India. 1951. First Five Year Plan document. Planning Commission.

———. 1956. Second Five Year Plan document. Planning Commission.

Jalan, Bimal., ed. 1993. *The Indian Economy: Problems and Prospects.* New Delhi: Penguin.

Mahajan, V. S. 1982. *Planning and Socialist Transformation of Indian Economy.* Vikas.

Narayana, N. S. S., ed. 2000. *Economic Policy and State Intervention.* Oxford University Press.

Rangarajan, C. 2000. *Perspectives on Indian Economy.* New Delhi: UBSPD.

Reddy, Y. V. 2003. *Economic Policy in India: Managing Change.* New Delhi: UBSPD.

Reddy, Y. V. and K. Koasbram. 1988. *Multilevel Planning in India: Processes and Perceptions.* Hyderabad: Centre for Economic and Social Studies.

World Bank. 2001. *World Development Report 2000/2001: Attacking Poverty.* New York: Oxford University Press.

TWO

Indian Agriculture Perspectives

Indian Agriculture

The agricultural crisis of the mid-1960s triggered by the severe droughts of 1965–6 and 1966–7 compelled policy makers to appreciate the strategic significance of agriculture in a poor industrialising economy. The need to assure food security led to the stress on agricultural growth, which was also seen as a means to remove poverty and ensure growth with social justice. There were still other concerns. Public investment is required to realise these aims. Public investment supplies the necessary infrastructure, including irrigation, research and extension, power, and transportation, to mobilise the growth potential of the agriculture sector. From the Fourth Five-Year Plan there was an emphasis on the Green Revolution, a technology-led growth process with an emphasis on the adoption of high-yielding varieties of wheat and rice with price subsidies and investment policies. A separate sub-strategy of institutionalising credit support through the banks to support the agricultural growth strategy was a critical plank of this policy. The insufficiency of resources devoted to agricultural growth in the first three Plans came into sharp focus with the food crises and dependence on US PL 480 imports. The focus of the new agricultural strategy changed to a concentration on increasing the use of new inputs, supported by subsidised finance through the banking system and procurement prices.

Centrality of Agriculture in the Indian Economy

The Indian economy is largely agrarian; the importance of agriculture hardly needs to be emphasised. Though the contribution of agriculture and allied sectors to the GDP has declined to 22%, the percentage of population engaged in agriculture and allied activities continues to be 67%. In view of the continued dependence of two-thirds of the population on agriculture, it continues to provide a ratchet to GDP growth. Growth in other sectors does not lead to employment on a significant scale. Agriculture has a multiplier effect on growth. Long-term growth of the agriculture sector is necessary to achieve self-reliance at the national level, attain food security for households, generate employment opportunities, and bring about equity in the distribution of income and wealth, resulting in a rapid reduction in poverty levels. Though some degree of independence from weather conditions has been attained from the time when the Indian economy was described as a gamble dependent on the monsoons, agriculture still plays a critical role in determining the macro-economic balance, especially in generating private consumption demand necessary for growth. The Fast-Moving Consumer Goods (FMCG) sector is largely dependent on the growth of agricultural income. The link between the agriculture sector and the growth of the economy makes growth in this sector vital for output growth, control of inflation, price and financial stability.

The sustainable growth of agriculture is essential to accomplish the following objectives:

- Put the economy on a high growth trajectory as envisaged by the Tenth Plan
- Ensure self-reliance and food security
- Make agriculture more remunerative for farmers
- Help in poverty alleviation, especially in cases of chronic as well as transient poverty
- Provide sustenance and livelihood in rural areas as agriculture is labour-intensive
- Generate employment in the non-farm sector through its forward and backward linkages
- It is important for the provision of raw materials, and as a consumer of finished products, industrial machinery, etc.
- Agricultural growth has a strong spillover effect on the economy in terms of its forward and backward linkages, demand linkages and employment linkages.
- The contribution of agriculture to economic growth in terms of capital transfers may decline but the sector's contribution due to the higher share of non-agricultural inputs in the input structure gets progressively strengthened.
- The eventual impact on poverty is far more significant than the initial impact. Reduction in prices of foodgrains, on which the poor spend most, itself leads to the containment of poverty.

The Current Problems Confronting the Sector

The following can perhaps be considered the most significant challenges, among the major issues confronting the agriculture sector in general, which have to be met if the objectives of sustainable and high economic growth are to be attained. "There appears a growing anxiety that the process of reforms has bypassed the agriculture sector. Accordingly, extending reforms to the farm sector and achieving robust growth in agriculture holds the key to reversing the Industrial slowdown". (Reddy: 2001)

The search for realization of the full growth potential of the agriculture sector leads to an analysis of the critical factors constraining agricultural growth.

1. Capital inadequacy – need for credit support from the banks
2. Decline in public investment in agriculture
3. Decline in agricultural productivity
4. Decline in research and development expenditure
5. Decline in irrigation watershed development
6. Minimum Support Prices (MSPs) for procurement of buffer stocks
7. Role of subsidies
8. Controls on domestic trade

In addition, the other area of concern is the preponderance of low value agriculture leading to low cost-benefit ratio and the inefficient use of natural resources.

1. Capital Inadequacy: Need for Credit Support from Banks

Agricultural development, in particular, calls for the creation of outlets for provision of institutional credit for production purposes. A conscious policy of augmenting the flow of institutional credit for agriculture has been pursued with vigour in post-Independent India. Recognising that Cooperatives, with local roots and possibilities of emergence of local leadership, are natural agencies for providing credit with mechanisms for monitoring the end use of credit, the government and the RBI have promoted the cooperative movement on a big scale with access to special credit arrangements, some of them on concessional terms. However, while Cooperatives have made tremendous progress, they have failed to come up to the high standards expected of them. They are plagued by a variety of problems. Poor mobilization of local resources, ineffective leadership, poor monitoring of the end use of credit and mounting overdues due to high loan defaults have crippled the cooperative sector. Still, the sector continues to meet most of the short-term and medium-term requirements of the agriculture sector through its extensive geographical spread of Primary Agricultural Societies, District Central Cooperative Banks and State Cooperative Banks. The long-term needs of the agriculture sector are being met through the State Cooperative Banks and Rural Development Banks at the apex level and the Primary Agriculture and Rural Development Banks at the state level. The share of Cooperatives in the dispensation of agricultural credit continues to be 67%.

Recognising the need to shore up their capital, the central government Budget for 2002–3 attempts to recapitalise the cooperative banks with financial support from the central and state governments – a provision of Rs. 100 crore has been made. The dismal performance of Cooperatives had led the policy makers to look to commercial banks, particularly the public sector banks, to step into the breach through their rural branches, which proliferated in the three decades following nationalisation. Commercial banks did bring a new approach to bear on the provision of credit for agriculture with their superior material and human resources. But soon, commercial banks also encountered problems of overdues and it was felt that their high cost structure could make them inappropriate agencies for being the purveyors of rural credit on a dispersed basis. Their share in agricultural credit is only 36%. It was this realization which led to the setting up of Regional Rural Banks (RRBs) in 1976. The central and state governments participated in the share capital of these banks; they were also linked to a sponsor bank which contributed up to 35% of their share capital. It sought to combine the kind of local knowledge presumed to be the special feature of Cooperatives with the professional ethos of a commercial bank. These banks, which at the outset adopted lower scales of compensation for their staff than their sponsor banks, were specially mandated to lend to agriculture and the weaker sections of at concessional rates of interest. They could initially manage to lend at concessional rates because of the access to subsidized refinance from their sponsor banks and National Bank for Agriculture and Rural Development (NABARD). But the RRBs were crippled soon enough by several factors, among which was a new compensation policy in pursuance of which they had to pay their employees on par with those of their sponsor banks. Their character as low-cost institutions specially designed to serve rural areas was thus lost irretrievably. They were also adversely affected by the problem of mounting overdues and uneasy industrial relations. A policy package was evolved for them which has had some success as 167 of the 196 RRBs are now making profits, but their share in the disbursement of agricultural credit is still only 7%. It was presumably because of the setbacks encountered in the channelization of credit through Cooperatives, rural branches of commercial banks and RRBs that the new concept of a Local Area Bank emerged. The concept was attractive in that it sought to involve local leadership in the mobilization of local resources for profitable lending in a compact area.

By the end of March 2003, only four Local Area Banks could be set up; only 10 branches have been opened in rural areas. They operate mostly in already banked centres. The total volume of business handled was less than Rs. 85 crore, and obviously the bulk of the business emanated from the district headquarters, where the head offices of these banks were located. Their impact in providing credit to the agriculture sector has been negligible. In the present day environment, public sector banks are less than enthusiastic about lending to any sector that is perceived as risky, as the new capital adequacy income recognition and stringent provisioning norms for any non-performing assets have created a psychosis in the minds of bankers. They achieve the minimum necessary but are not willing to extend agricultural credit beyond that. The ground level credit disbursed to agriculture by all agencies (commercial banks, cooperative banks and RRBs) was estimated at Rs. 64,000 crore during 2001–2 and is projected to reach Rs. 82,073 crore during the financial year 2002–3.

The flow of direct finance to agriculture and allied sectors from all financial institutions, including commercial banks, cooperative banks and RRBs, was Rs. 38,127 crore in 2001–2, whereas it was just Rs. 3436 crore in 1980–1. Thus there has been a more than ten-fold increase in the flow of credit to agriculture, implying a compound growth rate of 12.8% per annum. Indirect finance to agriculture and allied sectors, which was Rs. 3,384 crore in 1987–8 rose more than eight-fold to Rs. 28,346 crore in 1999–2000 i.e., at a compound growth rate of 19.4% per annum. The percentage of credit from the institutional sector – the Cooperatives and banks – as opposed to moneylenders has increased from 7.2% in 1951 to 61.2% in 1981 and 64% in 1991 as per the All India Debt and Investment survey. However the credit delivery scenario in the 1990s is unsettling, as there is deceleration in the disbursement of direct finance by scheduled commercial banks from 15.1% in the 1980s to 11% in the 1990s. Institutional credit to small and marginal farmers plays an important role in replacing informal credit market mechanisms due to the interlinkages arising between informal credit and other factors/product markets. The deceleration in the growth of loans for the small landholdings in the 1990s compared to the 1980s is indicative of a combination of better loan repayments (as most of the loans are small value crop

Table 2.1

Priority Sector Lending by Public Sector Banks also Reflecting Shortfall in Achievement of Agriculture Target of 18%

(Amount in Rupees, crores)

	March 1991	March 1992	March 1993	March 1994	March 1995	March 1996	March 1997	March 1998	March 1999	Sept 1999	March 2000	Sept 2000	March 2001	Sept 2001	March 2002	Sept 2002	March 2003
Net Bank Credit (NBC)	105632	112160	132782	140914	169038	184391	189684	218219	246203	251679	292943	308944	340888	354311	396954	422556	477899
Total PS advances	42276	44581	48653	53197	61794	69609	79131	91319	107200	111612	127807	134108	146546	153374	171185	178943	203095
% of PS adv. to NBC	40.02	**39.75**	**36.64**	**37.75**	**36.56**	**37.75**	**41.72**	**41.85**	**43.54**	**44.35**	**43.63**	**43.41**	**42.99**	**43.29**	**3.12**	**42.35**	**42.50**
Total agri. adv.	15857	18265	20020	21204	23513	26351	31012	34304	40078	40660	46190	48897	53685	56108	63083	65873	73507
% of agri. adv. to NBC	**15.01**	**16.28**	**15.07**	**15.05**	**13.91**	**14.29**	**16.35**	**15.72**	**16.28**	**16.16**	**15.77**	**15.83**	**15.65**	**15.63**	**15.81**	**15.59**	**15.34**
Advances to SSI	16783	17398	19388	21561	25843	29482	31542	38109	42674	41913	45788	45439	48445	47060	49743	48718	52988
% of SSI adv. to NBC	15.89	15.51	14.60	15.30	15.29	15.99	16.63	17.46	17.33	16.65	15.63	14.71	14.21	13.28	12.53	11.53	11.09
Adv. to weaker sections	10260	10881	11865	12779	13918	15579	16478	18134	19244	19608	21145	22096	24805	25815	28975	29986	32304
% of adv. to weaker sections to NBC		9.71	8.94	9.07	8.23	8.45	8.69	8.31	7.82	7.79	7.22	7.15	7.28	7.29	7.30	7.10	6.76

[Provisional data – based on half-yearly ad hoc data received from banks]

loans) as well as low disbursements. Small and marginal farmers continue to be both credit and demand constrained. Immediate steps are required to ensure that there is wider coverage of small and marginal farmers by institutional sources.

Agricultural credit constitutes an important part of priority sector lending by commercial banks. A target of 18% of net bank credit has been stipulated for domestic scheduled commercial banks for lending to agriculture. To ensure that the focus of the banks on credit flow to the direct category of agricultural advances is not diluted, a cap has been stipulated for the lending under the indirect category at 4.5% of net bank credit. Public sector banks have been formulating Special Agricultural Credit Plans (SACPs) since 1994–5 by fixing self-set targets for disbursement during a year (April–March). With the introduction of SACP, the flow of credit to the agricultural sector by public sector banks has increased substantially from Rs. 8255 crore in 1994–5 to Rs. 29,332.39 crore during 2001–2.

Data relating to the outstanding agricultural advances of public sector and private sector banks show that the amount of outstanding advances to agriculture in absolute terms has increased substantially over the years, although as percentage to net bank credit, it is below the stipulated level of 18% and hovers at 15% (See Table 2.1).

The tables given below show the relative changes that have occurred in borrowing by cultivators, institutional credit flow, private sector capital formation, the gross value of outputs, inputs and short-term credit, the non-performing assets in the priority sector and the recovery position of agricultural loans by Rural Financial Institutions (RFIs).

Table 2.2 Ratio of Direct Agricultural Credit (Disbursements) to Agricultural Gross Domestic Product (GDP), Total GDP and Total Credit

(in percentage)

	Agricultural Credit/Agricultural GDP	Agricultural Credit/Total GDP	Agricultural Credit/CS
1950–1	0.5	0.3	Not available
1960–1	3.3	1.3	Not available
1970s	5.4	2.1	10.8
1980s	8.3	2.6	8.5
1990s	7.4	2.0	6.4
2001–2	8.7	2.0	5.5

(Source: RBI Bulletin, November 2004.)

Table 2.3 Relative Share of Borrowing of Cultivator Households from Different Sources

Sources of Credit	1951	1961	1971	1981	1991
A. Non-institutional	92.7	81.3	68.3	36.8	30.6
i) Moneylenders	69.7	49.2	36.1	16.1	17.5
ii) Traders	5.5	8.8	8.4	3.2	2.2
iii) Relatives/Friends	14.2	8.8	13.1	8.7	4.6
iv) Landlords and others	3.3	14.5	10.7	8.8	6.3
B. Institutional	7.3	18.7	31.7	63.2	66.3
v) Government, etc.	3.1	15.5	7.1	3.9	5.7
vi) Cooperative Societies/ Banks	3.3	2.6	22.0	29.8	23.6
vii) Commmercial Banks, etc.	0.9	0.6	2.4	28.8	35.2
viii) Others	-	-	0.2	0.7	1.8
C. Unspecified	-	-	-	-	3.1
Total	100.0	100.0	100.0	100.0	100.0

(Source: All India Debt and Investment Survey, 1991–2, Salient Features, RBI Bulletin, May 1999.)

The flow of credit to the agricultural and rural sector has expanded impressively over time. The total short-term credit flow from all banks (commercial banks, RRBs, cooperative banks) had increased from about Rs. 2148 crore during 1981–2 to a level of Rs. 40,387 crore during 2001–2, while the term-credit given for financing investment activities by the farmers increased from Rs. 1601 crore in 1981–2 to Rs. 21,555 crore in 2001–2 (Table 2.3). However, an area of concern in rural banking is the declining trend observed in the coverage of borrowers in the agriculture sector by the commercial banks. The number of accounts with outstanding (direct) credit to agriculture by commercial banks declined from a peak of 20.7 million by March 1995 to 15.7 million by March 2002, i.e., by about 25%. Steps are required to reverse the trend and ensure that there is a wider coverage by the commercial banks of the small and marginal farmers and weaker sections of society.

Table 2.4 Decadal Average Shares of Institutions in Direct Agricultural Credit (Disbursement)

(in percentage)

	Cooperatives	RRBs	Commercial Banks
1970s	79.5	2.3	21.0
1980s	55.9	5.3	38.9
1990s	51.5	6.2	42.3
2001–2	44.0	11.0	45.0

(Source: RBI Bulletin, November 2004.)

Table 2.5 Institutional Credit Flow from 1997–8 to 2002–3 (Amount in Rupees, crores)

Particulars/Agency	1997–8	1998–9	1999–2000	2000–1	2001–2	2002–3	CGR (%)
I. Productions (ST) Credit							
Cooperative banks	10877	12514	14771	16528	18673	20247	13
RRBs	1396	1710	2423	3245	3769	4156	24
Commercial banks	8349	9622	11697	13486	17904	21873	21
Other agencies	18	57	74	55	41	5	
Sub-total (A)	20640	23903	28965	33314	40387	46281	18
II. MT/LT Credit							
Cooperative banks	3098	3356	3489	4190	4780	4049	5
RRBs	644	750	749	974	1053	1311	15
Commercial banks	7482	8821	13036	14321	15683	19160	21
Other agencies	92	30	29	28	39	9	
Sub-total (B)	11316	12957	17303	195113	21555	24529	17
III. ST + MT/LT CREDIT							
Cooperative banks	14085	15870	18260	20718	23453	242296	11
RRBs	2040	2460	3172	4219	4822	5467	22
Commercial banks	15831	18443	24733	27807	33587	41033	21
Other agencies	110	87	103	83	80	14	
Grand Total (A+B)	**31956**	**36860**	**46268**	**52827**	**61942**	**70810**	**17**

(Source: Annual Report, 2004, NABARD.)

Institutional credit plays an important role in encouraging private sector capital formation in agriculture and allied sectors. The private sector capital formation in agriculture and allied sectors increased from Rs. 276 crore in 1960–1 to Rs. 8,402 crore in 1990–1 and further to Rs. 22,181 crore in 1999–2000 (at current prices). The term-credit which accounted for about 10.9% of the private capital formation during 1960–1, increased over the period to 47% during 1980–1 and further to 65.5% during 1999–2000 (Table 2.3). It implied that more and more private sector capital formation is being financed by the credit from institutional sources.

Table 2.6 Private Capital Formation and Share of LT Credit (Rupees in crores)

Year	Private Sector Capital Formation	Investment Credit	Proportion (%)
1980–1	2843	1335	47.0
1990–1	8402	4208	50.1
1995–6	13066	8704	66.6
1996–7	15517	9470	61.0
1997–8	17444	11316	64.9
1998–9	19311	13264	68.7
1999–2000*	22181	14525	65.5

* Provisional

(Source: Report on Trend and Progress of Banking in India, 2001–2.)

Table 2.7 Gross Value of Outputs, Value of Inputs and Short-term Credit (Rupees in crores, 1993–4 prices)

Year	Gross value of Output	Value of Inputs	Short-term Credit	ST Credit as % to	
				Value of Inputs	Value of Output
1993–4	204874	27413	9752	35.6	4.8
1994–5	215334	29559	10606	35.9	4.9
1995–6	212244	31829	12560	39.5	5.9
1996–7	232833	30735	13330	43.4	5.7
1997–8	225746	31669	14030	44.3	6.2
1998–9	245413	34566	14642	42.4	6.0
1999–2000	246330	36596	16307	44.6	6.6

(Source: Report on Trend and Progress of Banking in India, 2001–2.)

Table 2.8 Non-performing Assets (NPAs) in the Priority Sector

Priority Sector Segment	Amount of NPAs	% to Total
Agriculture	7,311.4	30.76
Small-scale sector industries	10,285.0	43.28
Other Priority Sectors	6,169.3	25.96
Total	**23,765.7**	**100.00**

(Source: Report on Trend and Progress of Banking in India, 2001–2.)

Table 2.9 Recovery Position of Agricultural Loans by RFIs (Percentage of recovery to demand as at the end of June)

Agencies	1994	1995	1996	1997	1998	1999	2000	2001
SCBs	89	90	90	86	84	81	83	84
DCCBs	67	70	69	70	70	70	69	67
SCARDBs	57	62	61	62	61	62	62	58
PCARDBs	62	61	57	59	55	60	58	53
RRBs	46	51	55	57	60	64	68	71
CBs*	57	60	62	63	67	68	68	N.A.

* Direct agricultural lending by commercial banks

(Source: Annual Report, 2002, NABARD.)

Development of agriculture would depend to a great extent on improvement in infrastructure, which will increase credit absorption capabilities. To provide loans to state governments for the creation of rural infrastructure at reasonable rates, the Rural Infrastructure Development Fund (RIDF) was set up in 1995–6 under the initiative of the central government. Under the scheme, the central government through budgetary outlays contributes to the corpus funds of RIDF. Since the year 1995–6, public sector and private sector banks with shortfalls in lending to priority sector/agriculture have to contribute to the RIDF. So far, nine branches of the RIDF have been established, with an aggregate corpus of Rs. 34,000 crore. The RIDF is utilized to assist state governments in the completion of ongoing rural infrastructure projects. An issue flagged here is that loans through RIDF are indirect borrowing by state governments from banks and represent a diversion of funds earmarked for the agriculture sector. This mechanism represents at best a marriage of convenience, for both state governments and public sector banks; while the former are provided with ready access to funds, the latter are assured of steady returns on the investment. There is criticism that the RIDF mechanism is incentive-incompatible with the need for the stepping up of credit in the agriculture sector, and offers a soft option to state governments and a virtual exit option for banks.

In the case of RIDF-I to RIDF-VI, the rate of interest on deposits placed by banks in the Fund was uniform for all banks irrespective of the extent of their shortfall. Effective RIDF-VII, it was decided to link the rate of interest on RIDF deposits to the banks' performance in lending to agriculture. Accordingly, as a measure of penalty, banks receive interest from NABARD on contribution to RIDF at rates of interest inversely related to the shortfall in agricultural lending.

In the case of RIDF-VIII, these rates of interest ranged between 8% and 5% per annum. Furthermore, for ensuring parity in risk weights assigned to direct priority sector lending and RIDF, these have been fixed at par at 100%. It has also been decided that in the future interest on RIDF loans would be fixed by adding 2% to the prevailing bank rate. Still, the disbursements under the RIDF have been extremely disappointing.

Table 2.10 Expected and Actual Disbursements under Different Branches of RIDF (as on 31 March 2002)

RIDF Branches	Corpus	Amount Phased up to 31 March 2002	Amount Disbursed up to 31 March 2002	% of Disbursement	
				Sanction	Phasing
RIDF I	2000	1910.54	1760.7	92.2	92.2
RIDF II	2500	2619.57	2249.9	85.9	85.9
RIDF III	2500	2693.18	2183.1	81.1	81.1
RIDF IV	3000	2988.35	1863	62.3	62.3
RIDF V	3500	3568.38	1969.3	55.2	55.2
RIDF VI	4500	3872.32	1899.1	41.4	49
RIDF VII	5000	1479.09	1116.6	22	68.2
Total	**23000**	**19131.4**	**13042**	**55.7**	**68.2**

(Source: Report on Trend and Progress of Banking in India, 2001–2 and Annual Report of NABARD, 2001–2.)

2.11 Average Number of Accounts in Relation to Size

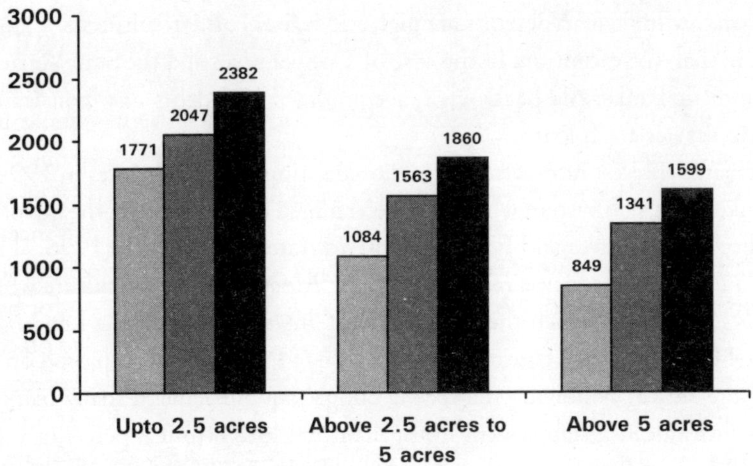

(Source: NABARD)

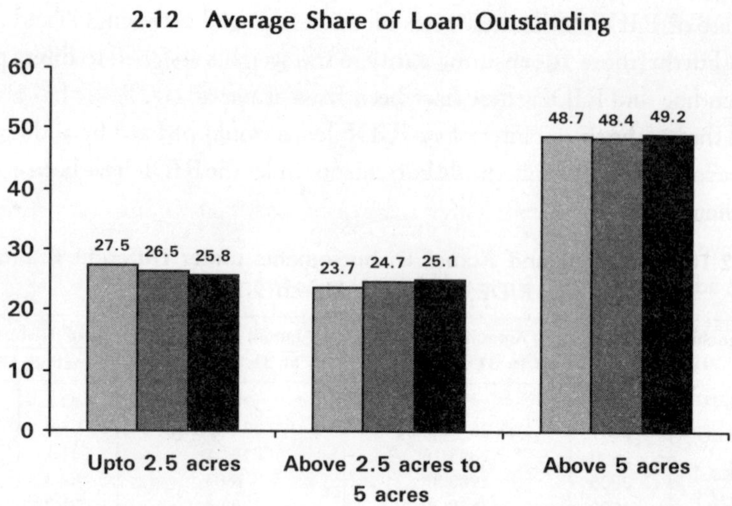

(Source: NABARD)

Interest rates are not an issue for banks; for farmers the timeliness and adequacy of credit is more important than the cost of credit. However, the growth rates of credit in the agriculture sector are impressive, but the sector continues to be credit starved. Even though credit to the sector has increased over the years, it is still not sufficient to meet all the needs of the sector. Historical reasons also contribute to the perception by banks of lending to this sector as risky, the transaction costs of bank loans are high, loan defaults are high and waivers of agriculturists' loans more the norm than the exception. In the case of Cooperatives and the State Agriculture Development Banks, the backlog of accumulated bad debts also constrains the ability to service fresh loans.

As regards interest rates, after the nationalisation of interest rates in 1994, they were linked to a slab system which was determined on the basis of the quantum of loan. For Cooperatives and RRBs the interest rates were freed in 1996. The cap of 12% for small loans was removed in year. Most loans to agriculture would be below Rs 2 lakh for which the ceiling rate of interest is the Prime Lending Rate (PLR). There has been a continuous reduction in PLR and this is passed on to the agriculture sector. Following the recent Budget announcement, many banks have further introduced a slab system for agricultural loans from 2 percentage points below PLR and 2 percentage points above PLR, keeping the ceiling for loans below Rs 2 lakh at PLR, recognising that the benefits of the softening interest rate regime were not being passed on to the farmers.

The RBI has taken a slew of measures for the expansion of agricultural credit. An innovative measure has been the introduction of the Kisan Credit Cards (KCC), which has been well received both by banks and borrowers. Cumulatively, 95.16 lakh KCCs had been issued by public sector banks since the inception of the scheme upto December 2002. All eligible farmers were to be covered under the KCC scheme within the next three years (i.e., by March 2004). All commercial banks have been instructed accordingly.

As an additional measure for furthering the interests of the farming community, a Personal Accident Insurance Scheme for the KCC holders has been introduced. The scheme provides a personal insurance package to the KCC holders to cover them against accidental death or permanent disability, upto a maximum amount of Rs 50,000 and Rs 25,000 respectively. The premium burden is to be shared by the banks and the KCC holder in the ratio of 2:1.

The high-level committee on agricultural credit to commercial banks, appointed by the RBI in December 1997, recommended several procedural modifications with regard to agricultural advances which included simplification of procedures/forms in respect of applications, agreements etcetera, discretion to banks on matters relating to margin/security requirements for agricultural loans above Rs. 10,000 etc. These have been implemented and have facilitated ease of access to credit by farmers from banks and enabled them to get timely and adequate credit from banks for meeting not only their production needs but also their household and/or post-harvest expenditure.

The other steps taken include expansion of the scope of lending to agriculture by commercial banks to incorporate lending through Non-banking Finance Companies (NBFCs), loans to agri-clinics and agri-business centres, loans for purchase of land by small and marginal farmers etc. The ceilings under priority sector of various activities have been enhanced (such as distribution of inputs for allied activities, supply of drip/sprinkler irrigation and other agricultural machinery irrespective of the location of the suppliers). To help farmers store their agricultural produce, the ceiling of produce (marketing) loans has been increased from Rs 1 lakh to Rs 5 lakh, and the period raised from six months to one year.

With a view to promoting investment in agriculture, particularly in high-tech areas such as aquaculture, floriculture, pisciculture, etcetera, all scheduled commercial banks have been advised to set up at least one Specialized Agricultural Finance Branch (SAFB) in each state to be set up by the conveners of the respective State Level Bankers' Committees (SLBCs). Public sector banks have opened 61 such SAFBs so far. However, their contribution does not appear to have been significant.

Irrigation needs much greater attention than it has been given. There has been a decline in the outlay for irrigation in the Tenth Plan; also a decline in public investment in agriculture has led to a decline in investment in irrigation facilities. This needs immediate redress. Of the various environmental and biochemical determinants of agricultural productivity, irrigation is often cited as the critical factor in as much as it raises cropping intensity, permits changes in crop patterns in favour of more productive crops and increases crop yields. It has therefore been referred to as the leading input for agricultural growth.

2. Decline in Public Investment in Agriculture

Public investment in rural infrastructure has great influence on agricultural potential – it can be a critical input or a critical bottleneck for the growth of our agricultural potential. Public and private investments are largely complementary. Public investment in large irrigation works, rural electrification, agricultural research and extension is important. Similarly, public investment in transport, storage and communication has also been crucial in bringing surplus output to the market and improving specialisation.

In recent years, the share of agriculture in the GDP has shown a decline; this by itself is not a cause for concern, as it is a feature of all economies in transition. As economies grow, the secondary sector gains in importance, and this in turn is displaced by the burgeoning services sector. There has been a significant decline in public investment in agriculture, and private investment has not been able to keep pace with the needs of this sector. This is also a significant reason for the drop in yields and output. Public investment in this sector is vital due to its positive ramifications. Irrigation, agricultural research and extension, soil-testing services, farm electricity, land reforms, institutional reforms, adequate availability of high yielding seeds etc. cannot be generated on their own or by farmers working through Farmers Service Associations. These have to be generated through public investment due to the positive externalities of public investment, which cannot be captured by private, cost-benefit analysis. There is a critical need for greater public investment in agriculture infrastructure. The decline in the growth rate of Gross Capital Formation (GCF) in agriculture is a cause for serious concern. GCF in Indian agriculture is declining: GCF in agriculture as a percentage of the total GCF in the country declined to 7.96% in 1999–2000 as against 15.44% in 1980–1.

A direct fallout of the decline in public investment has been a marked deceleration in input use, growth of technological innovation, decrease in the expansion of irrigation, stagnation in employment etc. There has to be a serious revival of public investment in agriculture to increase infrastructure so as to increase credit absorption capabilities in the agriculture sector.

3. Decline in Agricultural Productivity

The decline in the productivity of Indian agriculture is a worrying trend. The area under cultivation is restricted as there is a limitation on cultivable area. Hence agricultural growth has to be centred on productivity increases to keep pace with the growth in population.

The deceleration in yield growth was spread across both foodgrains and non-foodgrains and all crops during 1970–1 to 2001–2. Moreover, there was increase variability in agricultural production during the latter part of the 1990s, primarily due to fluctuation in acreage in the case of foodgrains.

The overall growth rate of agriculture in the 1990s has been low against the trend of growth in the 1980s. Based on all-crop Index Numbers of Agricultural Production (base: triennium-ending 1981–2=100), the growth rate based on semi-log (exponential) trend averaged 3.2% for the 1980s (1980–1 to 1989–90) and 2.4% for the 1990s (1990–1 to 1998–9).

Table 2.13

Period	Area	Foodgrains Production	Yield	Area	Non-food-grains	Yield	Area	All Crops Production	Yield
1970–1 to 2000–1	-0.03	2.52	2.13	1.46	3.31	1.66	0.35	2.83	1.93
1970–1 to 1979–80	0.44	1.91	1.06	1.10	2.15	1.00	0.59	1.99	1.03
1980–1 to 1989–90	-0.22	2.81	2.71	1.11	3.70	2.27	0.09	3.13	2.52
1990–1 to 1999–2000	0.07	1.98	1.30	1.29	2.77	1.08	0.41	2.30	1.19

(Source: Report on Currency and Finance, 2000–1, RBI.)

The Index Numbers for area and yield are available only till 1997–8. However, it is apparent that the decline in production in the 1990s is on account of stagnation in the area under cultivation for foodgrains, and deceleration in yield rates in respect of both foodgrains and non-foodgrain crops. In the 1990s, output expansion has decelerated in the case of rice, which recorded a growth rate of 1.7% based on exponential trend. Wheat production has continued to grow at a noticeable rate of 3.3% per annum. The yield improvements have been lower in the case of both rice and wheat in the present decade compared to that recorded in the 1980s. However, the trend growth rate in wheat output has been maintained in the 1990s mainly on account of renewed expansion in the area under this crop. While India has touched the international yield level in the case of wheat, the yield rate of rice is far below the world average. The coarse cereals output continued to suffer as the area under cultivation declined at a rate of 2% per annum in the 1990s. In the case of pulses, the trends of the 1980s have been maintained in respect of area, production and yield in the absence of any noticeable technological breakthrough. The production of oilseeds decelerated in the 1990s, but still recorded a satisfactory growth rate of 3.7% per annum. The expansion in area has tapered off in the case of oilseeds possibly indicating limits to the compositional shift in the face of endowment consideration. The trend of growth in the case of sugarcane has been by and large maintained. There has been some acceleration in the production of cotton in the 1990s, mainly as the area under this crop has expanded at a remarkable rate of 3% per annum, in contrast to the shrinkage in the 1980s.

Season-wise, the exponential growth rate of 3.4% in rabi foodgrain production witnessed in the 1980s was sustained in the 1980s. In fact, rabi production could have been higher but for a decline in productivity in the 1990s. Thus, the growth in the production of foodgrains was by and large confined to kharif crops. The kharif crops recorded an exponential growth rate of 0.7% during the 1990s as against 2.3% during the 1980s, reflecting, primarily, the impact of continued shrinkage in the area under cultivation.

The competitive strengths of Indian agriculture can be enhanced through improvements in productivity and efficiency levels; by adding more value to the activities of this sector, through increase in value added per hectare, more so on small and marginal holdings; improvement in productivity of inputs especially purchased inputs as fertilizer and irrigation water, and prevention of environmental degradation of land and water resources.

4. Decline in Research and Development Expenditure

Research and development has been largely neglected in Indian agriculture and forms only 0.3% of the country's agricultural GDP, as against the norm of 1%, which has also been endorsed by policy makers.

To keep pace with recent changes and to make Indian agriculture globally competitive we need to increase expenditure on research and development in agriculture and increase extension. Agricultural research systems need to be revitalised to develop new products through biotechnology and genetic engineering. Research and extension are vital for the growth of a vibrant and dynamic agriculture sector. Greater public investment is required in agricultural research and development; private participation in frontier areas like natural resource management and biotechnology is essential. Lab-to-land policies successfully experimented with in China should be operationalised. Plant breeding, agronomic research and, the efficacy of services that convey the knowledge of new varieties and improved techniques to farmers have to be stepped up.

5. Decline in Irrigation Watershed Development

Only 39.2% of the gross cropped area was under irrigation in 1998-9. The share of public expenditure on irrigation and flood control compared to total expenditure has declined over the years. The share which was 10% during the Sixth Plan period (1980–5) came down to 7.6% during the Seventh Plan period (1985–90) and was further reduced to 6.5% during the Eighth Plan (1992–7) period. During the Ninth Plan period (1997–2002) the share remained at around 6.5%.

Table 2.14 Development of Irrigation Potential and its Utilisation (in million hectares)

Irrigation Schemes	At the end of the Seventh Plan 1985–90	At the end of the Eighth Plan 1992–7	Ninth Plan Target 1997–2002	At the end of 1998–9*
Major & Medium Irrigation				
Potential	29.9	32.96	9.81	34.66
Utilisation	25.5	28.44	8.71	30.12
Major Irrigation				
Potential	46.6	56.6	7.24	58.11
Utilisation	43.1	52.32	4.93	53.54
Total				
Potential	76.5	89.56	17.05	92.79
Utilisation	68.6	80.76	13.64	83.66

* Provisional

Figures are provisional and subject to change as information from some of the states has not been received by the Planning Commission.

Note: Irrigation projects with a Culturable Command Area (CCA) of more than 10,000 hectares are classified as major projects and projects with CCA of more than 2000 hectares and upto 10,000 hectares as medium projects. Minor projects have CCA of less than 2,000 hectares.

(Source: Economic Survey, 2001–2.)

Watershed development requires high priority to augment irrigation facilities in rain-fed areas. Watershed development programmes should be more people-oriented and Panchayati Raj institutions should be actively encouraged to be involved in them to operationalise the 73rd amendment in spirit. The Panchayats should be given financial and administrative powers in this regard. Institutional reforms and stronger infrastructure are required. There has been an overexploitation of ground water in certain parts of the country, which represents a dangerous trend.

A watershed is a geo-hydrological unit, comprising of one or more villages, which drains into a common point. The process involves not only soil/water conservation and stabilization of vegetation but also the enhancing of the productivity of resources. The responsibility of planning, executing and maintaining the watershed projects, which usually run for a period of five years, is entrusted to local peoples' organizations/associations.

Subsequent to the issuance of the 'Guidelines for Watershed Developments', popularly known as Common Guidelines, in 1995, a number of studies were conducted to suggest improvements in the guidelines, make it contemporary, transparent and easy to follow. Accordingly, a revised set of Guidelines for Watershed Development (2001) was formulated by the Government of India, to ensure, inter alia, greater flexibility in implementation, removal of overlaps, greater role for women, establishing credit facility from financial institutions etc. There is a need for SHGs, water-user groups, greater participation by the people etc.

In order to seek additional income-generating activities, SHGs are being organized in such project areas. However, the continuation of such SHGs is affected by the availability of limited funds. Maintenance of assets created in such watershed projects also requires financial assistance by user groups. Besides, the livelihood activities to be undertaken in rural areas for the benefit of the landless people residing in the project area require provision of additional funds. The revised guidelines by the government provides for availing of credit facilities from banks/ financial institutions by Watershed associations/District Rural Development Agencies (DRDAs) for developmental work in the project areas.

Following the success of the Indo-German Watershed Development Programme introduced in Maharashtra in 1992, the Government of India had declared the formation of a Watershed Development Fund. Accordingly, NABARD has set up a Watershed Development Fund (WDF) with a corpus of Rs. 200 crore contributed equally by the government and NABARD.

With the introduction of variable interest rates on deposits of banks in RIDF depending upon the shortfall in lending to agriculture, effective RIDF-VII, NABARD has been advised to credit the margin available to it in excess of the normal usual margin of 0.5% in the WDF.

6. Minimum Support Prices for Procurement of Buffer Stocks

The food management policy of the Government of India has all along been geared to ensure food security and the Public Distribution System (PDS) is an important mechanism for achieving this objective. Buffer stocks of foodgrains were to be built up to cushion the country against any large shortfall in the production of foodgrains, and a PDS was set up to distribute foodgrains at an issue price generally lower than the market. The increase in support prices had contributed to a notable build-up of stocks of foodgrains with official agencies. Stocks are substantially higher than the norms prescribed for the Ninth Five-Year Plan. The narrowing of the price differential between the PDS prices and open market prices was reflected in the sluggish rise in offtake in recent years. Many recent empirical studies also suggest that there has been a secular decline in world commodity prices in the last few years. The international price of wheat is less than the domestic price and the Minimum Support Price (MSP).

The MSP mechanism was intended to encourage higher investment and adopt high-risk new technology and take care of the possible hazard of high input cost. Moreover, it is considered to be an effective instrument of changing the cropping pattern in the desired direction. However, the fixing of an MSP has thrown up an issue, namely, whether MSPs of crops should be fixed on the basis of import parity price or annual cost of production, a concern expressed in the Ninth Plan document. The MSP could impede the international competitiveness of exportable goods, and cannot remain unnoticed. The question is how to evolve a viable MSP policy that would provide adequate incentive to farmers without impacting on the international competitiveness of Indian products. The issue gains in importance as agricultural exports are going to be affected. Empirical studies have brought out the superiority of the option of variable levies on trade compared to buffer stocking in stabilising prices in a framework of liberalised trade. This option needs careful consideration, as it is becoming increasingly evident that stabilisation operations involving physical handling of foodgrains are expensive. The carrying cost of buffer stocks has been estimated to be rising at the rate of 15% per annum in the 1990s.

Our agricultural policies are rooted in an era of shortages as a consequence of which there are serious conflicts in domestic policies relating to production procurement, pricing and distribution. The domestic agricultural marketing system continues to be highly restricted and overly regulated.

The MSP has created perverse incentive structures. Currently the MSP, rather than being a base level support price, is treated as a preferred price offered selectively in some states by the Food Corporation of India (FCI) which operates as a buyer of the first resort. This has dangerous side-effects and leads to much inequity and waste, and encourages distorted cropping patterns. In practice, the price support system exists only for rice and wheat. Incentives in the form of price subsidies have led the Punjab farmer, for instance, to opt only for the cultivation and rotation of wheat and rice, leading to the neglect of dryland crops. The fallout has been the fall of the water table as a result of the commercialisation of ground water and over pumping, and detriment to soil fertility due to the excessive use of nitrogenous fertilisers. As prices are guaranteed, farmers also have little incentive to improve the efficiency of crop productivity. Procurement operations are confined to two crops: wheat and rice and four states: Punjab, Haryana, Andhra Pradesh and Uttar Pradesh. Thus the benefits of procurement are not passed on to all the states. The comparative advantage, which exists in the production of fruit and vegetables, is not being availed of by the farmers due to the distortion in incentives created by the price structure. Diversification can only take place if the government plays the role of an enabling agent. The policy of open-ended procurement at MSPs, in some cases, higher prices than those fixed by the Commission for Agricultural Costs and Prices, have led to an accumulation of food stocks. The carrying costs of these food stocks are prohibitive. Ironically, the poor for whom these are meant are often without access to them. Procurement prices are raised in response to political pressures and are disguised as populist measures; the reality however is quite different. The high prices offered for rice and wheat have placed these commodities beyond the reach and far above the purchasing power of the rural and urban poor. This is evident also from the low offtake after the introduction of the targeted PDS in 1997.

To sum up, the objectives of price policy have been marked by multiple, conflicting objectives and a lack of clarity. Agricultural price policies comprise an MSP to ensure that producers of certain commodities, mainly cereals, are not put to loss should the market price fall below a certain minimum level, i.e., to function as a cushion against price-induced risk, and ensure that there is no large shortfall in foodgrain production. The MSP, which was initially based on the paid out or variable cost of production, has now been enlarged to take care of the full cost of production. The principle of fixing MSPs on a cost plus basis got established. Procurement price enables producers of certain commodities to sell their produce at a price fixed in advance by the government. The distinction between MSPs and procurement prices was first blurred and later abolished. As a result of mounting subsidies, which follow from high minimum support policies and higher costs of procurement and distribution of foodgrains through the PDS, stocks are released at high issue prices thereby defeating the purpose of making foodgrains available to the weaker sections at below market prices. A concerted effort to use foodgrains for a massive watershed development programme as a food-for-work programme may yield high benefits to the economy. This approach assumes significance in the context of the fact that a sizeable population continues to be underfed and undernourished.

Table 2.15 Procurement of Wheat and Rice (Central Pool)

(in million tonnes)

Marketing year	Wheat		Rice	
	April Quantity	March Percent change	October Quantity	September Percent change
1995–6	12.33	3.9	9.95	-25.7
1996–7	8.16	-33.8	12.22	22.8
1997–8	9.3	14	14.33	17.3
1998–9	12.65	36	11.84	-17.4
1999–2000	14.14	11.8	17.27	46.5
2000–1	16.35	15.6	19.1	10.6
2001–2	20.63	26.3	21.28	11.4
2002–3*	19.03	–	12.23	–

* As on 5 February 2003.

(Source: Food Bulletin, Department of Food and Public Distribution, Government of India.)

Table 2.16 FCI's Economic Cost of Rice and Wheat

(Rupees per quintal)

	1999–2000	2000–1	2001–2	2002–3	2003–4 (BE)
Rice					
A. Acquisition cost	887.3	1014.04	1052.66	1072.69	
i) Pooled cost of grains	831.24	930.41	961.16	981.01	
ii) Procurement incidentals	56.06	83.63	91.5	91.68	
B. Distribution cost	187.5	166.43	151.61	133.68	
Economic Cost (A+B)	**1074.8**	**1180.47**	**1204.27**	**1206.37**	**1248**
Wheat					
A. Acquisition cost	685.51	716.6	739.13	757.64	
i) Pooled cost of grains	518.08	580.66	571.93	585.76	
ii) Procurement incidentals	117.06	135.94	167.2	171.88	
iii) Carry over charges to state governments	50.37	-	-	-	
B. Distribution cost	202	141.66	132.17	121.52	
Economic Cost (A+B)	**887.51**	**858.26**	**871.3**	**879.16**	**921**

(Source: Food Bulletin, Department of Food and Public Distribution, Government of India.)

7. Role of Subsidies

Subsidies in the agriculture sector have become a contentious and sensitive issue. All countries subsidise their agriculture; the European Union is a significant example in this regard. The total support extended to agriculture by the countries of the Organisation for Economic Co-operation and Development (OECD) was US$ 311 billion in 2001, i.e. a staggering 1.3% of the GDP of the OECD countries. In fact, the aggregate measure of support to Indian agriculture is low by the standards of the World Trade Origanisation (WTO)and the international norms do not require us to prune subsidies. In any analysis of subsidy in agriculture it is important to answer the basic question: subsidy for whom? Surely subsidies are meant for the poorer sections, and if the richer segments corner them and the benefits do not percolate down to the poor, there are inefficiencies in the system. An issue of even greater concern is that while public investment in the agriculture sector is declining, fiscally expensive subsidies are increasing. Other than the subsidy bill on buffer stock operations input subsidies are fiscally expensive. The share of fertilizer subsidies in the total explicit subsidies of the central government has increased from 35% in the 1980s to 49.8% in the 1990s; most of this goes towards supporting the fertilizer industry, which is also the case with the power subsidies which result in huge transmission losses, wastage and inefficiencies. Direct and indirect subsidies are now much more than the value of all investments in agriculture, and are growing. Subsidies do not create a long-term competitive advantage. Indirect subsidies, like fertilizer power and irrigation etcetera are not exactly farm subsidies, and lead only to uneconomic resource utilization. It is far more important to increase investment than to increase fertilizer and power subsidies; farm subsidies should be made more direct and linked to the line of sight of the farmer. The first step for reform must be to dismantle the high-cost–high-subsidy regime, which is diverting resources away from productive uses such as investment in research and extension and creating better agricultural infrastructure.

8. Controls on Domestic Trade

State intervention in the free movement of agricultural commodities has impacted the functioning of domestic markets. The inadequate marketing infrastructure is aided by the poor pre- and post-harvest practices. Some of the restrictions placed from time to time on the free movement of agricultural commodities are spelt out below:

- The occasional physical bottling up of marketable surplus of wheat to facilitate the procurement operations of the FCI through the MSP mechanism in Punjab, Haryana and western Uttar Pradesh
- The levy price (compulsory acquisition) system for rice and sugar to enable the government to procure the estimated requirements to feed the PDS and for buffer stocking impacted the efficient functioning of the markets for rice and sugar.
- The operations of the FCI and the PDS are perceived to be distorting the normal regional and seasonal variations of commodity prices and production decisions by farmers relating to both time and locations of sales of marketable surplus, especially in the north-west region.
- The regulatory authorities vested with the several commodity-specific Boards viz. the Cotton Corporation of India (CCI), the National Dairy Development Board (NDDB), the Jute Corporation of India (JCI) and the Tea, Coffee and Tobacco Boards
- Legal and institutional constraints on the free movement of agricultural produce should be removed. Although restrictions on the inter-state movement of goods have been partially eased, states are still attempting to impose controls. If

such controls are lifted and the number of *arthias*/intermediaries are reduced, great progress will be achieved.

- The Essential Commodities Act, 1955, the principal Act which controls production, supply, storage and movement, trade and commerce in a large number of agricultural commodities needs to be entirely dispensed with.
- The Agricultural Produce Marketing Acts also need a fresh look; provisions need to be inserted, as has been done in Karnataka, to allow private and cooperative sectors to take up the direct marketing of agricultural commodities from the farmers' fields without the intermediaries.
- Professionally-managed wholesale markets like the Rythu Bazaar of Andhra Pradesh should be encouraged.
- Value Added Tax (VAT), which is uniform, should be introduced as opposed to the maze of levies, octroi and taxes, which exist at present.
- There should be effective partnerships with banks to break the *arthia*- or middleman-funded informal credit system which promotes a nexus of vested interests.
- Agricultural futures markets should be encouraged as a market-based system to manage and control risk. They would definitely contribute to a more liberalized and open agriculture sector.
- Weather insurance to combat weather uncertainties and price fluctuation linked to weather is also an innovation worthy of attention.

In sum, what is clearly needed is a paradigm shift away from controls instituted in an era of shortages to leveraging competitive advantage in a free and open economy.

The potential of Indian agriculture is tremendous if only the correct policies are put in place. The obsession with food security (a PL-40 psychosis) led to restrictive trade policies both on the import and export of agricultural products, coupled with high protection to industry. The terms of trade for agriculture have improved in the 1990s, but the advantages of the improvement in the terms of trade have been counterbalanced by the increase in input subsidies coupled with control on output prices. This quixotic policy has struck a body blow to Indian agriculture and needs immediate redress. International prices are falling and keeping the prices high will only make agriculture uncompetitive and succeed only in pricing out of the market.

The WTO presents new opportunities; competitive advantage through diversification can be increased. The terms of trade can be so favourable as to make Indian agriculture a competitive force in the world economy.

The inclusion of agriculture in the WTO presents opportunities in the agriculture sector and offers the promise of enhanced exports. Estimates indicate that global trade policy reforms would yield three times the benefit to the developing countries than all the official development assistance they currently receive. Reductions in subsidies provided by the developed countries will raise the prices of agricultural products in the world markets, which will serve to make our products more competitive. Liberalization of agricultural trade worldwide and further improvements in market access will create new openings for our products. However, the downside is also significant: the developing countries, the European Union and the US are reluctant to open up their markets, and weaknesses in current provisions need to be addressed. There is need to ensure that sanitary and phytosanitary barriers to trade are not put in place as technical barriers to trade and that domestic producers do not face the threat of subsidized imports. As a consequence of the support regime being followed by some of the developed countries our exports do not get negatively affected by unfair competition from subsidy-driven production elsewhere.

Despite being a major producer of several agricultural commodities, India continues to be a minor player in international markets. India's traditional exports of tea, coffee, tobacco and spices are being threatened by other exporters eating into the market share, and by fluctuation in the prices of these commodities. Non-traditional exports such as flowers, fruits and vegetables represent sunrise areas of growth potential. Crop diversification will contribute greatly to agricultural growth prospects. We have to leverage competitive advantage by following a policy of diversification in fruits and vegetables. Despite India being the second largest producer of fruits and vegetables, less than 2% of this production is commercially processed as against 30% in Thailand, 78% in the Philippines and 83% in Malaysia. There is huge untapped potential for developing the food and agro industry. Marketing, infrastructure, storage and processing facilities are highly inadequate, leading to significant quantities of farm produce being wasted. A number of hi-tech segments have recently emerged in the agriculture sector, floriculture, aqua culture, vermiculture and Green House technology etcetera, all of which can be further developed to give a boost to the agriculture sector. Low value-addition and poor standards of quality make our products uncompetitive in the world markets; this is also due to the adoption of obsolete methods of processing agricultural products. These areas require immediate redress.

There is a significant need to reform marketing and distribution policies; heavy investments need to be made in establishing cold chains across the country through cold storages, transport facilities etc.

Policy Choices

Tenants, sharecroppers, small and marginal farmers account for a large proportion of the rural poor engaged in agriculture. What Indian agriculture needs are macroeconomic policies to encourage public investment in agriculture, and to redress the infrastructural and institutional bottlenecks that hamper agricultural growth. Policies which need reform relate to foreign trade, inputs such as fertilizers, irrigation and power, subsidies, communication, storage and transportation, and processing distribution and marketing. The economic reforms improved the terms of trade for agriculture. Earlier development resources (financial, physical, human) had been allocated largely to the industry sector; the share of agriculture was reduced commensurably. Indian agriculture is far from being integrated with world markets. This should be a priority. The potential for agricultural exports, of traditional as well as non-traditional products such as cut flowers and fresh fruits, is vast. However in the absence of adequate infrastructure, particularly for exports of perishables and for pre-shipment exports and quality grading, this potential may not be realized. At present, world trade in agricultural commodities is distorted by interventions of major exporting countries such as the European Union and the US. In the absence of trade barriers and domestic interventions, with stable exchange rates, domestic prices will follow the same trend as world prices. Integration with world markets rather than insulation from them would be more stabilizing in many commodities. Similarly within the country it is imperative to remove restrictions on the movement of produce across state boundaries. The composition of public spending should be towards rapid, broad-based agricultural growth by which it would subsume equity considerations and assure poverty alleviation. The scale and composition of public investment in agriculture needs restructuring. Growth-enhancing expenditure on research and development, agricultural extension, transportation, roads, bridges and markets/*mandis* is required, as against the investment in the leaky 'power' bucket with its transmissi and distribution losses or in irrigation which benefits few at the cost of many users. Community water users' associations need to be encouraged. Modern innovation and communication technologies offer innovative ways of extending new ideas and techniques to farmers;

the use of these needs to be optimized. There is a rationale for extending input subsidies for water, fertilizers or electricity only if the intent is to increase the use of those subsidies. If, however, the intention is merely to boost output, then an output subsidy would be more appropriate and should be considered. The flaw in all our subsidies lies in that they are not properly targeted. If the idea of subsidizing inputs is distributional to ensure that those small and marginal farmers have access to subsidies that would not otherwise have used the subsidized inputs, then the subsidies have to be effectively targeted so as to ensure that the poor farmers alone benefit from them and they are not hijacked by large farmers. We argue for direct income transfers to the lowest deciles rather than reliance on subsidies to subserve equity considerations. On the grounds of both efficiency and equity, agriculture requires greater focus and attention for economic growth with equity; reform of our agricultural policies is no longer a choice, it is a necessity.

1. Need to Step Up Public Investment in Agriculture

Public investment in agriculture sets the tone for overall investment in the sector. The role of the government in promoting agriculture is affirmed through its public investments. The sector has been suffering due to the decline in public investment, though private investment has shown an increase, it is mainly confined to minor irrigation mechanization and land-levelling. Public investment, on the other hand, being in medium and large irrigation works, is more broad-based. As the compositions are different, public and private investment cannot be treated as substitutes for each another. Agricultural performance witnessed a dip in the 1990s partly on account of the subdued public investment in agriculture and the lack of diversification. Declining public investment has affected overall real capital formation in this sector.

Resources have to be productively invested in roads, electricity generation and irrigation, which are by nature public goods, and therefore the responsibility of the State. Simultaneous efforts should be made to attract private investment in the agriculture sector for investment in the storage, post-harvest processing and marketing of agricultural products.

2. Steps to be Taken to Enhance Agricultural Productivity to Increase per Hectare Investment

The near plateauing of yields in the 1990s indicates that any further improvements in yields are difficult to accrue unless accompanied by new technological breakthroughs and the establishment of a proper mechanism for extension.

Structural bottlenecks are supply-side bottlenecks arising through the pattern of fragmented and small landholdings, which reduce yields per hectare. Issues of land degradation need to be addressed to increase the productivity levels of agriculture.

The only factor of production with a non-elastic supply is land. Land is a non-renewable resource base supporting all primary production systems. It also serves as storage for water, which supports plants and life. However, this most important natural resource has been neglected, and it faces continuous depletion, suffers from various kinds of erosion, degradation and deforestation. Tonnes of soil mass with major nutrients are washed away every year. Though there had been some sporadic attempts by central/state governments to address the problems of land degradation, it was not until the constitution of the National Wasteland Development Board in 1985 that a national-level integrated approach was initiated in this direction, leading to the launch of a Wasteland Development Programme (1989). This, however, did not bring out the desired result either of an integrated approach by various sectors or the participation of various stakeholders. In contrast to the Green Revolution strategy which achieved a breakthrough in the production of a couple of crops by concentrating on the fertile irrigated areas and on the relatively well-off farmers, the new strategy in the coming years should usher in growth which would have to be pervasive involving use of degraded land, dryland farming, optimal use of water and common property resources. For the total crop output to increase, a three-pronged strategy of area expansion, yield improvement and shifts in crop patterns is required.

3. Need to Enhance Research and Development Expenditure

There is an imperative need for technological upgradation in the agricultural sector. The promotion of diversified agriculture will need a greater concentration of resources on research and extension in new areas. Agricultural universities and agricultural research need revitalization; they hold the key to the growth of this sector. This is attested to by the development programmes launched to augment the production of pulses and oilseeds. Despite high rises in prices, due mainly to the gap between demand and supply, no perceptible increase in the production of pulses is recorded in the absence of technology.

4. Capital Adequacy to Boost Agricultural Production

Capital adequacy to boost agricultural production cannot be stressed enough. The lack of institutional credit for the agriculture sector constrains agricultural growth and development. Credit flow to the agriculture sector through banks needs to be stepped up.

Several measures have been initiated in the 1990s to augment the flow of institutional credit to the rural sector and enhance the efficacy of the credit distribution channel. The growth of direct institutional credit flow towards agriculture and allied activities, however, declined during the 1990s compared to the 1980s. Coupled with a shift in the composition of credit away from medium/long term loans, this could have affected capital formation. These developments indicate that banks may have targeted relatively risk-free irrigated areas and individuals with high net worth to provide priority sector agricultural loans. In comparison, rain-fed and drought-prone areas and relatively poorer households have had greater dependence on informal sources of finance. The deadweight of non-performing assets (NPAs) of agricultural advances has also affected the recycling of credit. The adherence to prudential norms of income recognition, asset classification and provisioning has made banks more conscious of risk. This could also have contributed, at the margin, to the deceleration in the flow of credit to agriculture.

It is important to understand that conventional banking practices do not work for the rural poor. The requirements of physical collateral and the enormous amount of paperwork place bank loans beyond their reach. Poor people cannot afford to risk their limited holdings of land or livestock while illiteracy creates further fear of paperwork. The Kisan Credit Card is an important innovation; more needs to be done to popularize it and make it accessible even to the tenant farmer and the landless labourers. At present it is restricted to farmers with landholdings. Similarly, efforts should be made to accept collateral substitutes or joint liability group models to assess the credit worthiness of the borrowers so that the poor without collateral are not completely beyond the pale of institutional credit facilities of the banks.

5. Irrigation and Watershed Development

Poor water management has been an impediment to agricultural development. Irrigation facilities must occupy a central place in Indian agricultural development strategy; these areas require greater attention. The increase in net irrigated area during the 1990s compared to the 1980s aided rabi cultivation of foodgrains. This has resulted in achieving a substantial growth in wheat production, which is essentially an irrigated rabi crop. The increasing share of rabi production in total foodgrain production has imparted some element of stability to agricultural production in India. This has far-reaching implications for the economy in general, since a stable and growing farm sector can contribute greatly to overall economic stability. Conjunctive use of surface and ground water resources is necessary. The use of in situ moisture management techniques such as mulching, and micro overhead pressurized irrigation systems like drip and sprinkler and Green House technology needs to be encouraged for greater efficiency in using water and improving productivity, especially of horticultural crops. Emphasis also needs to be placed on promotion of water-harvesting structures and suitable water conveyance systems in the hilly and high rainfall areas for rectification of regional imbalances.

The problems of irrigation development and water management in the agriculture sector are known problems. Participatory growth processes like meshing of public and private NGOs, voluntary agencies, Panchayati Raj institutions, the private, corporate sector networks and mutually beneficial partnerships for optimizing benefits are required. The strategy should start with a National Water Policy that would explicate key objectives like priority use by critical sectors, water pricing and cost recovery for development. Micro-credit expansion has not taken place in the agriculture sector. Shahidur Khandekar has explained that the Grameen Bank experiment is an effective institutional method for reaching the poor in the non-farm sector; one of the keys to its success has been the system of weekly repayment of loans. This has succeeded as most of the activities in the non-farm sector are of point-input continuous-output type. In contrast, agricultural operations are point-input point-output type. They can be made to yield continuous income only if the sale of crops is phased out over an extended period. The discipline of weekly repayments is still likely to come up against a variety of strong time preferences for current consumption. Finance is important, but it is not all. Appropriate policies are critical for creating an environment in which financial services can make a difference. Extension services are essential to enable farmers to make optimum and productive use of credit. All efficient functioning markets too are critical to small-scale farmers and entrepreneurs in obtaining the inputs they need to produce and market their products.

6. Minimum Support Prices, Procurement, Offtake and Buffer Stock Policies Need a Re-look

Domestic policies of pricing procurement and distribution need change. The PDS or the revised Targeted Public Distribution System (TPDS) needs another evaluation. Analysts have suggested that food stamps can be issued as an alternative model to plug the large-scale leakages and malpractices inherent in the system. The fair price shops can be brought under the supervision of local bodies such as the Panchayats to make food subsidies more effective as safety nets for the poor. Dispensing with inefficiencies in the procurement pricing and public distribution of foodgrains is required. A progressive correction is required in the prevailing perverse incentive structure for agriculture so that the excessively high MSPs that currently exist for rice and wheat do not continue to distort resource allocation in agriculture as a whole. Food habits have changed. According to a National Sample Survey (NSS) the monthly per capita consumption of cereals in India has declined from 14.4 kg to 12.8 kg in rural areas over the period 1987–97. This is despite the fact that at constant prices, the Monthly Per Capita Consumer Expenditure (MPCE) has risen by 6% in rural areas and by 13% in urban areas over the same period.

The all-India MPCE during 1997 was Rs. 459 out of which expenditure on food was Rs. 255 and on non-food items Rs. 204. In rural areas, the MPCE was Rs. 395, with expenditure on food items Rs. 232 and non-food items Rs. 163, while in urban areas the MPCE was Rs. 645, expenditure on food items Rs. 320 and non-food items Rs. 325. The urban-rural disparity in MPCE was only 12% in Punjab but 100% in Maharashtra. The average household size in the country was 5 in rural areas and 4.6 in urban areas in 1977, but the focus of the agricultural policy is still on rice and wheat production. The reality is that growth in agricultural production will require much faster diversification away from foodgrains alone to fruits, vegetables and processed foods.

7. Role of Subsidies

The issue of mounting agricultural subsidies is a contentious one. It impacts not only the agricultural sector but is also important in the context of fiscal consolidation. Explicit and implicit subsidies for this sector remain large and ill-targeted. The food and fertilizer subsidies are explicit subsidies. In addition, there are three main types of implicit subsidies in the form of subsidies to power, water – through public irrigation projects and credit under priority sector lending norms – and fertilizers. The excessive and unbalanced use of subsidized inputs can have an adverse impact on the performance of agriculture. Appropriate pricing and user charges of such inputs would release resources for improved public investment in new infrastructure projects and for the maintenance of the existing facilities. It is, therefore, important to reduce most of the agricultural subsidies and ensure better targeting of those that are essential for social welfare. However, the subsidy issue is made more complex in the light of falling international agricultural prices.

If these prices return to the mid-1990s levels, the need for subsidies will be correspondingly lower.

There is a need to refine government intervention to retain the competitiveness of Indian agriculture. If user charges can be enforced and fertilizer, power and water subsidies reduced, it will provide a significant public dividend where it is required and enable higher public investment in agriculture. The cardinal choice is whether we should continue with the existing high cost subsidy regime, warts and all, or whether we should take a serious look at our subsidy regime and opt instead to enhance public investment in agriculture.

8. Need to Dispense with Controls on Domestic Trade

The structural transformation of agriculture would need to take into account the structural rigidities emanating from government intervention and the policy initiatives taken to improve agricultural performance. Four initiatives can go a long way in this regard; firstly, strengthening private sector trade by abolishing restrictions on that trade; secondly, making the price stabilization mechanism more efficient by relying on international prices rather than on public procurement prices; thirdly, targeting food insecurity and removing all inefficient subsidies that are now captured largely by the elite; and lastly, making food operations more efficient by withdrawing from all those commercial activities which can be left to the private sector. It has to be recognized that in an open economy scenario government intervention will only serve to further distort prices. Significant cost reduction is needed in the transportation, storage and distribution costs of agricultural products.

Productivity needs to be enhanced; our economy cannot sustain high rates of growth in agricultural trade without enhancing the competitiveness of the farmer in domestic and international markets. The performance of Indian agriculture in the 1990s has often been attributed to the lack of reforms in the agricultural sector. Whereas this is not exactly true, more needs to be done for the agriculture sector, both in terms of sequencing and overall priority. For example, futures trading, particularly in foodgrains, should be promoted first so that dependence on MSP mechanism for price stabilization could be avoided. Similarly, the strengthening of public distribution needs to accompany the relaxation of the Essential Commodities Act, 1955 to ensure uninterrupted supplies of foodgrains to the poor at reasonable prices. As most of the vital reform measures in the agricultural sector, viz., the removal of inter-state restrictions on movement, storage of and trading in foodgrains, were initiated only recently, their impact is yet to be felt, particularly because of the fact that the states have a major role to play in their implementation. The policy of linking allocation of resources from the centre to the states with their performance in implementing agricultural reform measures is a step in the right direction.

The importance of the social objectives of banking and the efforts made by banks to achieve them can be better appreciated, placed in the context of the pre-Nationalisation position. Historically, commercial banking in India was started and developed by businessmen and industrialists whose activities were concentrated mainly in metropolitan cities and port towns. Banking was naturally concentrated in the big cities. As late as December 1967, the two metropolitan cities of Bombay and Calcutta accounted for about one-third of the total deposits and one-half of the total credit disbursed by banks. The ratio of credit to deposits was more than 100% in the metropolitan cities, which meant that whenever a branch was opened in a smaller centre it was with a view to garnering deposits for deployment in the business of the industrialists and businessmen of the urban, mainly metropolitan, areas. Branches of banks in small centres were treated as "deposit branches". At the end of 1967, the credit–deposit ratio was as high as 147.4% for Madras, 128.8% for Calcutta, 116.3% for Ahmedabad and 102.2% for Bombay, while for the country as a whole, the ratio was 69.3%. The study group I of the NCC on 'Organizational Framework for the Implementation of Social Objectives' was headed by Prof. D.R. Gadgil. This group, with the help of voluminous statistical data, pointed out that at the end of December 1967 in 13 districts there was no commercial bank office, in another 13 districts deposits were mobilized but not a single rupee was given by way of advances, in 63 districts per capita credit was less than one rupee and in 61 districts the credit–deposit ratio was less than 10%. Thus, in 550 of 336 districts in the country at that time, banking was virtually absent. The study group also pointed out that between April 1961 and March 1967, while deposit accounts with the banking system increased from 6 million to 14 million, advances accounts had contracted by 22,000 from Rs 10.78 lakh to Rs 10.56 lakh. This implied that funds were mobilized from an increasingly large number of customers, but they were used for the benefit of a smaller number of the people. The efficiency of banks was judged by the percentage of dividend declared. The industrialists/businessmen who controlled the banks used to declare high dividends to keep the small shareholders happy and utilize the funds to corner stocks of sensitive commodities such as cotton, oilseeds and oil to book profits. The opening of branches in smaller centres entailed heavy expenditure and would have had an impact on the profits of banks. The Board of Directors of private sector banks responsible to the shareholders would not have been able to convince the shareholders of the inevitability of lower dividends in the interests of serving the larger objective of spreading banking to all sectors, regions and areas. Thus, pre-Nationalisation, the banks had a restricted operational base. Agriculture, which contributed 40% to the national income at the time, received hardly 2% of bank credit, the bulk of which went to tea plantations. Commercial banks did not consider it their function to lend to agriculture. Even the expert committees which went into the problems of rural credit as the All India Rural Credit Survey Committee 1951–2, the V.L. Mehta Committee on Co-operative Credit, 1960, and the Informal Group on Institutional Arrangements for Agricultural Credit, 1965, headed by the then Governor of the RBI, M.P.C. Bhattacharyya, unequivocally asserted that commercial banks were not suited to lend to agriculture – nothing was more welcome to the private sector commercial banks.

References

Ahluwalia, M. 1978. 'Agricultural Performance and Rural poverty in India'. World Bank Staff Occasional Paper. Washington D.C.: The World Bank.

Desai, B. M. 1997. 'Agricultural Paradigm: A synthesis'. In *Agricultural Development Paradigm for the Ninth Plan under New Economic Environment*, ed. B. M. Desai. New Delhi: Oxford and IBH Publishing Co.

Government of India. 2000. National Agriculture Policy. Ministry of Agriculture.

Gulati, Ashok. 1998. 'Indian Agriculture in an Open Economy: Will it Prosper?' In *India's Economic Reforms and Development: Essays for Manmohan Singh*, ed. Isher Judge Ahluwalia and I. M. D. Little. New Delhi: Oxford University Press.

———. 1999. 'Towards an Agenda for Reforms in Agriculture'. NCAERIEG-World Bank Conference on Reforms in the Agricultural Sector for Growth, Efficiency, Equity and Sustainability, April 15–16.

Gulati, Ashok and Sudha Narayanan. 2002. *The Subsidy Syndrome in Indian Agriculture*. New Delhi: Oxford University Press.

Jalan, Bimal. 2001. Inaugural address delivered at the National Seminar on Value Addition in Indian Agriculture, Bangalore.

Mohan, Rakesh. 2002. 'A Decade after 1991: New Challenges Facing the Indian Economy'. 28th Frank Moraes Lecture delivered at Chennai on 26 July, organized by the United Writers Association and the Frank Moraes Foundation reproduced in the *RBI Bulletin,* November.

Mujumdar, N. A. 'Towards a New Paradigm of Agricultural Growth'. In *Financial Sector Reforms and India's Economic Development,* vol. 2, ed. N.A. Mujumdar. Academic Foundation.

Pursell, Garry and Ashok Gulati. 1995. 'Liberalising Indian Agriculture: An Agenda for Reform'. In *India: The Future of Economic Reform,* ed. Robert Cassen and Vijay Joshi. New York: Oxford University Press.

Rao, Hanumanth C. H. 1994. 'Reforming Agriculture in the New Context'. *Economic and Political Weekly,* vol. 29.

Reddy, Y. V. 2001. 'Indian Agriculture and Reform: Concerns, Issues and Agenda'. Presidential address delivered at the Conference of Indian Society of Agricultural Marketing, Vishakapatnam.

Reserve Bank of India. 2000–1. Annual Report.

———. 2001–2. Annual Report.

———. 2001–2. Report on Trend and Progress of Banking in India.

———. 2001–2. Report on Currency and Finance in India.

Vyas, V. S. 2001. 'Agriculture: Second Round of Economic Reforms'. *Economic and Political Weekly,* vol. XXXVI, no. 10.

——. 2002. 'Changing Contours of Indian Agriculture'. In *Facets of the Indian Economy,* ed. R. Mohan. New Delhi: Oxford University Press.

THREE

Commercial Banks: Strategic Opportunities

Evolution of the Banking System: First Phase

India had a fairly well-developed commercial banking system in existence at the time of independence in 1947. The RBI was established in 1935. While the RBI became a state-owned institution from 1 January 1949, the Banking Regulation Act was enacted in 1949 providing a framework for regulation and supervision of commercial banking activity.

The first step towards the nationalisation of commercial banks was the result of a report (under the aegis of the RBI) by the Committee of Direction of All India Rural Credit Survey, 1951, which is the locus classicus on the subject till date. The Committee recommended one strong integrated State-partnered commercial banking institution to stimulate banking development in general and rural credit in particular. Thus, the Imperial Bank was taken over by the Government and renamed the State Bank of India (SBI) on 1 July 1955, with the RBI acquiring the overriding substantial holding of shares. A number of erstwhile banks owned by princely states were made subsidiaries of the SBI in 1959 as a result of the reorganisation of the princely states. Thus, the beginning of the Plan era also saw the emergence of public ownership of one of the most prominent of the commercial banks. In 1962, the Deposit Insurance Guarantee Corporation was established to provide insurance cover to bank depositors.

The second evaluation of the role of banking in India was undertaken during 1966 as the private banks were still not providing the required support in the form of credit disbursal, more particularly in the unorganised sector. Each leading industrial house in the country at that time was closely associated with the promotion and control of one or more banking companies. The bulk of the deposits collected, were being deployed in organised sectors of industry and trade, while the farmers, small entrepreneurs, transporters, professionals and the self-employed had to depend on moneylenders who used to exploit them by charging high rates of interest. In February 1966, a scheme of social control was set up whose main function was to periodically assess the demand for bank credit from various sectors of the economy to determine the priorities for grant of loans and advances so as to ensure optimum and efficient utilisation of resources. The scheme, however, did not provide any remedy. Though a number of branches were opened in rural areas, the lending activities of the private banks were not oriented towards meeting the credit requirements of the priority/weaker sectors.

There was a feeling that though the Indian banking system had made considerable progress in the 1950s and 1960s, it established close links between commercial and industry houses, resulting in cornering of bank credit by these segments to the exclusion of agriculture and small industries. To meet these concerns, in 1967, the Government introduced the concept of social control in the banking industry. The scheme of social control was aimed at bringing some changes in the management and distribution of credit by the commercial banks. The close link between big business houses and big banks was intended to be snapped or at least made ineffective by the reconstitution of the Board of Directors to the effect that 51% of the directors were to have special knowledge or practical experience. The appointment of a full-time chairman with special knowledge and practical experience of the working of commercial banks or financial, economic or business administration was intended to professionalise the top management. The imposition of restrictions on loans to be granted to the directors' concerns was another step towards avoiding the undesirable flow of credit to the units in which the directors were interested. The scheme also provided for the takeover of banks under certain circumstances.

Political compulsions then partially attributed to the inadequacies of social control in 1969 led to the Government of India nationalising 14 major scheduled commercial banks which had deposits above a certain amount. The objective was to serve better the needs of the developing economy in conformity with national priorities and objectives. Repeating the earlier exercise, 11 years after nationalisation, the Government announced the nationalisation of 7 more scheduled commercial banks above the cut-off size. The second round of nationalisation created an impression that if a private sector bank grew to the cut-off size it would be under the threat of nationalisation.

From the 1950s a number of exclusively State-owned Development Financial Institutions (DFIs) were also set up both at the national and state level, with the lone exception of the Industrial Credit and Investment Corporation (ICICI) which had a minority private share holding. The mutual fund activity was also a virtual monopoly of a government-owned institution, viz., the Unit Trust of India. Refinance institutions in the agriculture and industry sectors were also developed, similar in nature to the DFIs. Insurance, both life and general, also became state monopolies.

Nationalisation

On 19 July 1969, the Government promulgated the Banking Companies (Acquisition and Transfer of Undertakings) Ordinance, 1969 to acquire 14 bigger commercial banks with paid-up capital of Rs. 2850 crore, deposits of Rs. 2629 crore, loans of Rs. 1813 crore and with 4134 branches accounting for 80% of advances. Subsequently in 1980, six more banks were nationalised which brought 91% of the deposits and 84% of the advances in public sector banking.

Under the Nationalisation Act, 14 of the largest privately-owned domestic banks, with deposits of at least 50 crore each were nationalised and the ownership transferred from private hands to the Government of India. In 1980, under the dispensation of the same Act, seven of the largest private banks were acquired each with deposits of at least 200 crore increasing the total number of nationalised banks to 20 by 1980. Thus the evolution of Indian banking in the post-Nationalisation era was imbued with the belief that the development of the banking system in India had to be inspired by a larger social purpose so as to subserve national priorities and objectives. For this it was necessary for the government to take direct responsibility for extension of and diversification of banking services and for the working of a substantial part of the banking system. The nationalisation of banks led directly to the oligopolistic dominance of public sector banks with respect to both deposits mobilised and loans extended. This dominance was achieved primarily by the expansion of these branches and the creation of an extensive branch network consciously undertaken by the government to extend banking to all parts of the country.

Prior to the nationalisation of banks, several rural and semi-urban areas remained under-served by banks. Traditionally, lending was largely collateral-based; there was a concentration of credit in a few sectors to the detriment of agriculture and small-scale industry. At the time of nationalisation, the socio-economic objectives were explicitly laid down and the banks were asked to contribute to the maximum possible extent towards the economic and social development of the country. Traditional banking ethics, it was held, were not compatible with the needs of economic development, and balanced development was not possible without strengthening the hold of commercial banks in the backward and neglected areas. Banks moved from security-oriented, collateral-based lending to Twenty-point-Programme oriented credit. The Banking (Companies Acquisition and Transfer of Undertakings) Act of 1969 was "An act to provide for the acquisition and transfer of the undertakings of certain banking companies in order to serve better the needs of development of the economy in conforming with national policy and objectives and for matters connected therewith or incidental thereto".

Objectives of the Nationalisation of Banks

The nationalisation of 14 major Indian scheduled commercial banks on 19 July 1969 was effected to impart a new ethos to commercial banking in India. The underlying philosophy of nationalisation was that "an institution, such as the banking system, which touches and should touch the lives of millions has necessarily to be inspired by a larger social purpose and has to subserve national priorities and objectives".

In simple language, this meant that banking is a service industry; its functioning affects millions of people. Therefore, the operations of banks should be in alignment with the national policy objectives of increasing production, diffusion of economic power, reduction of inequalities, removal of poverty, etc. Its operational implication was that banks should:

1. considerably expand their branch network in all parts of the country and not remain concentrated in urban and metropolitan areas
2. mobilise funds from all sections of society by framing deposit schemes appropriate to different segments of society
3. deploy funds in all productive endeavours – big or small – so that production effort becomes broad-based
4. pay particular attention to the credit needs of lakhs of people engaged in agriculture and small business enterprises, whose production and distribution effort contributes substantially to the national cake
5. through these measures reduce, if not remove, regional and sectoral imbalances in banking and through that in economic development

Scorecard of Performance

Have the banks moved towards attaining these objectives? What is the record during the last decade? What has been gained and what has been lost? An objective assessment of the achievements of the banking sector since nationalisation, without concealing its shortcomings, is being attempted. The Green Revolution generated a demand for credit, which the cooperative banks, riddled as they were with endemic weaknesses, were quite unable to meet. The commercial banks were envisaged as effective substitutes, which would make amends for the inefficiencies of the cooperative banks.

Prima facie, the balance sheet of gains and losses is an encouraging one; yet there are a few dark spots in the functioning of banks that cause concern. The unprecedented geographical expansion and functional diversification, remarkable social orientation, striking shift in lending policies from asset-base to production-base, imaginative deposit-mobilisation schemes tailored to suit the pockets of different sections of the society are all developments which prove, in unmistakable terms, that the banking system has undergone a major transformation from 'wholesale' banking to 'retail' banking. This change has been described as a change from banking of the 'classes' to banking of the 'masses'. It is known as a 'sea change'! The single most important factor influencing this phenomenal change was the nationalisation of banks. Nationalisation changed the complexion of commercial banking; it kindled hopes of making banks the catalysts of growth to bring about a rapid development of the rural areas. Banks responded magnificently, and the growth recorded by the banking system during the last decade has no parallel in the banking history of the world. This fast pace of change itself, however, created a number of problems like those of trained manpower, deterioration in customer service, declining profitability etcetera, which deserve careful attention.

Generally, the commercial banks, prior to nationalisation, considered it risky and unprofitable to lend to a large number of small borrowers in view of the high transaction cost involved in maintaining records, supervising the small loans, etc. Hence, productive sectors such as agriculture, small-scale industries, road and water transport operators, professionals, the self-employed, small businessmen, retail traders etcetera, were neglected by the commercial banks, even though people engaged in these activities were contributing substantially to employment generation and production of goods and services. Commercial banking thus remained an urban-oriented service.

Post-Green Revolution

The agricultural sector witnessed a technological breakthrough. High-yielding varieties of seeds, fertilizers and better irrigation meant substantially larger yields and the Green Revolution was in sight. Modern methods of agriculture required large amounts of credit to finance the increased doses of inputs. Cooperatives alone could not take up the challenge. No doubt, over the years, the credit provided by primary agricultural credit societies had increased. Even so, they could not have sustained and developed the nascent Green Revolution. A multi-agency approach to rural credit was, therefore, considered necessary. It was argued that commercial banks hold public money in trust; it must be used for public good in accordance with the national policy and objectives.

During December 1969, RBI introduced the Lead Bank Scheme on the recommendations of the F.K. Nariman Committee. In the post-Nationalisation period, there was substantial increase in the number of branches opened in rural/semi-urban centres, bringing down the population per bank branch. During 1976, RRBs were established (on the recommendations of M. Narasimham Committee report) under the sponsorship and support of public sector banks as the third component of the multi-agency credit system for agriculture and rural development. The Service Area Approach was introduced in 1989.

Evolution and Progress of Social Banking

Keeping in view the objectives of nationalisation, public sector banks (PSBs) undertook geographical, spatial and sectoral expansion of reach and services. Resultantly, the number of branches increased seven-fold (from 8321 to more than 60000 out of which 58% were in rural areas) and the number of people served per branch came down from 65000 in 1969 to 10000. Much of this expansion has taken place in rural and semi-urban areas. The expansion is significant in terms of geographical distribution. States neglected by private banks before 1969 now have a vast network of PSBs. The PSBs including RRBs, account for 93% of bank offices and 87% of banking system deposits.

While the 1970s and 1980s saw a high growth rate of branch banking network, the consolidation phase started in the late 80s and more particularly during the early 90s, with the submission of the report of the Narasimham Committee on Reforms in Financial Services Sector in 1991.

In these five decades since attaining independence, banking in India has evolved through four distinct phases.

The Foundation Phase

This phase spans the 1950s and the 1960s till the nationalisation of banks in 1969. The focus during this period was to lay the foundation for a sound system of banking in the country. As a result the phase witnessed the development of the necessary legislative framework for facilitating re-organisation and consolidation of the banking system, for meeting the requirements of the Indian economy. A major development was the transformation of the Imperial Bank of India into the State Bank of India in 1955 and the nationalisation of 14 major private banks in 1969.

The Expansion Phase

The expansion phase had begun in the mid-1960s but gained momentum after the nationalisation of banks, and continued till 1984. A determined effort was made to make banking facilities available to the masses. The network of branches of the banks was widened at a very rapid pace through the Lead Bank Scheme of the RBI to cover the rural and semi-urban population which had no access to banking hitherto and to bridge the spatial and functional gaps in the development of banking. Most of the new branches were in the rural and semi-urban areas reflecting the concern with achieving greater spatial distribution of branches. The banking system achieved a commendable measure of expansion, particularly in rural areas, despite several inhibiting factors such as inaccessibility, poor infrastructure and difficult living conditions. That the banks did it in spite of these constraints is a reflection of their dedication to broader national objectives and their social purpose. However, this weakened the lines of supervision, affected the quality of assets of banks, negatively impacted profitability and brought the competitive efficiency of the system to a low ebb.

The Consolidation Phase

The phase started in 1985 when a series of policy initiatives were taken by the RBI, which saw a marked slowing down in branch expansion. Attention was paid to improving the housekeeping, customer service, credit management, staff productivity and profitability of banks.

The Reform Phase

The major challenge of the reform phase has been to introduce elements of market incentive as a dominant factor gradually replacing administratively-coordinated planned actions for development. Such a paradigm shift has several dimensions, corporate governance being one of the important elements. The evolution of corporate governance in banks, particularly in PSBs, thus reflects changes in monetary policy, regulatory environment, and structural transformation, and to some extent, the character of the self-regulatory organisations functioning in the financial sector.

During the reform period, the policy environment enhanced competition and provided greater opportunity for the exercise of what may be called the genuine corporate element in each bank to replace the elements of coordinated actions of all entities as a 'joint family' to fulfil predetermined Plan priorities.

Greater competition has been infused in the banking system by permitting the entry of private sector banks, liberal licensing of branches by existing foreign banks and the entry of new foreign banks. With the development of a multi-institutional structure in the financial sector, emphasis is on efficiency through competition, irrespective of ownership. Since non-bank intermediation has increased, banks have had to improve efficiency to ensure survival.

The macro-economic crisis faced by the country in 1991 paved the way for extensive financial sector reforms which brought the deregulation of interest rates, more competition, technological changes, prudential guidelines on asset classification and income recognition, capital adequacy and autonomy packages; they also led to an expansion into the micro-credit sector.

The Branch Licensing Policy

The thrust of the new branch licensing policy was on opening branches in under-banked areas particularly in rural and semi-urban areas. The share of rural branches increased over time from a mere 23% in 1969 to 58.5% in 1991; there was a decrease in the number of people served per branch and an increase in bank deposits as a percentage of the national income. The result of the sharp order of branch expansion was a sharp growth of deposits with the system. The banking system services 300 million deposit accounts which, even after allowing for some measure of multiple account ownership, is a measure of its pervasive coverage. The cause of deposit mobilization is as much institutional as it is economic, and it is the availability of banking offices that helped the mobilization of deposits. The financial intermediation ratio and the financial interrelations ratio also rose sharply as a consequence. The objective of transforming banking from 'class banking' to 'mass banking' was also fulfilled through the institution of the priority sector norms.

In a development parallel to nationalisation, the concept of the priority sector was evolved in the late 1960s to focus attention on the credit needs of certain neglected and underprivileged sectors. The principal method chosen for directing the credit flow into the priority sector, including agriculture, was the stipulation that a proportion of the total NBC should be deployed in these sectors by specific target dates. Public sector banks were asked to extend credit to the priority sector to the extent of 40% of their total credit. The target for lending for agriculture and allied activities initially set at 15% of the total credit was steadily increased to 18%. These stipulations continue in recognition of the importance attached to these sectors.

Development of Rural Credit

Offering credit at concessional rates has been one of the elements of the strategy for the deployment of rural credit. The principal justification for charging lower interest rates to certain categories of borrowers has been that farm-based investment activity in the short run does not always yield returns which enable regular servicing of loans while at the same time meeting minimum consumption requirements. Since concessional lending affects the profitability of the RFIs, a policy of cross-subsidisation in commercial banks and refinance from the RBI was put in place simultaneously.

Prior to 1955, all commercial banks were privately-owned. In 1955, the Government of India, in accordance with the recommendations of the All India Rural Credit Survey Committee, took over the ownership of the Imperial Bank of India and reconstituted it as the State Bank of India (SBI) under the State Bank of India Act, 1955. Later in the same year the State Bank of India (Subsidiary Banks) Act was passed, enabling the SBI to take over seven banks of the princely states as its associate banks. The formation of SBI and its seven associate banks was undertaken with the objective of accelerating the pace of the extension and attainment of the priority sector objectives. Prior to the nationalisation of banks, the commercial banks had a policy of benign neglect towards agriculture on the plea that rural credit extension was best suited to the cooperative banks. The failure of Planning in general and in the agriculture sector in particular was attributed to this attitude of indifference on the part of the commercial banks. Thus a much larger role was envisioned for them. The working group on priority sector lending and the Twenty-point Programme set up by the RBI phrased it as under "the concept of priority sector lending is mainly intended to ensure that assistance from the Banking Sector flows in an increasing manner to those sectors of the economy which though accounting for a significant proportion of the National Product, have not received support of institutional finance in the past." The commercial banking system and particularly the PSBs at the behest of the RBI and the Ministry of Finance approached the task with evangelical zeal. As a result, the total credit extended by PSBs to agriculture, small-scale industries and other priority sectors increased from Rs 440 crore in June 1969 to Rs 47850 crore in June 1993. As a result, advances to the priority sector showed an increase from 15% in June 1969 to 43% in 2002. While priority sector advances of PSBs formed 43.1% of NBC as at the end of March 2002, the corresponding percentage for private sector banks was 40.9%. Priority sector lending by foreign banks amounted to 34.2% of the NBC for the same period. Thus all bank groups exceeded the targets under priority sector lending. There was a marginal improvement in the percentage of NBC going to the priority sectors in 2001–2 over 2000–1 in respect of PSBs and private sector banks. The percentage share of priority sectors in the NBC for PSBs and private sector banks was 43% and 38.2% respectively in 2000–1. The share of priority sector lending in the NBC of foreign banks improved marginally from 34.1% to 34.2%.

Post-Nationalisation Era

Post-Nationalisation, banks supported the programmes of the government. Since then, banks have been expected to be partners in the nation's progress towards the realisation of the goal of distributive justice. Equity and welfare considerations, willy-nilly, dominated their policies till 1991. In the initial years, banks were very enthusiastic to do their best. Priority sector advances had a significant element of concessionality and the unit costs of administering these loans were very high.

This contributed to sagging bottom-lines, and soon reduced the enthusiasm of banks. The banking system was plagued by problems of poor performance and low profitability. Through the dispensation of the priority sector, banks were mandated to ensure that at least 40% of advances flowed to designated sectors such as agriculture, small-scale industries and services. Within the 40%, a sub-categorisation of 10% was stipulated for lending to the weaker sections of society defined as the poorest of the poor. A further sub-category, small and marginal farmers, was made to ensure the flow of funds to agriculture. There was a specification that 18% of all advances should be for direct agriculture; this was further subdivided into a 4.5% ceiling for indirect finance flow to agriculture and 13.5% for direct flows. Thus a maze of regulatory prescriptions was created. The statutory pre-emptions were also high; as a consequence the PSBs felt stymied in their efforts at generation of profits.

Attitudinal Shift

Since 1991–2, priority sector targets have been imposed on the foreign banks at 32% with a 10% sub-target for exports and 12% for the small-scale industries sector. The new private sector banks have to fulfil priority sector obligations on par with the commercial banks. The initial enthusiasm for priority sector credit waned on account of several factors including the high administrative and operational costs of these loans. As priority sector loans were of small amounts, PSBs were not able to monitor their distribution and follow up the recovery of tiny loans. This only served to increase their costs on the one hand and diminish profitability on the other. Most of the loaning led to the creation of impaired assets as loaning was politicised. The commercial banks were squeezed in both ways by the high statutory pre-emptions of their deposits clubbing the statutory pre-emptions through Statutory Liquidity Ratio (SLR) and Cash Reserve Ratio (CRR) prescriptions, which in the late 1980s could vary from 52% to 56%. This left the banks with minimal amounts to do the actual business of banking. Priority sector loaning was administered at concessional rates of interest. This narrowed the margins of the banks and put pressure on their balance sheets. Most of the banks, unable to cross-subsidise priority sector lending or extend large loans and earn profits, found themselves incurring huge losses. As they were State-owned there was no immediate fear of collapse, but from a business point of view, this was becoming an unsustainable proposition.

Table 3.1 Advances to the Priority Sectors by Public Sector Banks

Sector	Amount Outstanding (Rupees in crores)				
	June 1969	March 2000	March 2001	March 2002	March 2003
I. Agriculture	162 (5.4)	45,296 (14.3)	53,571 (15.7)	63,082 (15.9)	73,507 (15.3)
i) Direct	40 (1.3)	34,247 (10.8)	38,137 (11.2)	44,908 (11.3)	51,799 (10.8)
ii) Indirect	122 (4.0)	11,049 (3.5)	15,434 (4.5)	18,174 (4.6)	21,708 (4.5)
II. Small-scale industries	257 (8.5)	46,045 (14.6)	48,400 (14.2)	49,743 (12.5)	52,988 (11.1)
III. Other priority sector advances	22 (0.7)	30,816 (9.7)	40,791 (12.0)	53,712 (13.5)	71,448 (15.0)
IV. Total priority sector advances	441 (14.6)	1,27,478 (40.3)	1,49,116 (43.7)	1,71,185 (43.1)	2,03,095 (42.5)
V. Net bank credit	3,016	3,16,427	3,41,291	3,96,954	4,77,899

(Source: Report on Trend and Progress of Banking in India, 2002–3, RBI.)

Widening Disparities

The priority sector lending dispensation had also been introduced with the objective of reducing disparities in the development of the various states of India. It was felt that the lack of credit was inhibiting the development of the backward states. Free flow of credit would help to redress this situation of unequal growth. However, bank-lending to the priority sector was hardly uniform in all the states. It was much lower in states like Bihar, Rajasthan and Uttar Pradesh. To attain the targets of 40% for the country as a whole, the banks were pumping in money into the developed states. This measure created perverse incentives and served to further exacerbate regional imbalances instead of helping to bring them down, as envisaged by the policy makers. The system of directed credit was a qualified success, as advances to certain sectors were no doubt stepped up, but it was at a cost. This was achieved at the cost of deterioration in the quality of the loan portfolio due to fixation of targets for sectoral lending and the need to achieve these targets. No attention was devoted to the quality of lending, pre-sanction appraisal or post-disbursement follow-up and supervision. The priority sector loans were more or less doles. Thereby the welfare function of the State was assigned to banks. The growth of overdues naturally led to erosion in profitability though there was a shift from security-oriented credit to purpose-oriented credit. 'Loan Melas' or 'Loan Mafi' culture was an overt manifestation of the rampant political interference in loaning decisions. This led to a complete subversion of the system.

Expansion or Evasion?

Though the recommendations of the Narasimhan Committee on the Financial Sector Reforms to reduce the priority sector commitments were not accepted within the given policy framework, the scope of the priority sector was considerably expanded. Hence everything and anything, from food processing, to venture capital finance, to large plantation financing, became grist to the priority sector mill. However, there was no relaxation in sub-targets or sub-sectoral ceilings. Despite widening the ambit of the priority sector, if the banks were still not able to fulfil their targets, they were permitted to deposit the amount of shortfall in the RIDF. The RIDF was operationalised through NABARD in 1995–6, to provide loans to state governments and State-owned corporations for quick completion of ongoing projects. Domestic commercial banks contribute to the fund on the basis of their shortfall in lending to the priority sectors/agriculture. The corpus of RIDF-I to RIDF-VIII amounted to Rs 28,500 crore as on 31 March 2002. For the first five years since its inception, the RIDF represented a win-win situation for banks and state governments. Banks which were not able to achieve the targets under agricultural lending could deposit their funds under the RIDF and earn interest on the deposits. The perennially cash-strapped state governments had access to a line of credit for state infrastructure projects through RIDF. NABARD was the gainer of a free float, as the drawing of funds from the RIDF was poor. The state governments were not able to complete project formalities, tendering processes of projects etcetera, in time, hence fund utilisation continued to be poor. The government has now made rates of interest on RIDF deposits inversely proportional to the shortfall in lending for banks, but the RIDF deposits still continue to fetch risk-free return as compared to the uncertain and riskier actual lending to agriculture. The rates of interest which were earlier a handsome 10.5% have now been brought down to 8.5% and are henceforward proposed to be pegged at the bank rate plus two percentage points.

Inherent Weaknesses

Directed credit suffers from well-known infirmities. Subsidised interest rates create an artificially high demand for such credit, accompanied by large-scale diversion of credit. Adverse selection, moral hazard, the difficulties of screening of borrowers, the hassles of enforcement of contracts, all these render directed credit unviable.

High overheads and administrative transaction costs are entailed in monitoring the numerous small-value transactions of the 'penny economy'. The moral hazard is ever-present and there is, to use Akerlof's phrase, always "a market for lemons". This has been reiterated time and again: concessionality in interest rates serves only to attract the wrong set of borrowers; for the genuine borrower not the cost, but the timely availability of credit is important.

Measures of Redress

The system should not be allowed to generate perverse incentives. The rates of interest should not be kept artificially low. These changes would reduce the incentives to cheat to qualify for priority sector lending and reduce the misuse and diversion of such loans. Another refinement in priority sector lending can be to set the loan quota for priority sector lending including quotas for its various sub-categories as agriculture and small-scale industries for the banking system as a whole rather than for each individual bank. While the total quantum of aggregate flows to the priority sector borrowers will remain unchanged it would serve to improve the efficiency of priority sector lending. It has recently been proposed that banks can be allowed to trade the priority sector lending liability among themselves. This trading arrangement will encourage cost reducing specialisation. For instance, one bank may specialise in lending to the small-scale industry, another to agriculture, a third to exporting industries, etc. It will also allow some banks, like the newly emerging private sector banks, to buy their lending obligations from other banks at a price; a level playing field will then exist among them while reducing their costs.

Policy Choices

The major policy question today is whether directed credit is justified on the grounds of either efficiency or equity considerations. For instance, directed credit for the poorer sections of society was introduced on the rationale that banks would not otherwise direct credit to socially-desirable directions. The provision of directed credit at concessional rates of interest was expected to break the stranglehold of 'the evil moneylender' and bring down the cost of credit, commensurably increasing the volume of credit. As financial markets are informationally imperfect, lenders lack the information to screen and monitor borrowers. As poor borrowers cannot furnish collateral security, there are difficulties in foreclosure and lenders tend to ration credit. The extension of banking to rural areas yields social benefits. Externalities of financial infrastructure and the high costs incurred in setting it up have been put forward as another reason for intervention. It is held that the provision of cheap credit is an important means of distributing income and wealth. There is finally the efficiency oriented argument. Banks have not completely succeeded in breaking the monopoly of moneylenders, and they have not made enough efforts to identify promising ventures overlooked by the private sector, due to information asymmetries. Are subsidising rural networks to pay for non-recoverable costs or does priority sector lending generate positive externalities? There is a need for policy debate on the issue through counter-factual studies.

Achievements and Shortfalls

Agricultural Credit Review Committee (Khusro Committee, 1989) confirmed that institutional credit to agriculture has expanded rapidly and rural households as an aggregate obtain 61% of their credit requirements from institutional sources (as against only 12% in 1951). There is a clear and dramatic correlation between household wealth and reliance on institutional credit. For example the poorest households (households with assets less than Rs 100) meet only 9% of their credit requirements from institutional sources. Just as striking is the fact that only 30% of rural families have obtained access to institutional credit. It is self-evident that medium and large farmers (those with holdings above five hectares) have pre-empted a large part of such credit and have consequently received large subsidies. It is also striking that the incidence of overdues is just as bad among the large farmers as it is among the small farmers. One of the possible reasons for this is that they corner agricultural credit and then re-lend it through the informal market.

As with agricultural credit, directed credit to the small-scale sector was extended on the rationale that small-scale firms were discriminated against by banks because of risk aversion and information asymmetries. It was felt that correcting such discrimination would improve both the aggregate output and the distribution of income as the small-scale enterprises are labour-intensive. Concessional credit for small-scale industry comes from institutional sources as it is part of the banks' priority sector target. Finance for small-scale industries is also provided by various DFIs. Majority of them like the State finance institutions are controlled by the state governments but receive subsidised refinance from either the Small Industries Development Bank of India (SIDBI) or the RBI. The SIDBI has evolved several schemes specifically to finance the small-scale industry's units though small firms, especially tiny firms, face an imperfect credit market and an imperfect capital market for well-known reasons. Small firms, particularly in urban areas, are served by the urban informal market which is both large and efficient. The portfolio quality and financial viability of many state-level DFIs has been severely compromised by concessional lending to small firms. The availability of refinance from higher-level institutions has encouraged poor project appraisal. The small-scale sector contains many modern enterprises, particularly at the larger end of the size distribution, which should be treated on the same commercial footing as medium and large-scale firms. The case for subsidies on market failure grounds is weak. This argument is premised on the basis of the institution of temporary subsidies.

Continued Relevance of Directed Credit

On the other hand, the Indian reality is that directed credit has now been subsidised for 35 years, a span of time sufficient to overcome market failures arising from high fixed costs, externalities and lack of competition. This is not to deny that there may still be a valid justification for subsidies in case of specific calamities, but there is certainly no case for permanent interest subsidies. The equity-based argument has also not stood the test of time. The well-intentioned argument of State-owned banks/DFIs reaching the most needy is far too often subjected to political influence. Politicised mandates place undue emphasis on credit outflows over recovery. Poor lending practices such as weak borrower-selection criteria, little or no monitoring and subsidised interest rates weaken the State-owned institutions financially and compel them to be in perpetual dependence. In short, the intent is not to establish a sustainable financial institution that will continue to provide a stream of services to the poor over the long term, but to create credit disbursement channels. Populist, subsidized credit schemes have not been successful; in the past it was easier for banks to cross-subsidize their loss-making branches. This, in the changed context is not a credible alternative for banks. The disbursement of credit through the priority sector has not met with much success. It has proved very difficult to prevent cheap credit being cornered by relatively affluent farmers. It has also been established that the mere provision of credit remains at best an inferior instrument of poverty-alleviation in comparison to other alternatives. It has also been argued that as the very poor lack asset-backing they lack debt-capacity – the ability to service their debts. In view of their circumstances, direct credit transfers and public employment schemes are better options. The targeting of poor borrowers by banks has generally been found to be quite unsuccessful. This begs the question that if concessionality is removed, is there any validity in the continuance of the policy of directed credit? The conclusion is inescapable: directed credit with a sharper sectoral focus will have to continue. Interest rate reform is necessary. Concessionality in rates of interest should be removed; ease of access to credit for the priority sector should however continue and the continuance of this dispensation at the level of policy will help to facilitate this process. Concessional/subsidised interest rates have led to the creation of repressed financial markets. These have not only served to distort credit allocation and the distribution of loanable funds, they have also impeded deposit mobilisation efforts. They have created perverse incentives for rich borrowers to pre-empt credit and for lenders to acquiesce in this process; this offers a level of comfort to lenders as otherwise the interest rates are too low to cover the risks of lending to poor borrowers. The financials of these institutions are weak and they have become mere disbursement windows with a total lack of financial discipline. Directed credit should be retained only for the needs of agriculture. Small-scale industry must be placed beyond the pale of the priority sector. The reform of directed credit is necessary but it is hedged with many complexities involving a plethora of institutional and sequencing issues and necessitates the cooperation of the state governments.

Financial Innovation

The Kisan Credit Cards (KCC) is one outstanding example which has considerably reduced transaction costs and has arguably facilitated credit delivery. The KCC scheme introduced in 1998–9 has increased the farmer's access to credit from institutional sources. The objective of the scheme is to provide adequate and timely assistance from the banking system to farmers to enable them to meet all their cultivation needs including purchase of inputs in a flexible and cost-effective manner. The scheme is being operated by cooperative banks, RRBs and scheduled commercial banks throughout the country. Loans disbursed under the KCC are also eligible for personal accident insurance cover of Rs 50,000 for accidental death and Rs 25,000 for permanent disability. Till the end of September 2002 the total number of Kisan Credit Cards issued was 285 lakh, of which the cooperative banks issued 175.9 lakh cards, followed by PSBs with 87.9 lakh cards and RRBs with 21.2 lakh cards.

Microfinance

Microfinance has emerged as another cost-saving measure to facilitate the channelisation of priority sector credit. In recent years, microfinance has gained growing recognition as an effective tool in improving the quality of life and living standards of very poor people. The Bank Rakyat Indonesia is a successful model of a commercial bank in microfinance which presents several lessons for India. In the context of the broader financial sector reforms that will lead to the State divesting control over the banking system, the earlier models of dispensation of priority sector credit will be increasingly difficult to sustain and microfinance appears to be the best option, given the fact that the needs of agriculture, small and marginal farmers and the poor cannot be wished away.

Indonesian Experience

The Bank Rakyat Indonesia (BRI) presents several parallels with the Indian banks and deserves thorough scrutiny. After gaining independence in 1946, the Government of Indonesia created five State-owned commercial banks, each with a separate mandate. BRI came into being in 1950 with the merger of two older, state banks: Bank Perkreditan Rakyat (established in 1895) and the Algemeneene Volkscrediet Bank (established in 1934). BRI's predecessors were credit and savings institutions that catered to middle-class Indonesians particularly in rural areas. Under the new Government, BRI's purpose was to provide rural banking services with an emphasis on the promotion of agricultural development. Today, BRI is one of the largest banks in Indonesia, with a countrywide network. It has 325 branch offices and 3595 unit desas. It provides a range of services – corporate banking, commercial banking and microfinance. In recent years, BRI's micro-finance operation, also known as the unit desa system has gained attention.

This was not always the case. The BIMAS (Bimbigan Massal or mass guidance) programme was a complete failure. During the 1970s the Government of Indonesia declared self-sufficiency in rice production as one of the national goals, as a way to improve rural living standards and incomes and reducing the nation's dependence on rice imports. In 1973, the Government introduced BIMAS, an agricultural extension service and credit programme to encourage farmers to use new technologies and inputs in rice production. BIMAS channelled subsidized government credit, tied to purchasing various inputs such as improved seeds, fertilisers and pesticides to rice farmers in rural Indonesia. Given its mandate, BRI undertook implementation of the credit programme under BIMAS. Unit desas were established at the village level to operate as retail "windows" of the BRI district-level branch offices. Each unit desa served 18 villages on an average and had four staff members, a unit chief, a credit officer, a bookkeeper and a cashier. One among the factors which contributed to the failure of the BIMAS credit programme was the lack of autonomy. The staff of unit desas had little control over their operations. For example, although the staff gave loans and collected repayments, they had no authority over the selection and approval of borrowers. Officials in the Department of Agriculture and other local government agencies, under orders to ensure achievement of certain specified annual targets executed the assigned task. In sum, the responsibilities for loan approval and loan collection rested with different individuals, thus holding no one responsible for the quality of loans made and their repayment. This situation, combined with the pressure to, willy-nilly, achieve mandated targets, led to the problem of severe arrears, worsened by crop failures. The low interest rates on loans and deposits led to the creation of a repressed financial market. The interest rates on BIMAS loans, fixed at 12% a year was well below the inflation rate (34%) in 1974. The deposit rate on the savings scheme was 15%.

The low interest rates and the narrow spread between the lending and deposit rates had three consequences. First, cheap loans attracted rich farmers to BIMAS, which effectively blocked the participation of poorer farmers and encouraged corruption. Second, lending and deposit activity did not generate adequate revenue to cover operating expenses, and the unit desa system began incurring large operational deficits that had to be covered by the government, leading to an increase in the administrative subsidy provided to the unit desas from US$ 4 million in 1976 to US$ 24 million in 1983. Finally, low interest rates on savings and the weak design of the savings scheme failed to attract enough deposits and kept the unit desas dependent on government allocations for loanable funds year after year. There was no financial accountability. The unit desas operated as a window to the district-level branch office, they did not maintain complete financial statements; instead they kept partial records that were incorporated into the financial statements of the district-level branch offices. The inability to track the performance of the individual units removed all financial controls.

In 1974, BRI's management made an attempt to move away from lending-under-mandate to a more customer-oriented service. Two new non-agricultural loan products, Kredit Mini and Kredit Midi were introduced. They were not tied to any input packages; moreover the staff of the unit desa had a greater role in loan approvals. These loans, however, still carried loan ceilings, government-determined, borrower-selection criteria and mandated interest rates of 12% a year. Kredit Mini and Kredit Midi enjoyed more popularity than BIMAS loans and a better repayment record, but they were unable to offset the steep decline in BIMAS lending. Not surprisingly, the combination of decreased lending activity, non-recovery of over one-third of the money lent out and declining revenues led to mounting losses that made the unit desa system increasingly a burden. During the early 1980s, lower revenue from oil exports reduced a major source of funds that had kept the desa operations going so far. The transformation of the unit desas took place within the context of overall financial sector deregulation.

In June 1983 the Government of Indonesia suspended ceilings on loans, removed controls on interest rates for both deposits and loans, and prioritised savings mobilization. These changes provided an opportunity for BRI's management to explore new services and products; the unit desas were revamped. Decision-making was depoliticized and responsibility for the performance of the unit desas was placed in the hands of the BRI's management. Organisationally, the position of the President-Director was created. He/she would be solely responsible for the unit desa banking system thus leading to the accountability of the system at BRI's head office. Thus, due importance was accorded to operations at the head-office level. Structurally, unit desas separated from the district-level branch offices into autonomous financial entities. Each unit desa now prepared its own financial statements that allowed management to clearly identify the financial health of the unit. Each unit became a separate profit centre and reconfigured its bookkeeping and accounting system to reflect this change. For example, each unit desa prepared an individual balance sheet that reflected a loan-loss reserve based on anticipated delinquencies and a proportion of the government grants received as equity. District-level branch offices supervised the unit desas, for which they received a service fee from the units and managed liquidity for the units under their jurisdiction. Staff accountability was closely associated with the performance of the unit desas. Direct responsibility for loan approvals and repayments rested with unit desa staff, particularly loan officers. The unit's performance guided staff recruitment and incentives. For example, an incentive bonus that distributed 10% of a unit desa's annual profits among staff was introduced. Internal supervision and audit capacities were also strengthened. The number of internal supervisors and auditors was increased from one per six unit desas to one per four. A standard audit manual provided simple and clear guidelines on supervision rules. Most importantly, perhaps, supervisors, auditors and unit desa managers underwent a periodic training programme, over three years on reporting and supervision techniques. Greater supervision led to early detection of problems and early remedy. The unit desas' products changed along with their structure and organisation. New products were designed to meet the needs of clientele and promote profitability.

The first and most fundamental problem with the BIMAS loans was that they were too cheap. Low interest rates had blocked the outreach of these services to the poor, leading to corruption and operating losses. Investment capital loans were introduced under a new scheme called KUPEDES with higher interest rates. These interest rates screened out wealthier farmers who could obtain cheaper loans elsewhere. Borrowers had the flexibility to use the loans for their own purposes as long as they could prove their ability to repay the loan. Schemes such as TABANAS and SIMPEDES, which are basically savings schemes, were piloted by the BRI. The bold steps yielded dramatic results; even during the period of the South-east Asian crisis the unit desas served effectively as a safety net for the poor and continued their operations of serving the rural poor with savings and loan products. BRI supervises the unit desas and the BKDs, which are village sub units.

The case of BRI is cited as an example as it demonstrates that, like other successful micro-finance institutions (MFIs), a state-owned bank can achieve the goal of reaching the poor sustainably as long as it operates under the same best practice principles. Considerable and prolonged backing in financial and human resources was required by BRI to save the unit desas from collapse after the failed BIMAS experiment – this was extended mainly by the Indonesian government. BRI operated within a liberal financial sector policy that allowed it to design its own products and price them according to cost recovery principles. It also enjoyed complete operational autonomy without any government mandates on reaching lending targets or population groups. There was a large investment in professionalizing the human resource base through staff training, merit based recruitment and performance incentives, and clear and transparent financial reporting and accountability. Strong political support and financial and human capital are critical in certain situations; these aspects of reform come up against political expediency where populism prevents economic rationality. The political opposition to reforming state-owned development banks, particularly on issues such as removing interest rate subsidies and rigid targeting of certain population groups as beneficiaries may prove insurmountable. So far, given their resource base and scale of operations the commercial banks have played a very limited role in microfinance.

Regional spread of banking makes banks ideal for the dissemination of microfinance. The total number of branches of scheduled commercial banks at the end of June 2003 stood at 66,514. Branch expansion of commercial banks has recorded an average annual growth of nearly 1% over the last five years. The share of rural branches declined marginally to 48.7% as at the end of June 2003 from 49% as at end-June 2002 reflecting the branch rationalisation policy wherein loss-making rural branches at centres served by two commercial bank branches (excluding that of RRBs) may be closed by mutual consultation. There was a marginal rise in the share of urban branches, whereas the proportion of metropolitan branches stayed at the same level as earlier.

The state-wise distribution of branches shows that all regions witnessed a rise in the number of branches over the period July 2002 to June 2003, although in absolute terms, the additions to bank branches have been declining over the last few years. In line with the regional distribution of the national income, the southern and central regions accounted for the highest percentage of bank branches. In fact, the southern region experienced the opening of the maximum number of branches during the year, particularly in the states of Andhra Pradesh and Karnataka. The northern region also experienced a significant increase in the number of branches opened during the year, particularly in Punjab (31) and Delhi (26).

Usefulness of Social Banking

The outreach of the Indian banking system has seen rapid growth in rural areas. Insofar as all the scheduled commercial banks (SCBs) including RRBs are concerned, 48% of their total branches (32,303 branches, which translates to a population of about 23,000 per branch), 31% (13.67 crore) of their deposit accounts and 43% (2.55 crore) of their borrowal accounts are in the rural areas. Such an unprecedented expansion of the formal financial infrastructure has reduced the dependence of the rural populace on the informal moneylending sector from 68.3% in 1971 to 36% in 1991. (All India Debt and Investment Survey, 1991).

However, there continue to be wide gaps in the availability of banking services in the rural areas, as the SCBs have covered only 18.4% of the rural population through savings/deposit accounts and even a lower percentage of 17.2% of the rural households by way of loan accounts. Though the Primary Agriculture Credit

Societies (PACS's) with about one lakh outlets have a deep and wide presence in rural India, their impact in terms of extension of deposit and credit products has not only been minimal but also concentrated in only a few states. The decline in the productivity of the rural branches of the commercial banks, fragility of the co-operative credit structure and weakness of RRBs witnessed since the early 1990s, have further accentuated the problem of inaccessibility of banking services for a large part of the rural population. Furthermore, as the banking sector has shown propensity towards the larger size accounts, the number of loan accounts of small borrowers with credit limit range of less than Rs. 25,000 has decreased from 5.88 crore in 1991 to 3.69 crore in 2003.

The perception of bankers towards directed credit is one of extreme caution and wariness due to the risk of default and the high costs of small and multifarious transactions. Banks also confront socio-economic and cultural barriers which prevent their entry into microfinance. The institutional mission of banks precludes such forays. Their organisational structure makes it difficult for them to integrate microfinance within a larger bank culture and structure that is not geared towards a high volume. Most commercial banks are ill-equipped, in terms of financial methodology, to reach and retain low-income clients who require small amounts of capital. Human resources are a major constraint – issues of recruitment, training and performance-related incentives require specialised consideration and effort because micro-finance operations are labour-intensive and require special people skills. Multiple transactions required by the penny economy are not perceived to be cost-effective, far less profitable. The traditional bank mechanisms and overhead structures make it difficult for banks to minimise processing costs, increase staff productivity and rapidly expand micro-finance loan portfolios – efforts necessary to cover costs and earn profits. Ensuring compliance with regulatory norms may also prove a hassle. Fulfilling reporting and regulatory requirements to reflect micro-finance operations calls for new procedures that both commercial banks and government regulators have yet to develop.

Despite these operational constraints, commercial banks have several organisational and structural features that lend themselves to successful micro-finance operations. They are regulated institutions fulfilling conditions of ownership, financial disclosure and capital adequacy to help ensure prudent management. Many have the physical infrastructure, including branch networks, to enable them to reach a large number of micro-finance clients. They have well-established internal controls and administrative and accounting systems to keep track of large number of transactions. The ability to offer loans, deposits and other financial products make them attractive to micro-finance clients; access to their own sources of funds, equity capital resources mobilised through deposit mobilisation and profits make them financially independent of external support. Yet the banks are reluctant to tread on these uncharted shores. Micro-finance methodologies are so different from conventional banking that they are generally not understood by most middle-level bank managers and are sometimes considered as a secondary activity. For over five decades, banks have been reaching borrowers below the poverty line, providing them with financial services and helping them to improve their circumstances. Banks consistently achieve their priority sector lending targets; the credit extended to the poor in absolute terms has also shown an increase. To achieve these goals, banks have had to make many compromises and trade-offs. The imperative to develop viable and sustainable institutions has placed great pressure on organisational productivity and efficiency, but this has had to be balanced against social objectives. The goal of combating poverty in the most effective way has also necessarily been compromised, as it is clear that banks seeking to become financially sustainable cannot spend the time and resources with clients that MFIs and more holistic development organisations might prefer. Nevertheless, the achievements of banks in terms of financial performance and impact on poverty have been impressive.

While questions have been raised about the usefulness of 'social banking' in India on the grounds of its efficiency, recent evidence of the Indian rural branch expansion programme between 1990 and 1997 suggests that the programme made a significant dent on rural poverty and increased non-agricultural output. Access to finance has been considered to be a critical factor in enabling people to transform their production and employment activities and come out of poverty. Financial development, in this context, may enable the poor to obtain access to credit, and consequently improve their economic performance. Accordingly, in many emerging and developing countries, where a significant proportion of the poor remain cut off from access to credit, government intervention in the banking sector is perceived to channelise credit to the needy sectors of the society. The evidence of the success of such interventions in reducing poverty has, however, been limited. There is some recent evidence that the branch expansion programme in India undertaken since the nationalisation of banks has had a positive impact on poverty and non-agricultural output. Using data on 16 major Indian states over the period 1961–2000, the following has been observed by Burgess and Pande: branch licensing rule succeeded in encouraging commercial banks in opening branches in backward rural locations, rural banks managed to reach the rural poor, and commercial banks offered opportunities for households to save. The saving accounts provided households with means of accumulating capital which could be used to invest in various productive activities. It thus seems that social banking programmes as employed by the government served to redistribute resources to the rural poor. This would suggest that expanding access of finance to the poor, in rural settings can generate significant social returns.

Thus the arrival of bank branches in unbanked locations seems to have been in part responsible for diversification into non-agricultural production and employment, a reduction in rural poverty and a reduction in rural inequality. There appears to be both a direct effect that comes through the growth of the non-farm sector and an indirect effect that comes through agricultural wages. Impacts on rural poverty are driven by the social elements of the programme, namely expansion into unbanked locations and priority sector lending. When banks are left to their own devices they place branches in already banked locations and as on non-priority sector lending – they appear to bypass the poor.

The grassroots-level organisations like the SHGs have several features which are also found in traditional moneylending systems. Ironically, these are grounds on which the institutional credit system falters. Transaction costs are low for moneylenders; they know their clients and can therefore practice price discrimination in the loans extended by them. Their lending rates vary between zero to any other astronomical levels judged appropriate by them on the basis of their assessment and prior knowledge of the borrowers as a credit risk. They are available at all times and for all purposes; and above all as they have known the borrowers for generations; they know how to recover the money lent. All these features are present or can be easily incorporated in the SHGs but are absent in bank lending in the rural areas. Banks are governed by their rules and regulations and 'one size fits all approach to loans'. It is a fact which has to be recognized that if it had not been for nationalisation, banks might not have ventured into rural lending at all. Due to specific directions, mandated priority sector lending and the easy availability of refinance, banks are extending credit in rural areas, which, left to themselves, they might never have done.

Banks should not be allowed to withdraw, even partially, from rural banking. The reasons for this view are that the geographical spread, functional reach and vast infrastructure of the banks created during the 30 to 35 years since nationalisation would become a wasteful investment.

The architects of the social banking experiment in India appear, in part, to have been justified in stressing social elements in their attempts to use state control of banking as an engine for poverty reduction. Commercial banks appear to be best equipped to increase the scale of microfinance. The financial infrastructure, extensive branch network, inherent financial strengths, well-established operating procedures, capacity to offer diversified loan and investment deposit services, all equip them to give a thrust to microfinance. This also meshes with the philosophy of social banking. The issue then is largely of the willingness of commercial banks to come forward and adapt to the needs of the poor through innovative ways.

References

Burgess, Robin and Rohini Pande. 2002. 'Do Rural Banks Matter? Evidence from the Indian Social Banking Experiment'. International Monetary Fund.

Das, D. K. 1998. *Indian Economy after Fifty Years.* Deep & Deep Publications.

Dutta, R. 2001. *Second Generation Economic Reform in India.* Deep & Deep Publications.

Joshi, P. N. 1980. *Decade of Nationalised Banking.* Commerce Publications.

Monga, G. S. and R. K. Sinha. 2001. *Nationalisation of Banks: Retrospect and Prospects.* Deep & Deep Publications.

Narasimhan, M. 1992. The Financial System Report. New Delhi: Nabhi Publications

Reserve Bank of India. 2003–4. Trend and Progress of Banking in India.

Srinivasan, T. N. *Eight Lectures on India's Economic Reforms.* Oxford University Press.

FOUR

The Regional Rural Banks

To ensure the success of the developmental initiatives adopted in the first 25 years of independence it was felt, in the early 1970s, that despite the wide banking network, a critical gap still exists in rural areas, particularly in meeting the credit needs of the rural poor. To find a solution for this, the Government of India established Regional Rural Banks (RRBs) through the Regional Rural Banks Act of 1976 to bridge the gap in the flow of credit to the rural poor. Despite the various measures taken by the Government and the RBI through social control and the nationalisation of 14 major commercial banks, a large proportion of the rural poor remained outside the banking fold. The Government of India appointed a working group on rural credit (popularly known as the Narsimham Committee) in July 1975. The Narsimham Committee observed that the cost of structure of commercial banks, the attitudes of their employees and the lack of a professional banking approach in the cooperative credit structure were the true difficulties in rural credit. It also observed that the deposits collected by banks in rural areas was not totally deployed in the rural areas. Keeping this in view, the Narsimham Committee recommended the creation of a new set of regionally-oriented rural banks which would combine the local feel and familiarity with problems of cooperative banks with the business acumen of commercial banks.

Background

The Government of India accepted the recommendations of the Narsimham Committee and accordingly the President of India promulgated the ordinance of Regional Rural Banks, 1975 on 26 September 1975. It was subsequently replaced by the Regional Rural Banks Act, 1976 on 9 February 1976. The mandate of these rural financial institutions was:

- to take banking to the doorsteps of the rural masses, particularly in areas without banking facilities
- to make cheaper institutional credit available to the weaker sections of the society, who were to be the only clients of these banks
- to mobilise rural savings and channelise them to support productive activities in rural areas
- to generate employment opportunities in rural areas
- to bring down the cost of providing credit in rural areas

The New Model

The RRBs have a special place in the multi-agency approach adopted to provide agricultural and rural credit in India. These banks are state-sponsored, regionally based and rural-oriented. Partnered by the central government (50%), the state government (15%) and the commercial banks (35%), the number of RRBs rose from just six in 1975 to 196 by 1987. They covered 476 districts. They financed only the weaker sections of the rural community – small and marginal farmers, agricultural labourers, small traders, and so on. Along with commercial banks, they participated vigorously in poverty alleviation schemes (IRDP) and disadvantaged area programmes (drought-prone areas, desert development etc.). RRBs quickly became an important and integral part of the rural credit system. However, their financial viability was initially overstretched by policy rigidities coupled with a lower capital base in an environment of inadequate infrastructure and deeper social and economic disparities.

The Rationale

The rationale for their establishment thus derived partly from the weaknesses of the cooperative banks and partly from the inadequacies of the commercial banks. They were set up with the primary goal of meeting the crop production credit needs of the rural poor, particularly the small and marginal farmers, rural labourers, rural artisans and others who had very little access to the formal credit system that was in place in the early 1970s. Despite nationalisation and the creation of an extensive network of branches in the rural areas by commercial banks, the commercial banks had not succeeded in significantly stepping up advances to the agricultural and rural sector. Gaps in the coverage and efficiency of the cooperative banks had become evident. Attempts to restructure the cooperatives into financially viable, self-sustaining institutions had met with limited success. Post-Nationalisation and the Green Revolution, the demand for credit for machinery, fertilisers and seeds had far outstripped the ability of the cooperative and commercial banks to fulfil it. There were weaknesses embedded in the cooperative federal structure. Due to the lack of professionalism and lax management, the cooperative banks were not successful in the mobilisation of deposits. The post-disbursement supervision over credit was also weak, leading to mounting overdues. The overdues significantly contributed to their limited ability to avail of refinance from the higher tiers. Thus, financially, they were in a precarious position and could not contribute to the rural economy. The commercial banks worked on elaborate transfer-pricing and cross-subsidisation mechanisms, which also prevented any effective contribution. The increasing demand for credit in the rural areas remained largely unmet. Their invention marked a stepping-stone along the road to disillusion with the cooperative movement in favour of the commercial bank route to rural development.

The Narsimham Committee observed that the cost structure of commercial banks, the attitudes of their employees and the lack of a professional banking approach in cooperative credit structure were the real obstacles in the growth of rural credit. It was felt that

> ...in a country of the size and regional diversity as ours, no single pattern, be it commercial banking or cooperative credit can be expected to meet all the emerging requirements in all areas. A degree of adaptation and improvisation is called for and the range of institutional alternatives widened. It is in this context that we have come to the conclusion that that a new type of institution is necessary. Many, if not most of the rural bank branches are what the banks call deposit centres rather than advance centres. In other words, while commercial banks have been relatively successful in mobilising deposits in the rural areas their credit dispensation in most rural branches is not adequate for them to generate sufficient income to make these branches viable. While from the narrow accounting point of view, this may well be so, it raises another set of questions and issues, namely that the rural branches of banks which by definition operate in the economically weaker sections of the country, far from being the media of transmission of funds from the central money markets to the agricultural economy are proving to be instruments for the reverse transmission of funds from the rural areas to the urban and metropolitan centres. Clearly this trend needs to be arrested and funds garnered for the rural areas deployed in the area itself.

Hence the conceptualisation of RRBs as institutions which would combine the local feel and familiarity with the rural problems which the cooperatives possess with the degree of business organisation, ability to mobilise deposits, access to central money markets and the professionalism of the commercial banks.

The first five RRBs were set up on 2 October 1975 on the basis of an ordinance which was replaced by the Regional Rural Banks Act in 1976. The number of RRBs increased to 85 as at the end of 1980 and to 188 as at the end of 1985. The last RRB to be set up was the Godavari Gramin bank in April 1987 taking the total to 196. These 196 RRBs have 14,497 branches covering 427 districts and are spread over 23 states. Each RRB's area of operations extends over one to three districts with the exception of those in the North-eastern states and a few other regions where the number ranges from four to nine districts. The number of branches per RRB also ranges from 8 to 223. The Committee to Review Arrangements for Institutional Credit for Agriculture and Rural Development (CRAFICARD) stated that "The RRB is more suitable for adopting individual approach than the rural branch of a commercial bank, in view of its low cost profile, wider network of its branches in remote/rural areas, the local feel of its staff and its image as a small mans institution."

This was the policy and institutional background to their establishment.

RRBs have played a key role in rural institutional financing in terms of geographical coverage, clientele outreach, business volume as also contribution to the development of the rural economy. A remarkable feature of their performance over the past three decades has been the massive expansion of their retail network in rural areas. From a modest beginning of six RRBs with 17 branches covering 12 districts in December 1975, today, there are 196 RRBs with 14,446 branches working in 518 districts across the country. RRBs have a large branch network in the rural area forming around 43% of the total rural branches of commercial banks. The rural orientation of RRBs is evident from the fact that their rural and semi-urban branches constituted over 97% of their branch network.

Structure of RRBs

The RRBs are sponsored by public sector banks with the exception of three sponsored by private sector banks – two by the Jammu and Kashmir Bank Ltd and one by the Bank of Rajasthan Ltd – and one sponsored by a cooperative bank: the

Uttar Pradesh Cooperative Bank Ltd. The share capital of each RRB is required to be subscribed by the central government, state government and the sponsor bank in the ratio of 50:15:35. The authorised share capital per bank is at present Rs 500 lakh. The management of each RRB is vested in its Board of Directors, consisting of eight directors, excluding the chairman who is on deputation from the sponsor bank. Apart from appointing the chairman, the central government nominates three directors, while the state government and the sponsor bank nominate two and three directors respectively. As per the present dispensation, one non-official is nominated by the central government and another by the sponsor bank. It has also been the practice that out of three directors to be nominated by the Government of India, one director each is from RBI and NABARD. The senior officials of each RRB such as the chairman and the general manager are on deputation from the sponsor bank. This diverse group is engaged in the pursuit of varying objectives. Consequently, the Board of the RRB is not able to lead and provide necessary direction for the growth of the RRB. The critical element of corporate governance is absent. Each RRB recruits its other staff as per its requirements. From the inception of the RRBs, the staff were paid salaries and allowances on par with the state government employees of comparable hierarchy. The RRB employees went in appeal to the National Industrial Tribunal (NIT). The Tribunal gave an award in terms of which the pay and allowances of the staff of the RRBs were placed on par with that of the commercial banks. This award effectively destroyed their low-cost character. The establishment costs and the overheads of the RRBs were not commensurable any longer with the business they were able to generate or the profits being earned by them. Weaknesses were inbuilt in the structure of the RRBs.

Paradigm Shift

The advent of financial sector reforms in the early 1990s emphasised the need for a self-supporting, 'stand-alone' viable institutional structure in the banking industry. RRBs were, therefore, permitted to finance the non-farm sector, and later, the non-target group to the extent of 40% in the first step and subsequently upto 60% so as to enhance the profitability and viability of these institutions, thus doing away with the emphasis on agricultural sector and the people with small means.

Their clientele till the early 1990s was restricted to small and marginal farmers, agricultural labourers, artisans and small entrepreneurs. They were mandated to extend credit on concessional interest rates to the lowest deciles of the population. The RRBs administered supply-driven programmes of subsidised credit, designed to place modern agricultural inputs in the hands of poor farmers.

The narrow interest spreads available were barely sufficient to provide a reasonable margin to cover transaction and also risk costs as interest rates were administered.

The area of operations of the RRBs is confined to one to two, three contiguous, and in a few cases, more than three districts. The majority of the RRB branches are located in remote rural areas with inherent operational and administrative constraints and scarce business potential.

Problems Hounding RRBs

The small size of advances led to very low levels of business per branch, coupled with poor recoveries of loans, as loans were 'behest loans' and an extension of political patronage. The high costs incurred in recovery efforts were not in proportion to the amounts garnered through the recovery drives. The Service Area Approach (SAA), as per which, a clear area of operation was demarcated for each bank branch, was designed to ensure that an adequate level of service was provided in a defined area to 15 to 25 villages attached to a bank branch. While theoretically, the service area promised an assurance of service and ease of access to bank facilities and bank credit, in practice, it created monopolies as it denied the freedom of choice to customers of the banks. Even if they received indifferent service, they had little option but to bank with banks in their particular service area as decreed by the administrative fiat. The banks were also unhappy as they lost their known customers and business. The RRBs were affected as their area of operations was further inhibited by SAA. Thus in this scenario of shrinking business opportunities the implementation of the NIT award from 1 January 1997 which put RRB and commercial bank staff on par in terms of salary and allowances led to marked increase in staff costs and the realisation on the part of the RRB sponsor banks that their costs could become insupportable in the long run.

The Agricultural Credit Review Committee under the chairmanship of Prof A. M. Khusro (1989) recommended an amalgamation of the RRBs with the respective sponsor banks to enable their branches to continue as rural branches of commercial banks and enjoy the advantage of larger resources through cross-subsidisation possibilities. However this recommendation was not accepted. The Committee on the financial system under the Chairmanship of Shri M. Narsimham (1992) recommended that the RRBs be allowed to engage in all types of banking activities to improve their viability though their focus would continue to be on the target group. While recommending the setting up of rural subsidiaries of the commercial banks, the committee had left the option to the RRBs and their sponsor banks of determining whether the RRBs should retain their separate identity or be merged on a voluntary basis with their sponsor banks proposed rural subsidiaries. The recommendations could not be implemented. A set of short-term measures were introduced in December 1993 to help salvage the RRBs. The introduction of the new economic policies and the acceptance of international benchmarks and standards of capital adequacy, income recognition and provisioning norms lent to a sharper edge to the need to do something about the loss-making RRBs.

Reforms

The first package of measures was tailored to improving business returns for RRBs. These comprised redesigning the advances mix of these banks, improving their spatial spread, expanding their range of business and the services offered by them to their clients. Financing outside the target group which was permitted up to 40% of fresh lendings from September 1992 was increased to 60% of fresh lending from January 1994. The loss-making branches were allowed to be relocated/merged with nearby branches subject to certain conditions, or converted into satellite offices. The area of non-fund/ancillary business was enlarged to include purchase/discount of demand drafts and cheques, issue of drafts/mail transfers, guarantees and rupee travellers' cheques under working arrangements with sponsor banks, introduction of safe deposit lockers. Freeing of 70 RRBs with loan disbursals of less than Rs 2 crore from service area obligations were additional measures. To make the RRBs viable on a sustainable basis, it was felt that they could be rebuilt by cleansing their balance sheets on a stand-alone basis, improving their financial position while maintaining their regional and rural character. In 1994–5 it was decided that 50 RRBs would be taken up for restructuring during the year. Fifty RRBs were identified based on financial parameters, regional representation and geographical spread for comprehensive restructuring. Forty-nine RRBs were selected and provided with equity support of Rs 30 crore shared by all the three shareholders viz, the Government of India, state governments and sponsor banks for cleansing their balance sheets as well as for providing them with liquidity support and share capital. Separate modalities were worked out for the fiftieth RRB, the Tripura Gramin Bank, on account of its huge losses.

Policy Changes and Challenges

Beginning 1994, RRBs, through successive selections, have been placed under a comprehensive financial and managerial restructuring programme. The main features of the restructuring programme included the upfront augmentation of capital, cleansing of balance sheets and provision of additional liquidity, performance obligations and monitoring through the Development Action Plans prepared on the basis of the Memorandum of Understanding entered into with their sponsor banks and NABARD with measurable financial targets. The target/non-target group mix in the loan portfolio was relaxed to 40–60 with a view to improving their returns and later abolishing the target/non-target group altogether by making the commercial bank priority sector norms applicable to them. Prudential norms of income recognition and asset classification were adopted, the roles and responsibilities of different agencies engaged in supervisory oversight over the RRBs were clearly defined. Liberalisation in their portfolio, broader avenues for investment and fund management were attempted by expanding the scope of lending by allowing loans against gold ornaments, consumer loans etcetera, expanding non-fund-based business activities such as issuance of guarantees, travellers' cheques, provision of locker facilities etcetera, relaxing restrictions on investment of surplus non-SLR funds and later placing them on par with commercial banks with regard to priority sector lending. RRBs were allowed to set their lending rates for all types of borrowers and also permitted to relocate their loss-making branches to centres having "commercial" potential in the rural areas, marketplaces etcetera, and allowing them to experiment in terms of mobile branches, satellite offices, etc. Greater autonomy for sponsor banks in the appointment of the chairman and the general manager of the RRBs, greater devolution of decision-making powers to the Boards of the RRBS in business and staff-related matters. Upgradation of managerial and staff skills of RRBs, rationalising the access to DICGC by permitting RRB claims only if recovery in each account was at least 25% net of subsidy were the other restructuring measures initiated. The share capital of the RRBs was augmented and modalities for funding for cleansing up the balance sheets of the RRBs were worked out.

Comprehensive Restructuring

This restructuring exercise threw up some interesting facts: the RRBs in the north focussed on deposit mobilisation, recovery and investment, but neglected advances and organisational processes, the SBI-sponsored Gorakhpur Kshetriya Gramin Bank is a standard example which relied solely on investment and thus showed consistent profits. Thus some RRBs neglected lending in favour of investments; RRBs in the south followed a more holistic pattern in the strategies they adopted which consisted in the main of improvements in resource mobilisation, recovery, investments, advances, systems and procedures, image-building and customer services. For the financial year 1995–6 the Government of India made a further provision of Rs 300 crore, to be matched by an equal amount from the other shareholders. A number of policy measures for the development of RRBs on viable lines were introduced, covering their financial aspects, structural improvement, operational measures, human resource development, monitoring and review mechanism, organisational development initiatives etc. The impact of these measures was considerably augmented through fresh infusion of public capital into the RRBs during the late 1990s, to make up for the accumulated losses of the past. These measures coupled with the pressure to attain viability from the sponsor banks NABARD and RBI led to a turnaround for the RRBs. In 1996–7 when the stringent provisioning norms were first introduced most of the RRBs were incurring losses, by 2001 as many as 172 out of 196 banks in the country were earning current profits.

Relevance

The RRBs continue to be important in rural institutional financing in terms of geographical coverage, clientele outreach, business volume and contribution to the development of the rural economy. In line with macro-economic trends, deposit mobilisation by RRBs has been slowing down in recent years.

The data pertaining to the 196 RRBs for 2001–2 and 2002–3 indicate that there has been an overall decline in the number of profit-making RRBs in 2002–3. The performance of the loss-making RRBs witnessed a sharp downturn during 2002–3. On the expenditure front, both the interest expenses as well as operating expenses of the loss-making RRBs witnessed a sharp rise, the latter owing largely to the rise in the wage bill. The increase in operating profits of the profit-making RRBs in 2002–3 was largely offset by the significant losses of the loss-making RRBs. As a consequence, the loss-making RRBs, in terms of their net profit to total assets, fared poorly than in the previous year leading to a decline in the ratio for RRBs as a whole.

Table 4.1 Performance Indicators of RRBs (as on 31 March 2003)

(Rupees in crores)

Particulars	2001	2002	2003
Branch Network (No.)	14,311	14,390	14,433
Share Capital	195.66	195.81	195.85
Share Capital deposit	2054.33	2080.62	2112.74
Reserves	1270.86	1782.40	2357.41
Deposits	38271.87	44539.15	50098.34
Borrowings	4064.46	4524.37	4798.69
Investments	27636.14	30531.73	33063.42
Loans & advances outstanding	15816.30	18629.22	22157.85
Loans Issues	8823.22	10570.67	12641.00
RRBs earning Profit (No.)	170	167	156
Amount of Profit	676.48	699.93	733.97
RRBs incurring Losses (No.)	26	29	40
Amount of Losses	75.86	92.05	214.68
Accumulated Losses	2792.59	2694.06	2752.25

(Source: Annual Report, NABARD)

Table 4.2 Viability Status of RRBs (as on 31 March 2003)

(Rupees in crores)

Category	Number	Profit/Loss	Accumulated Loss	NPAs
Sustainably viable	97	623.95	--	1,518.91
Currently viable	59	110.01	1,183.50	955.96
Loss making	40	-214.67	1,541.66	724.88
Total	**196**	**519.29**	**2,752.16**	**3,199.75**

(Source: Annual Report, NABARD)

Aggregate deposits of RRBs increased from Rs 4151 crore in 1990 to Rs 56,350 crore by March 2004, owing mainly to their geographical spread and the opening of new branches in unbanked areas. The advances of RRBs increased from Rs 3554 crore to Rs 26,114 crore during the above period. Notwithstanding the sharp increase, RRBs advances constituted just around 2% of the banking systems credit portfolio. The share of RRBs in total agriculture credit (given by scheduled commercial banks, cooperatives and RRBs) has remained at around 9%, despite their strong rural outreach. The average per branch advances increased from Rs 25 lakh in March 1990 to Rs 154 lakh in March 2003. There are wide state-wise differences in credit deployment by RRBs.

During the year 2003–4, 163 RRBs earned profits amounting to Rs 953 crore while 33 RRBs incurred losses to the tune of Rs 184 crore. Ninety RRBs had accumulated losses as on 31 March 2004. Aggregate accumulated losses of RRBs amounted to Rs 2725 crore during the year 2003–4. Of the 90 RRBs with accumulated losses, 53 RRBs had eroded their entire owned funds and also a part of their deposits (i.e. to the extent of Rs 1,660 crore or 11.75% of the total deposits of these banks).

The percentage of recovery to demand has progressively improved in the RRBs from as low as 57% as on 30 June 1997 to more than 75% as on 30 June 2003. The percentage of gross NPAs, which was as high as 27.8% as on 31 March 1999, declined to 12.6% during the year ending 31 March 2004. NPAs in absolute terms stood at Rs 3299 crore as on 31 March 2004. 103 RRBs had percentage of gross NPAs less than the national average, while 93 RRBs had NPAs more than the national average. The Credit-Deposit (CD) ratio stood at 46.3% as on 31 March 2004. There were 50 RRBs with a CD ratio of more than 60% as on that date while 87 banks had a ratio of less than 40%.

Success of RRBs

The RRBs have succeeded in attaining financial viability; they need, however, to buttress this attainment. Financial strengthening and organisational development need to grow in tandem. The RRBs can forge mutually-beneficial relationships with other institutions operating in the rural economy. For instance, in the case of private banks unable to meet their agriculture lending targets, the RRBs can sell their attainments in the sector through securitization of debts, trading in agricultural loan credits or otherwise; thereby the RRBs can secure additional funds to raise lending volumes and agricultural lending will increase substantially. RRB branches should now be effectively converted into profit centres.

Table 4.3 State-wise Working Results of RRBs (as on 31 March 2003)

(Rupees in crores)

State	No. of	Profit Earning		Loss Incurring		Net Accumulated		Loans &	NPAs		Recovery	
	RRBs	No.	Amt.	No.	Amt.	Profits	Losses	Advances O/s	Amt.	%	Jun '02	Jun '03
Andhra Pradesh	16	15	90.65	1	-2.31	88.34	40.17	2953.54	272.55	9.23	70.19	70.96
Arunachal Pradesh	1	0	0	1	-11.19	-11.19	22.35	32.69	25.83	79.02	18.27	22.61
Assam	5	4	4.74	1	-3.25	1.48	103.82	468.18	83.91	17.92	50.73	58.86
Bihar	16	8	48.04	8	-60.66	-12.62	526.38	1143.86	232.09	20.29	56.35	60.17
Chhattisgarh	5	3	5.46	2	-5.60	-0.14	150.07	331.34	57.65	17.40	63.82	69.02
Gujarat	9	9	24.01	0	0	24.00	25.79	631.19	86.88	13.76	73.53	76.53
Haryana	4	4	46.89	0	0	46.89	17.09	676.22	48.98	7.24	83.17	84.73
Himachal Pradesh	2	2	4.11	0	0	4.11	0	196.32	12.79	6.51	78.07	80.79
Jammu & Kashmir	3	1	9.92	2	-15.82	-5.90	99.68	161.13	20.79	12.90	59.75	63.85
Jharkhand	6	2	3.90	4	-23.60	-19.70	121.67	337.09	97.17	28.83	39.33	44.94
Karnataka	13	12	76.98	1	-0.96	76.02	0	2548.37	270.04	10.60	75.99	75.53
Kerala	2	2	29.84	0	0	29.84	0	1204.28	116.92	9.71	83.93	84.99
Madhya Pradesh	19	16	16.99	3	-5.49	11.50	256.59	1323.44	187.68	14.18	70.06	72.49
Maharashtra	10	6	4.17	4	-18.52	-14.35	130.32	685.18	154.04	22.48	67.24	64.44
Manipur	1	0	0	1	-2.15	-2.15	14.23	13.87	4.86	35.03	49.93	51.80
Meghalaya	1	1	3.10	0	0	3.10	0	40.62	13.63	33.56	51.16	54.30
Mizoram	1	1	0.29	0	0	0.29	5.58	33.73	10.33	30.64	50.00	61.23
Nagaland	1	0	0	1	-0.16	-0.16	1.58	4.33	0.62	14.41	50.72	61.17
Orissa	9	4	13.15	5	-43.97	-30.82	459.83	1407.97	223.13	15.85	66.34	67.38
Punjab	5	5	35.44	0	0	35.44	0	350.17	18.39	5.24	91.35	92.71
Rajasthan	14	12	38.99	2	-7.29	31.70	196.72	1376.98	115.88	8.42	77.19	80.05
Tamil Nadu	3	3	18.33	0	0	18.33	0	529.24	23.05	4.36	88.11	89.28
Tripura	1	1	2.05	0	0	2.05	139.02	178.09	65.30	36.67	34.97	44.56
Uttar Pradesh	36	34	240.75	2	-5.21	235.53	157.39	3985.91	813.96	20.42	66.99	70.04
Uttaranchal	4	4	7.56	0	0	7.56	1.97	179.56	15.81	8.81	81.74	79.30
West Bengal	9	7	8.60	2	-8.48	0.12	281.97	1364.00	227.44	16.67	65.15	69.33
All India	196	156	733.96	40	-214.66	519.29	2752.16	22157.84	3199.75	14.44	71.52	73.53

(Source: Annual Report, NABARD)

At present, the branch profit and loss statement does not take into account many costs. Thus the management and staff have no way of assessing their own performance. Given the strategic objectives of development plans, each branch profit and loss account would need to reflect the cost of funds including borrowings from the head office at an appropriate transfer price, secondly the cost of operations, including staff salaries, benefits, incentives, rent and utilities, telecom, stationery, light fees etc. The performance measurement and monitoring systems put in place are critical. RRB plans should include an accounting and reporting system which makes the financial and outreach performance transparent to the top managers as well as to each branch manager. The performance budget should include targets for both sustainability and access. At the same time it is essential that there be measurable indicators of performance relevant to RRBs' strategic objectives. These measures could include profits of the branch, RRB as a whole, portfolio quality, in terms of keeping the non-performing assets below a specified level, Deposit growth with sub-targets for small deposits and advances growth, with sub-targets for advances to poor borrowers (small advances) and women borrowers. Keeping in view the objective of becoming financially self-sustainable in a more competitive environment there should be an understanding of the minimum business size that is required at the level of the RRB as a whole as well as for an RRB branch. If the existing business volume is below the minimum viable level, a credible business plan should be prepared to show how it will attain that level. New products should be designed for consumption; loan products, medium and long term loans for agriculture and allied activities and loans for non-farm sector activities, including processing, manufacture and services. New distribution channels could be included in the effort to transform each branch into a profit centre. The promising distribution channels could be through the E-choupals, the Kisan Credit Cards, rural telephony, SHGs particularly of poor women for both deposits and loan, mobile branches moving on a weekly schedule from village to village shandy/haat branches and tie-ups with local input suppliers (fertiliser dealers or produce buyers) as commission agents. The RRBs will have to innovate and learn new skills to survive. Training and development of staff for new product design, performance budgeting, computerisation for strong MIS effective customer service at the branch, at the customer's doorstep, through simplified appraisal processes and minimal documentation would enable RRBs to exploit their niche markets in the rural areas, for growth and progressive development.

The Impact of Policies

The policies introduced during the reform period starting in the early 1990s have been instrumental in reorienting the RRBs towards financial viability. These policy changes have enabled the RRBs to explore new markets and operating procedures with the objective of attaining sustainable viability. While policies allowed the relocation of branches, improved remuneration and incentives for RRBs' staff and opened up lending and investment avenues on commercial considerations, with the operating policy environment there has been a marked change in the macro-economic environment; a decline in market deposit rates from 14–15% to 4–5% has led to the closure of safe investment options. This is forcing the RRBs to again look at lending opportunities to build up their portfolio. As the branches are mostly in rural areas the RRBs find they have to lend to their low income clients if they have to build business. They have to offer increasing discerning clients a better product and portfolio choice. The popular products are the KCC loans, lending to the non-priority sector and in the small industries and business segment. Product design along with operating efficiency are critical to the success of the RRBs as viable rural financial institutions, the refinements effected in these areas will also enable them to bridge the perceived contradictions between their ability to leverage their outreach for viability thereby ensuring that there is no outreach/viability conundrum.

Working Group Recommendations

The Government of India had appointed a working group to suggest amendments to the RRB Act, 1976, under the Chairmanship of Shri M.V.S. Chalapathi Rao, to examine and review the progress in dispensation of rural credit especially through RRBs, examine the legal, regulatory and policy framework of RRBs and make detailed recommendations for making the RRBs an effective instrument for development and growth of the rural economy. The Committee found that of the 196 RRBs, 79 had attained a positive net worth (including recapitalisation deposits) as on 31 March 2001, 172 RRBs had made profits in the financial year 2001 by investing, only 24 RRBs made losses in the financial year 2001. However in the financial year 2002, perhaps more than 50 RRBs would incur losses on account of the decline in yields due to past payments for the National Industrial Tribunal award. Most of the loss-making RRBs are in the east and the north-east. The credit deposit ratio was 41% while that in the east and the north-east was below

20%. RRBs accounted for a mere 7% of rural formal sector advances; 60% of the advances had been extended to non-target group borrowers. NPA levels continued to be high; 18% gross with eight RRBs which had NPA levels higher than 50%. For RRBs advances extended to the agricultural sector amounted to 45.1% of all advances as on 31 March 2002 as compared to 45.65% the previous year. RRBs have sustained large financial losses in rural lending due to high administrative costs, heavy overdues and an unsustainable interest rate structure.

Policy Choices

The new Act, while enabling a whole range of changes, should not adopt a one-size-fits-all approach to the RRBs. Some of the major recommendations of the working group relate to further broadening the scope of activities the RRBs can pursue. RRBs should be able to finance the entire range of the rural economy; at present the bulk of the finance is extended to agriculture, as per this recommendation. RRBs should be allowed to finance infrastructure and infrastructure-related activities such as manufacturing, construction, trade and services, and extend finance to SHGs, cooperatives and individuals, to ensure that their area of operation is adequately serviced; they must be mandated to ensure that 60% of their deposits must be lent in their own area or be deposited under the RIDF. All RRBs should be able to offer other financial services, life and non-life insurance products as agents of insurance companies, market mutual funds etc. It has recommended a capital investment of over Rs 2270 crore and RRBs need to achieve a return on equity, as prescribed by the Committee, of at least 15%. This will require non-performing assets to be brought down to less than 1.5% on a steady basis, which will be possible if operating expenses are severely curtailed changing the capital structure and the ownership pattern of the RRBs. A differentiated ownership structure based on the financial health of the RRBs has been suggested.

The group has categorised RRBs into four subsets, depending on the strength of their balance sheets. Category A RRBs are those with a ratio of NPA greater than 1.5%, which have been in profits for the last three years and whose profit position is perceived to be sustainable. It has been recommended that such RRBs should be allowed to access the capital markets to raise additional capital and be open to changes in their ownership structure, which could be affected through the initial public offer (IPO) route. Category B RRBs are those which have attained

NPA greater than 0.5% and less than 1.5%. State and central governments can partially disinvest from these RRBs. Though they have reached current profitability but suffer from an overhang of past non-performing assets, such RRBs can graduate to the capital markets. Category C RRBs are those whose NPA is greater than zero but less than 0.5% can continue as per current ownership. These RRBs are struggling to attain current viability but have to bear the burden of the sins of the past in the form of huge accumulated losses. Category D RRBs are those with NPA less than zero, which need a strategic owner but which are clearly beyond redemption or rehabilitation and should immediately be taken up for liquidation as their continued existence is a threat which can jeopardise the interests of their hapless depositors.

The group has recommended the adoption of the concept of a 'Sponsor Institution' with a minimum shareholding pattern of 51% – this level will ensure adequate commitment and powers to intervene for the sponsor institution. Loss-making RRBs should be restricted to narrow banking, i.e., they can only accept deposits, offer microcredit through the SHGs and invest their surplus funds in SLR deposits and surplus in the RIDF. Open ownership of the RRBs has been proposed enabling any entity including the private sector to become the 'Sponsor Institution', defined as the 65% plus owner this dispensation, which allows the sponsor banks who are interested in retaining ownership to enhance their stake in the RRBs to 65%. It also enables those of the sponsor banks who wish to opt out to disinvest in favour of other banks, private parties, employees and the local community. Changes in ownership should not be mandated to allow the necessary flexibility to RRBs to adopt the route which appears to be best suited to their circumstances. It has further recommended that the area of operation of the RRBs be extended to cover all the districts which are uncovered by the services of the RRBs. Professionalism has to be introduced in the RRBs with a rationalised restructuring of the Board and all norms as per the Banking Regulation Act, and RBI rules therefrom including capital adequacy norms, NPA provisioning, income recognition and asset classification. Avoidance of risk concentration connected and related lending should be made applicable to the RRBs mutatis mutandis, as these are internationally accepted and sound banking practices.

Rating Models

RRBs are part of the financial system and will, at a later date, have to be rated. Hence all prudent and accepted banking practices have to be introduced for the

RRBs in a phased manner. The supervisory structure, business patterns of the RRBs, management and development of human resources, licensing of the RRBs, capital structure, devolution of some of the powers of the Government of India to RBI, strengthening the Boards of the RRBs to introduce effective corporate governance, appointment of auditors, imposition of penalties, etcetera are all areas which require attention. RRBs should be enabled to merge with each other as per merger procedures prescribed by the Companies' Act and the RBI, not necessarily approved by the Government of India. RRBs may also be allowed to take over the business of rural/semi-urban branches of any commercial bank at negotiated terms. RRBs should be allowed to be liquidated and wound up as per the Companies' Act, with the RBI and not the Government of India's approval. To prevent RRBs with high NPA from continuing to accept deposits and put depositors' money at risk, a provision has been suggested whereby the amount of deposits an RRB can accept has been limited to a multiple of its net owned funds. This limit will decline in proportion to the worsening asset quality of the RRB and will spur the RRB to initiate necessary action for redress like merger of RRBs with their respective sponsor banks, conversion of RRBs into subsidiaries of sponsor banks on a region-wise basis and the creation of a national-level rural bank. In the era of amalgamation, we should allow the sponsor banks to merge the RRBs region-wise, this will lead to greater efficiency and it is sound economics. The broad objective of the policies should be to put in place a forward-looking strategy which would encourage an orderly shift in focus from the provision of subsidised agricultural credit to the systemic development of rural financial markets with financially sustainable institutions that support the needs of agriculture and non-agricultural rural activities. Accordingly, there must be a corresponding shift in emphasis to the adoption of policies conducive to efficient, market-based financial intermediation, impacting development and building resources and institutions.

Microfinance is the natural niche of the RRBs through their large presence in the rural areas and it has been demonstrably proved to be the most effective for eradication of poverty. Successful micro-finance institutions are primarily local organisations that are reaching a significant number of the poor and these are commercially viable. It has been suggested that microfinance would be a valuable niche market which the RRBs could do well to exploit given their extensive presence in the rural areas and their strong resource base vis-à-vis that of the NGO sector. Microfinance is defined as the provision of credit savings and financial services to very poor people. Providing these services to very poor households leads to opportunities for the poor to create, accumulate and own assets, and for smooth consumption. Microfinance has been pioneered by specialised NGOs and commercial banks such as BRI-unit desa (Indonesia) Grameen Bank (Bangladesh) K-Rep Kenya and Prodem/BancoSol (Bolivia), among others. They have demonstrated that populations traditionally excluded by the formal financial sector can, in fact, be a market niche for innovative banking services that are commercially sustainable. Microfinance represents a significant departure from earlier exercises in providing credit to the poor through financial institutions (often public institutions) at subsidized rates with very little or no recovery defaults.

Promise

Potentially, RRBs are a valuable tool for enhancing rural economic development particularly as they are the point of entry for the bankable poor to the vast commercial banking system in India. Their importance derives from the fact that on account of local recruitment, they are familiar with the rural economy and have the ability to mobilise low cost deposits from a clientele that commercial banks are not able to reach adequately. In fact, RRBs have a relatively high covariance risk because typically, they are located in only one agro-climatic zone and that too generally in backward areas. As conceived, their focus was on rural areas with branches located on the basis of population coverage and development criteria rather than commercial considerations, and subject to varying degrees of local interference in decision-making. As a percentage of their total portfolios they were assigned a disproportionate responsibility for lending to the poorest of the poor and to the weaker sections of the society by administering government-sponsored poverty programmes. Consequently they have been beset by inadequate economies of scale, weak commercial cultures and militant trade unions. Historically, they have been identified with "dedicated" rural commercial banking, but now are subject to a diffused governance structure due to their ownership pattern, and are also often managed by relatively junior banking professionals. As a system, they continue to battle administrative controls and the fiat of their parent banks, NABARD and the Government of India, though, technically operational controls have been shifted to their sponsor banks. Technical competence is low and needs to be scaled up. The success of the RRBs in a deregulated environment will depend on their ability to sustain low transaction costs and concentrate on deposit mobilisation, continuous monitoring of credit and availability of supporting infrastructure.

Endnotes

The RRBs, set up with the intention of extending credit to the rural poor, have succeeded in the objective of taking banking services to the villages, but have failed to make a clear dent on credit to the rural poor during the past 30 years of their existence. This has to be viewed in the context of the policy framework for rural development adopted in India with a focus on income and employment generation and poverty alleviation. The renewed emphasis on agricultural and rural development by the Government of India would lead to a growing demand for different types of financial services in the rural areas, as the financial needs of the rural economy become diversified. The present structure of rural credit may not be able to fully cater to the same. The cooperative credit structure suffers from many infirmities and, hence, the RRB network will have to be leveraged to benefit the rural areas. RRBs, therefore, have to provide a larger share of credit disbursed, calling for much larger resource mobilisation as also greater efforts for their institutional strengthening. Thus, on the one hand, the concept of RRBs has to be pursued in the interest of the rural economy and on the other, the RRBs have an opportunity to cash in on the gap between demand and supply of banking services.

After nearly three decades of existence, the RRBs are facing many constraints warranting an overhaul and a serious consideration on the part of the policy makers for their strengthening. In order to reposition the RRBs as effective instruments within the existing legal framework, a number of options have been explored, which includes merger/amalgamation, change of sponsor banks, balance sheet strengthening, maintaining minimum capital, governance and management issues, regulatory and supervisory aspects and methods for improving profitability of RRBs. These options are not mutually exclusive, but complementary to each other. In the context of the need to increase rural credit and deliver better services in the rural areas there is a sense of urgency to reposition the RRBs in the financial system. Only then can RRBs meet the expectations of becoming vibrant rural financial institutions capable of meeting the growing requirements of rural India.

Merger Consolidation

To improve the operational viability of RRBs and take advantage of the economies of scale (by reducing transaction cost etc.), the route of merger/amalgamation of RRBs may be considered, taking into account the views of the various stakeholders.

The merged entities will have a larger area of operation and the merger process will help in strengthening some of the weak RRBs. The following options are available:

- Merger between RRBs of the same sponsor bank in the same state
- Merger of RRBs sponsored by different banks in the same state.

The process will bring down the number of RRBs and make it more convenient for the sponsor banks to manage the affairs of the RRB. Merger of RRBs with the sponsor bank is not provided for in the RRBs Act, 1976 and further, such mergers would go against the spirit of setting up of RRBs as local entities and for providing credit primarily to weaker sections.

RRBs in their original form were designed to be the micro-finance institutions to bridge the gap between those served by cooperatives and commercial banks and the large unserved population in the rural areas. In spite of being formed with a clear mandate and a defined objective, the RRBs moved away from their original mandate and became miniature versions of commercial banks. Over time, with ageing staff, branch rationalization (including shifting to more convenient locations) and a focus on profitability and a strong balance sheet, these banks have deviated from their social mandate. However, even today, as experience would show, in comparison to commercial and co-operative banks, RRBs offer the best fit for undertaking micro-finance operations on a much larger scale considering their close understanding of the local people and geography. Today 196 RRBs together, cover 516 districts and serve a client base of close to Rs 6.27 crore.

References

Hume, D. and P. Mosly. *Finance against Poverty,* vol. II. New York: Routledge.

NABARD. 2003–4. Statistics on Regional Rural Banks.

Reserve Bank of India. 2005. Report of the RBI Internal Working Group on Regional Rural Banks.

——. 2003–4. Annual Report.

——. 2003–4. Report on Trend and Progress of Banking in India.

——. 1976–2002. Report of the Working Group to Suggest Amendment in the Regional Rural Banks Act.

Sinha, S. S. 2001. The Regional Rural Banks Outreach/Viability Conundrum Report. Gurgaon: EDA Systems.

FIVE

The Cooperative Banks: Promise vs. Performance

Background to the Establishment of Cooperative Banks

The cooperative movement in the country originated as a measure against rural poverty, aggravated by the chronic indebtedness of the farmers and practice of usury at its worst by the moneylenders. Agriculture had largely been capital-starved and was exposed to the exploitative tendency of usurious moneylenders. There was an urgent need to evolve a systematic mechanism for enhancing the credit flow to agriculture. Agrarian disturbances in 1875 in the Deccan against moneylenders necessitated the enactment of Taccavi Legislation by the Government, and also led to the concept of the cooperative approach. The Northern India Taccavi Loan Act, 1875, the Land Improvement Loans Act, 1883, the Agriculturist Loans Act, 1884 etcetera were all enacted to facilitate the availability of credit to farmers. In 1892, Sir Federick Nicholson recommended the establishment of rural cooperative credit societies on the German pattern. The Famine Commission (1901) recommended the introduction of cooperatives in the country. In 1904, the Cooperative Credit Societies Act was enacted by the Imperial Government to facilitate the organisation of credit cooperatives and confer upon them special privileges and facilities, the scope of which was subsequently enlarged by the more comprehensive Cooperative Societies Act of 1912. Under the Government of India Act, 1919, the subject of cooperation was transferred to the then provinces, which were authorized to enact their own cooperative laws. Under the Government of India Act, 1935, cooperatives remained a provincial subject. Presently, the item 'cooperative societies' is a state subject under entry 32 of the State List of the Constitution of India. Cooperative Societies Acts enacted by state governments are now in place in the respective states. In order to administer the operations of cooperative societies where membership was from more than one province, the Government of India enacted the Multi-Unit Cooperative Societies

Act, 1942 which was subsequently replaced by the Multi-State Cooperative Societies Act, 1984 under entry 44 of the Union List.

The founders of Planning in India considered cooperation an instrument for the economic development of the disadvantaged, particularly in the rural areas. The non-exploitative character of the cooperatives, voluntary nature of membership, the principle of one man one vote, decentralized decision-making and self-imposed curbs on profits eminently qualified them as an instrument of development, combining the advantage of private ownership with public good.

Cooperative banks were the first institutions that were set up with a view to providing credit to agriculturists at low rates of interest to free them from the clutches of the moneylenders and to ensure that 'credit' reaches the farmers to enable them to meet their production needs and so increase production and productivity in the rural areas. These objectives of policy remain unchanged.

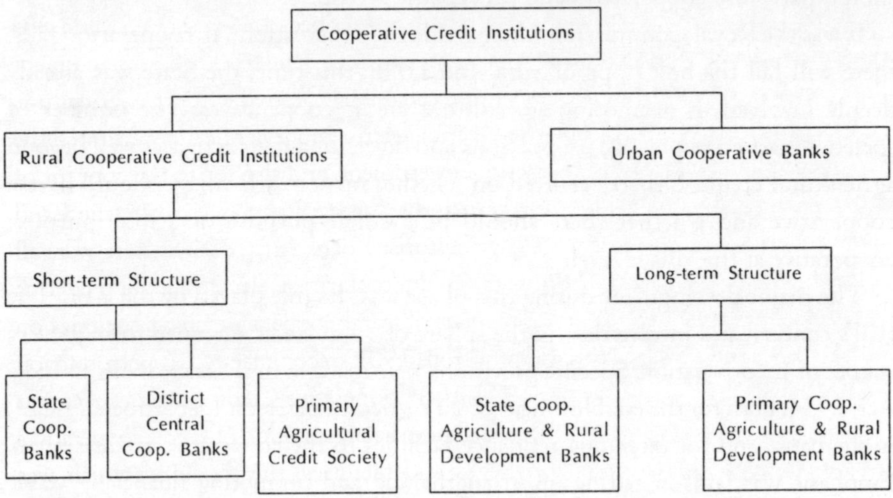

History of the Cooperative Banks

Development of the Cooperative Movement

The Indian cooperative movement was initiated by the government to align the rural credit system with the objectives of development planning. It spread and diversified with the encouragement and support of the government.

The passage of the Cooperative Credit Societies Act in 1904, and the enactment of a more comprehensive Cooperative Societies Act in 1912 marked the beginning of a government policy of active encouragement and promotion of cooperatives. This thinking gained wide acceptance and was adopted as a policy by provincial governments and thereafter, 'cooperation' became a provincial subject in 1919. The persistence of government interest in cooperatives and the importance attached to them was reflected in the appointment of three different committees to review their growth and functioning.

The classic study by Frederic Nicholson, followed by the Edward Law Committee on cooperative legislation, confirmed and reiterated the need for the State to actively promote cooperatives. A decade later, the Maclagan Committee (1915) advocated that "there should be one cooperative for every village and every village should be covered by a cooperative". The Royal Commission on Agriculture in India, which submitted its report in 1928, suggested among other things, that the cooperative movement should continue to focus on expanding rural credit and that the State should patronise cooperatives and protect the sector.

It was the Royal Commission which made the observation "if cooperation fails, there will fail the best hope of rural India". By this time, the State was already deeply involved in promoting agricultural credit cooperatives. The number of societies reached impressive proportions and diversified their activities well beyond agricultural credit. Debates centred on whether or not each village should have a cooperative and whether there should be a single-purpose or a multipurpose cooperative at the village level.

The major development during this phase was the role played by the RBI. The RBI's concern and involvement in the sphere of rural credit stemmed from its very statute of incorporation. Specific provisions were made in the Reserve Bank of India Act, 1934, both for the establishment of an Agricultural Credit Department (ACD) in the bank, and for extending refinance facilities to the cooperative credit system. Emphasis was laid on setting up, strengthening and promoting financially viable provincial cooperative banks, central cooperative banks, marketing societies and primary agricultural credit societies in each province. The RBI, from 1942, also started extending credit facilities to provincial cooperative banks for seasonal agricultural operations and marketing of crops.

There was a lull until 1945, when the Agricultural Finance Subcommittee and the Cooperative Planning Committee were set up by the Government of India. By then, there were signs of sickness in the Indian rural cooperative movement. A large number of cooperatives were found to be saddled with the problem of frozen assets because of heavy overdues in repayment. The Subcommittee's recommendation that the frozen assets of the members of such cooperatives be liquidated, by adjusting the claims of the society to the repaying capacity of the members, marked the beginning of State interference in the management of cooperatives and the consequent erosion in the credit discipline of the members. The Cooperative Planning Committee identified the small size of the primary cooperative as the principal cause of failure. It also advocated State protection from competition to the cooperative sector.

After Independence, rapid and equitable economic development became the central focus of State policy. Cooperatives in general and rural financial cooperatives in particular took centre stage. Taking cognisance of the weakness of the cooperative system, the All India Rural Credit Survey (AIRCS) not only recommended State partnership in terms of equity, but also partnership in terms of governance and management. Other recommendations included linking credit and marketing cooperatives and enlarging their area of operation. The recommendations of the AIRCS stopped just short of the government running the cooperatives.

State policy came to be premised on the view that the government should ensure adequate supply of cheap institutional credit to rural areas through cooperatives. The thinking then was that if the institutions that were meant to deliver such cheap institutional credit failed, there either had to be reorganisation of existing institutions, or creation of new types of institutions.

NABARD was created on the recommendation of the CRAFICARD (Sivaraman Committee, 1981). The State's heightened interest in and concern for the performance of cooperatives in the country was obvious. The focus, however, was on expanding and reorganising the State-supported structures, without addressing the tasks of restoring and strengthening autonomy, mutual help and self-governance that are the cornerstones of genuine cooperatives.

The State gave primacy to cooperatives as the sole means of delivering institutional credit to rural areas, and injected large amounts of funds directly. Higher-tier cooperative banks were encouraged to accept public deposits and borrow from other financial institutions. However, the system was soon found to be burdened with growing overdues. In keeping with the national priority of financing the rural sector adequately, the involvement of commercial banks was first suggested as a measure of social control. The involvement of commercial banks was thereafter institutionalised through the nationalisation of major commercial banks in 1969.

During the post-Nationalisation period, there was an unprecedented penetration of commercial banks in the rural sector. This trend, however, was accompanied by rigid policy directives right down to the micro-level on cost of credit, purposes, categories of borrowers, geographical areas, etc.

As the financial involvement of the government in cooperatives increased, its interference in all aspects of the functioning of cooperatives also increased. The consequent interference with the functioning of the cooperative institutions, often compelling them to compromise on the usual norms for credit worthiness, ultimately began to affect the quality of the portfolio of the cooperatives.

Instead of tackling the root cause of their weaknesses, the State took responsibility for strengthening the institutions, by infusing additional capital and a 'professional' workforce. Both the State and the workforce then began to behave like 'patrons', rather than as providers of financial services. Whenever any professional organisation is in trouble, it usually finds its own solution by re-negotiating the terms with its financiers and re-visiting its operating strategies. However, in the case of the rural financial institutions, the State has always provided a 'solution', irrespective of the need of the recipient organisation, thereby donning the role of a 'patron'.

In due course, political expediency also led to laxity in ensuring quality of credit and its repayment. The Government of India's 1989 scheme for writing off the loans of farmers greatly aggravated the already weak credit discipline in the cooperative system, and led to the erosion of its financial health. It also set an unhealthy precedent and spawned a series of schemes by the state governments, announcing waivers of various magnitudes, ranging from interest write-offs to partial loan write-offs. The competitive populism adopted by the political class has severely impaired the credibility and health of the cooperative credit structure.

The State has used cooperatives to channel its development schemes, particularly subsidy-based programmes for the poor. As these institutions have a wide reach in the rural areas and also deal with finances, the choice was natural. The trend, however, also made cooperatives a conduit for distributing political patronage. This and the sheer magnitude of resources and benefits channelled through the societies makes control of decision-making and management attractive to parties in power for accommodating their members, to influence decisions through directives, and for individual politicians to be on the management boards of the cooperatives.

Concerns about these trends and the need to overcome them began to be voiced around this time. The Agriculture Credit Review Committee (Khusro Committee, 1989) for the first time talked of the importance of encouraging thrift and savings among the members of the cooperatives. It also emphasised the need for better business planning at the local level and strategies to enable cooperatives to be self-sustaining. To this end, the Committee was also in favour of serving non-members, if it made business sense. In a sense, there were larger macro-economic changes on the anvil in the economy. The 1990s witnessed more concerted attempts both by the government and by non-official organisations and co-operators to explore ways to revitalise the cooperatives.

During the last 15 years, there has been an increasing realisation of the destructive effects of intrusive State patronage, politicisation, and the consequent impairment of the role of cooperatives in general, and of credit cooperatives in particular, leading to a quest for reviving and revitalising the cooperative movement.

Several committees (notably those headed by Chaudhry Brahm Perkash, Jagdish Capoor, Vikhe Patil and V.S. Vyas) were set up to suggest cooperative sector reforms during this period. The Brahm Perkash Committee emphasized the need to make cooperatives self-reliant, autonomous and fully democratic institutions, and proposed a Model Law. Subsequent Committees have all endorsed this recommendation and strongly supported replacing existing laws with the proposed Model Law. They have also recommended revamping and streamlining the regulation and supervision mechanism, introducing prudential norms and bringing cooperative banks fully under the ambit of the Banking Regulation Act, 1949. To facilitate the implementation of these reforms, they proposed that governments provide viable cooperative credit institutions with financial assistance for recapitalisation.

Progress in implementing these suggestions has been very tardy because of the states' unwillingness to share the costs and their reluctance to dilute their powers and to cede regulatory powers to the RBI. The passage of the Mutually Aided Cooperative Societies Act by the Andhra Pradesh government in 1995, however, marked a significant step towards reform. Following the example of Andhra Pradesh, eight other states (viz. Bihar, Chhattisgarh, Jammu and Kashmir, Jharkhand, Karnataka, Madhya Pradesh, Orissa and Uttaranchal) have passed similar legislation to govern and regulate mutually aided cooperatives.

In all cases these new laws provide for cooperatives to be democratic, self-reliant and member-centric, without any State involvement or financial support. They provide for cooperatives registered under the old law to migrate to the new Act. The old Acts were not repealed, nor was there any serious effort to encourage and facilitate the conversion of old cooperatives to come within the purview of the new Act. Most existing cooperatives, therefore, continued to adhere to the old law.

Cooperative Banking Structure

For historical reasons, two parallel wings of cooperative credit institutions have come into existence and developed: one for purveying short-term and medium-term credit to the cultivators and the other for dispensing long-term credit at first for debt redemption and subsequently for investment in agriculture.

The apex level cooperative credit institutions both in short-term (ST) and long-term (LT) structures are expected to play a leading role in the development of the respective cooperative credit structure. Cooperative banks have a three-tier inter-penetrative structure with Central Cooperative Banks at the apex, District Central Cooperative Banks at the middle-tier and Primary Agricultural Credit Societies at the lowest level. As a measure of institutional strengthening, NABARD provides refinance against the loans extended by these cooperative banks. Cooperative banks are now envisaged as one-stop shops for meeting the needs of production credit, investment credit, indirect finance and actual credit flow to the farm sector.

The ST credit structure available in most parts of the country has been a federal one with a three-tier system. As on 31 March 1999, the ST structure had more than 92,000 Primary Agricultural Credit Societies (PACS's) at the village level, 367 District Central Cooperative Banks (DCCBs) at the intermediary district level and 29 State Cooperative Banks (SCBs) at state level, including the newly-formed Sikkim State Cooperative Bank, meeting all types of credit needs of the rural sector whose coverage extend to the remotest parts of the country. In smaller states and union territories having a two-tier structure, the credit requirements of the PACS are being directly met by the SCBs.

The short-term cooperative credit structure (CCS) has a federal three-tier structure with PACS's being the grassroot-level institutions, the Central Banks at the District level (DCCBs) and the State Cooperative Banks (SCBs) at the state level. In the North-eastern states and smaller states, there are no DCCBs and the SCB purveys credit through its affiliated PACS's (and so the CCS is a two-tier system). In this section, we focus on the characteristics, in terms of scale, diffusion, structure and performance of the CCS at the national level, and bring out the regional diversities.

There are 1,12,309 PACS's, which works out to roughly one PACS for every six villages in the country. The societies have, therefore, a wider spread and reach in rural India than the commercial banks and RRBs. The CCS, moreover, has more than twice the rural outlets and 50% more clients than commercial banks and RRBs put together. There is, however, a wide variation in the density of cooperative outlets. While the density is high in states like Maharashtra and Kerala, it is very low in the north-eastern region.

The total membership of the PACS is reported to be around 12 crore. Scheduled Castes, Scheduled Tribes and small farmers, are reported to account for about 36% to 37% of the PACS membership as per NAFSCOB. Only half the members are borrowers – this proportion being less than average among small and marginal farmers and least among Scheduled Castes. These figures, it must be reiterated, are only indicative.

Even in terms of basic functions, there is a considerable diversity across states. In some regions there are a few pure thrift and credit societies that generate resources only from members and do not have financial transactions with non-members. In Maharashtra, apart from the regular PACS's, there are around 22,000 thrift and credit societies (called path sansthas). In states like Kerala, PACS's collect deposits from members as well as non-members in a significant way. 62% of the PACS's in the country are viable, 30% are potentially viable and 8% are either dormant, defunct or under liquidation. Here again, there are considerable variations across states.

There are also differences in the nature of the CCS. Most states, for instance, have different structures for purveying long-term and short-term credit while Andhra Pradesh has a single unified structure for providing both long-term and short-term loans. Most states have a three-tier structure, comprising PACS's, DCCBs, and SCBs. While in Gujarat, the SCB conducts most of its transactions with lower-tier organisations and does not have any branches outside of its head office, in Maharashtra the SCB undertakes full-fledged banking activities through multiple branches that operate like branches of any other commercial bank.

The LT cooperative credit structure has only two tiers, one at the state level and the other at the taluka/tehsil level. Some states have a unitary structure with the state-level banks operating through their own branches. As at the end of March 1999, the long-term credit structure consisted of 19 State Cooperative Agriculture and Rural Development Banks (SCARDBs) with 745 Primary Cooperative Agriculture and Rural Development Banks (PCARDBs) in respect of federal structure and around 1500 branches in the unitary structure in eight states. Three SCARDBs had, however, a mixed structure, incorporating both the unitary and federal systems (Assam, Himachal Pradesh and West Bengal). An integrated structure providing all types of agricultural credit (both short-term and long-term) under 'single window' credit system is available in Andhra Pradesh. In the north-eastern region, only three states (Assam, Manipur and Tripura) are served by the LT structure. Generally, in the states not having the LT structure, separate sections of the State Cooperative Banks look after long-term credit needs together with other rural financial institutions i.e. branches of RRBs and rural/semi-urban branches of commercial banks.

Structural Weaknesses

The cooperative credit movement in India has not been able to keep pace with contemporary rural financial institutions despite sound principles and long existence. The cooperatives have neither remained 'member-driven' enterprises nor had their leadership in quite a large number of cases proved to be professional, transparent, accountable and functionally effective. The vital link in the ST cooperative credit system – viz. the PACS's at the grassroots level – had generally been very weak. Most of them have been too small in size to be economical and viable, and a large number of them have been dormant existing only on paper. They suffered from infrastructural weaknesses, operational inefficiencies and structural flaws. They do not appear as real financial institutions that inspire confidence in their existing and potential members, depositors and borrowers.

Financial Inadequacy

The Agricultural Credit Review Committee (ACRC), 1989 had brought out that the net margins at the level of PCARDBs and PACS's worked out to 1 percentage point and 3.21 percentage points respectively, below the margins required for viable operations. The ACRC further observed that the net margin could be even worse, if the costs on overdues and bad debts were added.

The ACRC had recommended that the credit system might regulate the interest rates in a manner that the institutions could pay for the costs of resources raised as well as for servicing of deposits and supervision of advances with an adequate cushion to ensure their growth and survival.

In response, the SCBs and DCCBs were given freedom from the interest rate regulations with regard to deposits and advances effective 18 October 1994, subject to the prescription of a floor lending rate of 12%. Likewise, the ARDBs were given the freedom to decide their interest rates on advances to ultimate borrowers from 1 August 1995.

The fact that cooperative banks continued to operate on such a prima facie non-viable keel bears testimony to the absence of a business-like approach in running these institutions and securing management of the required quality. The observations of the All India Rural Credit Review Committee (1969) still stand good:

> ... cooperatives are getting so used to subsidies and protection of various types that cost considerations tend to be almost wholly ignored in the formulation of policies and programmes... The most prominent example of this approach is reflected in the attitude of the cooperatives towards rates of interest charged to their borrower. There is a tendency to emphasise the need for low rates of interest to the relative neglect of other important considerations such as building-up reserves and employing staff of the right quality.

Deposit mobilisation efforts have been made by cooperative banks which traditionally offer slightly higher interest rates on their deposits. In the post-liberalisation era, while other banking institutions have scaled down their interest rates on deposits, the cooperative banks have continued this practice without much regard for the prevalent market conditions. In the absence of proper investment planning and because of the inability to exercise high-yielding investment options, many cooperative banks were not able to earn adequate returns to meet even the service cost on deposits.

Viewed in the context of the Government of India policy of increasing agricultural credit three-fold during the Tenth Plan period so as to double the agricultural production in the country, the surpluses available with the cooperative banks need to be channelised towards loans and advances to agriculture in accordance with the national objectives and priorities. The demand for agricultural credit has yet to reach the saturation level.

At present the three-tier short-term credit structure is in existence in 15 states whereas a two-tier structure with SCBs directly lending to PACS's is working in 12 states that are small states. The three-tier structure has evolved over a period of time and the cooperative banks at the state and district level have been performing an important role in the resource mobilisation and financing of both agricultural and non-agricultural cooperatives besides providing leadership to the cooperative institutions in the respective regions.

Other major factors responsible for the deterioration in the performance of cooperative credit institutions are the low volume of business/low resource base, the low borrowing membership, lack of democratisation and professionalism, high incidence of overdues and almost stagnant recovery performance. They also suffer from the fallout of overlap of control, i.e., by the state government through the Registrar of Cooperative Societies and by the RBI/NABARD since most of the states have not yet adopted the Model Act or enacted suitable amendments in the State Cooperative Societies Acts and bylaws to tackle this problem.

More than 60% of the resources of PACS's are in the form of borrowings from higher financing agencies and have remained rather fragile. The deposits mobilised by these cooperatives are very small and even these are partly retained with DCCBs/ higher tiers. Poor recovery performance and incidence of high overdues has drastically reduced the eligibility of new members to borrow and has resulted in low paid-up share capital which in turn directly determines their borrowing capacity. The limited resources translate into low business levels, though the demand for credit had been continuously increasing. There is a need for strengthening resources, especially the capital base of cooperatives.

The long term structure has a negligible resource base of its own as it raises term resources for its operations through borrowings supplemented by their owned funds comprising share capital, reserves and very little of deposits. The SCARDBs have been permitted to mobilize fixed deposits since 1997 for periods not less than12 months subject to aggregate deposits accepted and outstanding, at any point of time, not exceeding the net-owned funds of the SCARDBs as revealed in the previous year's balance sheet.

One of the major factors affecting the ability of cooperatives to function as member-driven organisations is the lack of democratic management in letter as well as in spirit. As the cooperatives are essentially a people's movement, there is a need to restore the democratic character of cooperatives both in management and business processes and to suggest ways to improve their borrowing membership, at the same time reducing the State's interference in the management and business processes of cooperatives.

Dual Control

'Cooperation' is a state subject under the Constitution, governed by the respective State Cooperative Societies Acts. The cooperatives are at present under the control of state governments in all matters relating to registration, membership, election, financial assistance, loaning powers, business operations, loan recovery and audit. Some aspects relating to banking activities are regulated and supervised by the RBI/NABARD under the Banking Regulations Act, 1949 (AACS). There is thus no clear demarcation of regulatory powers, which at times results in cross directives from the controlling agencies, affecting the working of cooperatives, and leading to undermining the performance of cooperative banks.

To remove the overlapping controls and endow functional autonomy and operational freedom on cooperatives, there is an urgent need to prepare specific action plans. These plans should redefine the relationships clearly, the roles and responsibilities and areas of regulation through delegation of powers in respect of all the stakeholders viz. the state government, the RBI, NABARD and apex bank/ cooperative institutions. Banking functions should be brought completely under the Banking Regulations Act to be regulated by the RBI.

The provisions of the Banking Regulations Act should override the provisions of the State Acts/bylaws/rules which run counter to it. This will lead to a clear demarcation of the areas of activities of cooperative banks which will fall under the domain of the RBI vis-à-vis the Registrar of cooperative societies.

Role of Cooperatives in Providing Agricultural Credit

The main players in the field of agricultural credit in the formal sector include the commercial banks, the RRBs and the rural cooperatives. The rural credit cooperatives in the country are in an impaired state. Several factors have led to the impairment of the cooperative credit structure, but it would be advisable to understand the magnitude of the problem first. The cooperatives once dominated the rural credit market in the institutional segment (with a share of around 65%, going by the All India Debt and Investment Survey, 1991), but now have a significantly smaller role.

Data for the past decade indicates a fall in the share of cooperatives in the rural credit market, from around 62% in 1992–3 to about 34% in 2002–3 in spite of an increase of just under 10% per annum in the absolute disbursement on a compounded annual basis. The shares of different institutional sectors in providing credit to the rural areas are shown in the table below.

Table 5.1 Flow of Ground-Level Credit to Agriculture (both ST and LT)

Rupees in crores

Agency	1992–3	1997–8	2000–1	2001–2	2002–3
Coop. Banks	9,378	13,975	20,718	23,524	23,636
Percentage share	62%	44%	39%	38%	34%
Regional Rural Banks	831	2,040	4,219	4,854	6,070
Percentage share	5%	6%	8%	8%	9%
Commercial Banks	4,960	15,831	27,807	33,587	39,774
Percentage share	33%	50%	53%	54%	57%

(Source: NABARD)

Two trends emerge from the overall flow of credit to agriculture from the commercial banking sector. The number of rural branches of commercial banks has gone down marginally as part of the branch rationalisation programme. The second trend is that even though the commercial banks almost meet their targets for lending to the priority sector, they have moved more towards larger customers. The average size of direct loans to agriculture in the portfolio of the commercial banks was Rs 13,500 in 1997, and this is Rs 31,585 now. The average size of loans of the PACS, in comparison, is currently only Rs 6640 per borrower, according to the data tabulated above.

Continuing Relevance of Cooperative Banks

The cooperative banking structure has a unique position in the rural credit delivery system of India. The cooperative banking sector, which has existed for about a century, has made significant strides in the field of rural credit. Since then, the cooperative credit institutions, both in the short- and the long-term structures, have continued to play their crucial role in the dispensation of credit for agriculture and rural development. Over the years, they have remained the prime institutional agencies with their vast network, wide coverage and outreach extending to the remotest parts of the country. Both the short-term and long-term cooperative credit institutions are basically farmers' organisations primarily meant to meet their credit-related requirements.

The cooperatives were the only institutions providing institutional credit to agriculture till the commercial banks emerged on the scene in a big way, particularly, after their nationalisation in 1969, and social banking became their major thrust. Until the late 1960s, farmers and the rural borrowers could look to only one institutional credit agency in the cooperative sector to meet all their credit needs, whether related to seasonal agricultural operations, investment in land or redemption of debts.

Cooperative credit institutions have been accredited with playing a significant role in the deployment of credit for agriculture and rural sector. Today they cover 69% of the rural credit outlets and their share in rural credit works out to about 45% of the total credit for rural sector in the country. In purveying production and investment credit, it accounts for 57% and 29%, respectively.

The economic and financial sector reforms in India were initiated in 1991, as a step towards a broader process of international economic integration and the globalisation of financial markets. Progressive deregulation of interest rates, downscaling of statutory reserve requirements and infusion of additional capital followed as essential features of the process.

The prudential norms were recommended by the Basle Committee on Bank Supervision (BCBS) as a measure for assessment of the financial soundness through a set of common denominators and operational parameters for banks having trans-national operations. Though the cooperative banks operate at the district level and the state level, the prudential regulations have been extended to them with a view to emphasizing the need for them to function on sound lines at par with other banking institutions. Therefore, a review of the financial sector could be treated as complete only if it covers the important segment comprising the cooperatives. The overall picture of the cooperative sector is not too healthy. Its continued fragility does not augur well for the flow of credit to the rural sector. It is, therefore, necessary to assess the financial and other operational inputs required to restore the momentum of their growth on sound lines.

It has been emphasised from time to time that the vitality and viability of the cooperative credit system should be preserved to enable the cooperatives to function as effective agencies for dispensation of rural credit. Cooperative credit institutions accounted for the significant share of about 45% in the total direct institutional credit disbursed for agriculture and allied activities. The revitalisation and strengthening of cooperative institutions at all levels should, therefore, be considered not only desirable but also expedient to enable them to function as effective purveyors of rural credit. They should upgrade their services and technology to provide instant, efficient and affordable services. Fostering a healthy banker–client relationship is essential for the sustainability of banks through greater business volumes and improved productivity.

Banking is primarily an intermediation of funds between the 'savers' in the form of deposits and the 'users' in the form of loans and advances. For this intermediation to be successful on a continuing basis, there is need for a profitable trade-off between returns to the savers and costs to the borrowers supplemented by an appropriate spread of margin adequate enough to sustain the operations of the intermediary viz. the bank. Given the keenness to offer maximum returns to depositors while extending credit to the preferred clients at lower rates, the difference between the cost of raising deposits and borrowings and the returns on loans and advances, which constituted the interest spread/margin, was becoming increasingly narrower. Low margin was a problem afflicting the banking institutions both in the commercial as well as cooperative sectors.

Cross-subsidisation through concessional refinance made available by higher financing agencies and fine-tuning of the internal efficiency were the only means available to the cooperative banks to optimise their interest spread. The maneuverability in this regard was particularly limited for cooperative banks given the smaller area of operation and the nature of credit retailing undertaken by them, combined with the fact that cooperatives traditionally offered slightly higher interest rates to their depositors. Also, with the increasing presence of commercial banks in the field of agricultural credit enjoying greater patronage of the bigger cultivators, cooperative banking was constrained further in the scope of increasing their volume of business. Absence of modern banking services and well-trained professional staff were other constraints inhibiting their internal efficiency. As a result, the cooperative banking system at the grassroots level in particular was prima facie not financially sound.

The cooperative credit system has been recognised as the major institutional agency for provision of agricultural credit – both for production and investment purposes. The Committee on Banking Sector Reforms (Narsimham Committee II) states that "consideration be given to delayering of the cooperative credit system with a view to reducing the intermediation costs and providing the benefit of cheaper NABARD credit to the ultimate borrowers."

The appropriateness of the structure has been a necessary point of reference for the studies on cooperative institutions. All the major national-level studies such as the All India Rural Credit Survey (1954), Committee on Cooperation

(1960), All India Rural Credit Review Committee (1969), Committee to Review Arrangements for Institutional Credit for Agriculture and Rural Development (CRAFICARD, 1981) and the Agricultural Credit Review Committee (ACRC, 1989) have dealt with this question.

Cooperative banks borrow from and lend to their own members. Ideally, they should be self-sufficient as far as financial resources go, but in the majority of cases they are not able to generate sufficient funds to emerge as 'stand-alone' economically viable institutions. The factors affecting the financial health of the cooperatives are:

Poor Resource Base: Recapitalization is necessary to retain the micro-finance intervention capability of cooperatives but it is very difficult. The financial performance of the cooperative banks is not uniform in all states. In some states such as Andhra Pradesh, Maharashtra and Gujarat, they are very strong, while in Uttar Pradesh and Bihar their condition is perilous; thus, the heterogeneity of the system prevents the design of an "across the board" capitalization initiative. State governments are also not financially strong. It may also be difficult to find the money to capitalize the cooperative banks. The Capoor committee had clearly brought out that there are three issues involved in the question of recapitalization/ cleaning of balance sheets of cooperative banks. The first one is as to who should contribute to these resources, to what extent and in what form? Whether the owners, state government alone can bear the recapitalization burden is a moot point. Secondly should all the cooperative banks be taken up for restructuring financial assistance, recapitalization, rehabilitation or only a select group of cooperative banks? In the case of exercise of the latter option what should be the criteria for selection and what conditions should be imposed? And what would then be the fate of the remaining banks? A third issue is how to ensure that a requirement of this type does not recur in the future, i.e., it remains a one-time measure. A timeframe of five to seven years should be imposed, since sops beyond reasonable period would end up propping up even inherently unviable units, which would survive in the long run and be a strain on the system. Once this viability study is complete and the amount of fresh funds infusion estimated, further steps may have to be considered. Viability of member cooperatives' PACS's would largely determine the viability of the central cooperative banks at the district level in which the PACS's federate. The banks may be taken up for rehabilitation carefully on a selective basis even if the process of selection is time consuming. The revitalization package for cooperative banks may be a four-dimensional programme encompassing financial, operational, organisational and systemic aspects.

High Transaction Costs: With negative margins, the organization structure leads to high transaction costs. There are two ways in which the organizational structure can be simplified.

1. As suggested by the Khusro Committee (Agricultural Credit Review Committee) the short-term and long-term structures should be integrated at all levels, primary, intermediate, district and state level apex. Andhra Pradesh is the only state which has effected this integration of the short-term and long-term structure.
2. The Narsimham Committee has recommended delayering to reduce the high intermediation costs and to ensure provision of cheaper NABARD credit to the ultimate borrower. As a first step the State Cooperative Bank and CCB should consider skipping one tier and lend directly to the PACS's and the ultimate borrowers where the intermediate levels are weak.

There will be a reduction in the interest rate for the ultimate borrower due to a reduction in the level of intermediation, and secondly it will be possible for NABARD to provide refinance even in cases where one tier of the structure is not able to borrow on account of ineligibility due to the high percentage of overdues.

There is also a possibility of achieving cost economies, for instance the District Central Cooperative Banks are eligible for refinance from NABARD only after consolidating the demand of individual DCCBs and obtaining the credit limits. State Cooperative Banks in turn adds part of its own funds to the refinance and lends it to the DCCBs. The DCCBs repeat the same process for their member societies like the Primary Agricultural Credit Societies. SCBs and DCCBs get 2% margin for their role. If DCCBs are able to obtain funds directly from NABARD the cost of funds to the PACS's would come down significantly especially as State Cooperative Banks at present also take into account the internal resources of DCCBs and also their own non-overdue cover position in computing costs. Besides the possibilities of cost economies this will lead to an improvement in resource position with cheaper and less cumbersome procedures for raising the resources.

As far back as 1981 CRAFICARD had recommended the two-tier structure for cooperative banks. This has tangible benefits. As already discussed, it will reduce the cost of credit by cutting down one tier and lower the cost of credit for the ultimate borrower.

As with most issues there is a counter-argument also. This is premised on the view that as it will be necessary for these banks to open more branches so as to absorb the trained staff of the tier that is being skipped; the increased costs of overheads will negate any savings due to cutting one tier. Secondly, as Central Cooperative Banks are nearer to the Primary Agricultural Credit Societies and are relatively autonomous, they are in a position to render better services than State Cooperative Banks. The clinching argument against dispensing with one tier appears to be that the cost of funds to PACS's may not be reduced beyond 0.25%.

Major Recommendations of Various Committees

There are some positive benefits also in restructuring the rural cooperative credit institutions. The major recommendation of various committees from Khusro (1986) to Capoor (2000) to Vasudevan (2005) are:

1. Integrating the short-term and long-term wings of the cooperative credit structure
2. Rationalization by removing one of the structures/tiers to enable exploitation of scope and scale of economies in the rural structure.
3. It would also address the imbalances in the cooperative credit structure. While PACS's are moribund higher tiers, as SCARDBs, DCCBs and SCBs are healthy. In the short-term structure, outstanding loans and overdues are higher at the retail levels, which are the primary levels, leading to a choking of the credit flow at primary levels where it is most needed, while the higher tier continues to enjoy financial health and solvency. These imbalances have only served to weaken the cooperative credit structure over time.

The persistent and increasing burden of overdues contributes to the high cost per unit of business. The overdues and NPAs have crippled financial solvency and cramped the productivity and profitability of the cooperatives. The transaction costs of the cooperative banks are also very high. Transaction costs mean management expenses, establishment and staff costs and administrative costs which add to overheads and the cost of funds. Poor recovery of loans and lower levels of loan business result in large losses from slate to low financial viability. Low profitability, high and growing NPAs and low capital base are the real problems of the sector.

Lack of business diversification is another problem. The cooperatives are not able to offer all types of financial services on par with commercial banks, regional rural banks and now local area banks. Money transfer facilities are of crucial importance in the rural economy, but the cooperatives are not able to meet these needs. They are hampered by their inability to cater to credit needs for all purposes for a single asset. The restricted area of activities and operations is also a factor, which contributes to their low profitability.

Lack of professional management inhibits growth. Excessive state/central controls as cooperatives being a state subject leads to a very high degree of bureaucratization, leading to a lack of democratic functioning within the cooperative societies which more often than not results in complete supercession of their Boards. The Registrar of cooperative societies enjoys overwhelming power in the present system. The Mutually Aided Cooperative Societies Act is a landmark legislation as it restricts the role of the Registrar. Under this Act, cooperatives registered under the Cooperatives Act can register afresh, i.e., re-register, provided they return and reimburse the shares held by the government and enter into a memorandum of understanding with it regarding the existing loans. The adoption of the essential features of the Model Cooperative Societies Act as recommended by the Chaudhry Brahm Perkash Committee will enable bringing in necessary amendments in the State Cooperative Societies Acts and help to turn the cooperatives into member-driven professional business enterprises.

Suggested Solutions

What do the cooperatives need to emerge as strong efficient viable institutions? First, recapitalization support as the base-level institutions, being cash-starved, are completely moribund. However, recapitalization alone will not be enough to strengthen the structure. Recapitalization may buttress them financially but there will soon be a case of throwing good money after bad if this is not coupled with legislative changes going hand-in-hand with managerial and organizational restructuring.

Dual control must go in the cooperative banks. The government shareholding ranges from 17% to 87%. The government can buy shares in cooperatives and become a member. As a shareholder, the government has the right to appoint one or more members on the Board of Directors of the cooperatives. In addition, cooperative legislation in India empowers government to appoint managers in the cooperatives.

There is a marked deceleration in credit flows to around Rs 22706 crore of short-term credit and Rs 5108 crore of long-term credit, due to mounting overdues which have cramped the processes of credit recycling.

The PACS's are the weakest link in the cooperative credit structure and they should be reorganized. These weak and inefficient PACS's should be merged with stronger societies. Multipurpose societies should be encouraged. The maxim of 'one village, one society' should be retained as far as possible. Managerial weaknesses need immediate redress to ensure functional autonomy. Proper personnel policies should be adopted. Leadership is also important, and finally, any financial institution is first as strong as the men who staff it. If they do not live up to the institution, it is the institution that falls from grace.

Positive Achievements

Despite all these handicaps, cooperative banking has made significant strides in the field of rural credit. From a meagre credit share of 2.7% during the early 1950s, the share of agricultural credit purveyed by the cooperative banks has increased to as much as 45% by 1999. Notwithstanding the massive expansion of rural branches by commercial banks since their nationalisation during 1969, the cooperative banking sector continued to have the largest network of rural credit institutions. Their significant role in increasing agricultural production through the provision of both production and investment credit needs no emphasis. Of late, their role in supporting the rural non-farm sector has also been growing.

The Forgotten Alternative

Despite impressive strides in the mobilisation of deposits and channelisation of rural credit, a large number of cooperative credit institutions are far from being strong and self-sustaining business enterprises. Low resource bases and the consequent heavy dependence on higher-tier and refinancing agencies, an inadequate volume of business much below the break-even level, poor recovery management with attendant afflictions such as increasing non-performing assets and recurrent loss of assets have been some of the factors contributing to their financial and operational weaknesses. The absence of professional and business ethos and duality of control have been other important causes.

The financial position of most of the Scheduled Cooperative Banks (SCBs) and CCBs does not show any perceptible improvement. The accumulated losses of CCBs have increased to Rs 4442 crore in 2002–3 from Rs 3217 crore in 2000–1. The percentage of recovery to demand for SCBs and CCBs declined to 79% and 61%, respectively, in 2002–3 from 84% and 67%, respectively, in 2000–1. As on 31 March 2003, the gross NPAs to gross credit of SCBs and CCBs increased to 18% and 22%, respectively, from 12.7% and 18.3%, respectively, as at the end of March 2001. Many of these short-term rural cooperatives did not meet the minimum capital and reserve requirements stipulated under Section 11(1) of the Banking Regulation Act, 1949 (AACS).

State Cooperative Agriculture and Rural Development Banks (SCARDBs) and Primary Cooperative Agriculture and Rural Development Banks (PCARDBs), which constitute the long-term rural cooperative credit structure, have a negligible resource base of their own, and mostly raise resources through borrowings. Their poor recovery performance has affected their ability, particularly at the primary level, to cater to the credit needs of new and non-defaulting members. This has also resulted in low paid-up share capital, which constrains their borrowing capacity, and the consequent limited resources have inevitably led to low business levels.

The PACS's as the grassroots-level arm of short-term cooperative credit, mediate directly with individual borrowers, grant short-term to medium-term loans and also undertake distribution and marketing functions. There were 1,12,309 PACS's as on 31 March 2003, with about 120 million members. A large number of PACS's, however, face severe financial problems primarily due to significant erosion of their own funds, deposits, and low recovery rates. Various policies have been adopted to improve the financial health of the PACS's. NABARD, in particular, has been extending funds to develop the infrastructure of PACS's.

Policy Choices

The performance of cooperatives at present is not rousing and yet, right from the inception, the 'mantra' or guiding policy has been that cooperatives have failed yet cooperatives must succeed. They have also been referred to as the 'forgotten alternative'. The failure of the cooperatives is attributed to multifarious reasons: excess government intervention based on share capital contribution, huge transaction costs, lack of professionalism, lack of effective leadership and so on. Several committees have studied the cooperative system in depth and suggested several measures for restructuring and revamping them. These measures were largely cosmetic and did not address the basic structural weaknesses. While some of the measures failed due to half hearted efforts in implementing them, others have resulted in complicating the cooperative structure. New institutions were created instead of adapting the existing system to the situation.

The revival of cooperatives is a must for a variety of reasons. Firstly, a lot of effort has been expended in building up a wide network of cooperatives in the rural areas, which will be wasted if the system is allowed to perish under the weight of its own contradictions. PACS's are nothing but SHGs. If PACS's can be revitalized they can function with the same efficiency as SHGs. SHGs seem to be the answer to restricted availability of credit to weaker sections and non-viability of institutions. Cooperatives, on account of being a natural niche for the dispensation of microfinance, and some DCCBs such as DCCB, Bidar in Karnataka that exploits the natural affinity which members of cooperatives have with weaker sections, have made tremendous headway in this regard.

Endnotes

Obviously, unless the causes of the serious and growing impairment in several dimensions are tackled, cooperatives cannot be expected to arrest their declining role in providing agricultural credit, let alone play a significant role in achieving the targeted rapid expansion of credit to the farm sector. As noted earlier, several committees and concerned cooperators have suggested measures to revive and revitalise the CCS, so that cooperatives become an effective medium for meeting the savings and credit needs of small and marginal farmers, rural artisans and other underprivileged sections of rural society.

Reviving and revitalising the CCS is essential, both on functional and ideological grounds. In functional terms, cooperatives already have a wider and deeper reach in the countryside than other financial institutions. Experience has shown that the latter serve mostly the better-off segments of borrowers that have a sufficiently large asset base. They are reluctant to cater to the small and marginal farmers and other underprivileged sections, on grounds that lending to them is far too costly and risky to be profitable.

Cooperatives, of the mutual thrift and credit type, are the only form of organisation by which economically disadvantaged individuals and groups could, through voluntary collective action, overcome their disadvantageous position in an unequal market and promote their well being. Organisations, in which members know each other first hand, are closely linked through kinship and other social relations, and have a strong mutual stake in proper use of the common credit pool; credit would be put to good use. Costs of administration and risks of default in repayment could be reduced. No less relevant is the moral appeal of cooperatives as a counter and an alternative to individual or corporate enterprise, for mobilising and using economic resources for owners' profit.

Recognising the important role that the cooperative network can play in delivering credit to sections of the rural population, which cannot be, or are unlikely to be, reached through commercial and rural banks, all the earlier-mentioned committees are unanimous on the steps needed to realise their potential. They emphasise the need to (a) restore democratic management in the societies by holding free and fair elections regularly; (b) reduce the scope for government interference in their management to a minimum; (c) rationalise staff and improve their professional ability; and (d) create a climate conducive to prudent management of resources and efficient management and recovery of dues. Some suggest a delayering of the cooperative structure, increasing the service area of primary cooperatives to make them viable, and even making DCCBs and PACS branches of the SCBs.

Having perused the reports of earlier committees, the task force agrees with their central approach and thrust that the CCS needs:

- special financial assistance to wipe out accumulated losses and strengthen its capital base
- institutional restructuring to make for democratic, member-driven, autonomous and self-reliant institutions
- radical changes in the legal framework to empower the RBI to take action directly in matters and to the extent deemed appropriate for prudent financial management of banks
- qualitative improvement in personnel in all tiers and at all levels through capacity building and other interventions, leading to an increase in overall efficiency.

References

Capoor, J. Report of the Task Force to Study the Co-operative Credit Sysem and Suggest Measures for its Strengthening. Reserve Bank of India.

Deshmukh, P. G. 2002. *Working of Co-operative Banks in India: Overview and Prospective.* New Delhi: Kanishka Publishers and Distributors.

Government of India.1951.The First Five Year Plan: A Draft Outline. New Delhi: Planning Commission.

Pant, Joshi, Deepali. *Co-operatives: A Re-look.* New Delhi: Yojana.

Reserve Bank of India. 2003–4. Report on the Trend and Progress of Banking in India.

Report of the Committee on Banking Sector Reforms, Chairman, M. Narasimham, New Delhi.

Vaidyanathan, A. 30 December 2004. Committee on Task Force on Revival of Cooperative Credit Institutions.

SIX

Institutional Microfinance

Towards Growth with Equity

Growth with equity – the larger mandate of Social Banking – continues to be our goal. Banks can leverage their financial strength to extend credit and their network of branches can reach out to micro-finance clients.

Increasingly, micro-credit institutions are being considered as an alternative to government intervention in rural credit. The substitution of the existing rural credit system with a microcredit-based system is being recommended. In India, two-thirds of the population is still engaged in agriculture or related activities. As the distribution of land is skewed due to adverse land-person ratios, the majority of farmers have an inadequate resource base for production. Hence, small, marginal, landless or near-landless rural population depend on credit for their livelihood. Keeping the importance of credit for agricultural development and alleviation of poverty in view, Social Banking was adopted in 1969. Social Banking has been described as "the reservation of entitlements for previously disadvantaged groups". As per the philosophy of Social Banking, the initiation and direct involvement of the banks is central to the strengthening of the credit delivery system for agriculture and poverty alleviation. These policies to some extent led to an improvement in the access of bank credit to the rural poor on concessional rates. On the whole, the impact was not as great as envisaged. Firstly, efforts aimed at improving the distribution of formal credit and increasing access to the poorest of the poor and the landless to credit were defeated as credit remained concentrated in the hands of the mid-level cultivator and the landed population. Secondly, poor repayment of the loans resulted in the creation of non-profit making assets. Thirdly, the banking system could not fully adapt to the task of poverty alleviation, as bank loans lacked the component of consumption credit. Despite these shortcomings, the direct involvement of the banking system in affirmative action for increasing the flow of credit and for eradication of poverty is envisaged. Access to financial services is essential for the poor. Financial services enable the poor to maximise the returns on their surplus, smoothen their consumption and reduce their vulnerability to the risks that they face on a day-to-day basis. The poor use various forms of financial services to meet their needs. They borrow not just for productive purposes like business and agriculture but also to fulfill a number of consumption/ lifecycle needs related to births, weddings, funerals, deaths, etc. Their savings are in the form of cash and assets that can be liquidated at a future date. While small loans and savings provide timely relief to them and help them to cope with sudden income shocks or emergencies, larger loans and investments can be used to diversify income sources and invest in existing businesses to increase revenue and the scale of operations.

Demand–Supply Gap

Studies have provided estimates of the outreach of the formal financial system. Data from the All India Debt and Investment Survey, 1992 indicates that the share of the non-institutional agencies (informal sector) in the outstanding cash dues of the rural households is as high as 36%. The disaggregation of this data further reveals that the credit dependence on informal sources was higher in the case of lower asset groups. The dependence on the informal sector was as high as 58% for households with assets lower than Rs 5000. Financial services could enable the poor to leverage initiative and help build assets and income. However, banks do not directly lend down market. Hence, low income groups are beyond the pale of the formal financial system. This makes a discussion of level of interest rates and terms of finance irrelevant. The fundamental problem remains an exploration of ways to increase access to credit. The difficulty arises as financing needs and the economic characteristics of low income households and formal financial institutions are widely divergent. Formal financial institutions require stable income from which principal and interest on the loans advanced can be recovered. Small borrowers have unsteady income streams and are often not in a position to offer collateral. Most of the poor do not have access to the banking system for the purposes of savings either. Micro-finance institutions can enable such linkage through the SHG Bank programme where savings of the group can be deposited in banks. The transaction costs of savings in formal institutions were as high as 10% for the rural poor. This was due to the small average size of transactions and distance of the branches from the villages. As a result, a large number of the poor depend on the informal mechanisms of savings like chits, bishis, matkas, savings with local traders and merchants and savings with deposit mobilisation finance companies (non-banking finance companies). Some of the finance companies may be unregulated and result in fraudulent operations.

As a result of the low access to institutional (formal) sources of financial services, the poor resort to informal sources of credit to which there is easy access. The dependence on informal sources increases with the increase in the level of poverty. Informal systems may be inefficient and even exploitative due to their monopoly position. Interest rates in the informal market vary from 3–10% a month. Vegetable vendors are known to borrow at even 10% a day to finance their daily working capital needs. The poor, who save through informal mechanisms, face high risks to their precious savings. Many forms of savings, especially savings with local merchants and traders, are reported to have a negative interest rate.

In rural areas, the transactions between various parties (banks, traders, input dealers, and farmers/consumers) are predominantly cash-based and are very low in value. In this regard, it is interesting to note that bank loans up to Rs 25,000 constituted 89% of the total number of loan accounts of rural branches involving hardly 12.5% of total loans outstanding as on 31 March 1998. The cost of cash-based transactions is high. The cost of cash-handling infrastructure for a bank branch includes the cost of setting up the branch, the cost of manpower and the cost of cash security. This cost increases with a decrease in the value of transactions and decrease in the denomination of currency transacted.

Constraints of Formal Financial Institutions

The basic issues confronting banks relate firstly to the non-tracking of borrowers, as the banks lack the knowledge of grassroot-level realities in the villages. Secondly, non-repayment of bank loans serves as a disincentive to further lending. Formal lending to the poor through the banks is beset by two other difficulties: (1) Pre-sanction appraisal screening is not effective. The banks are not able to distinguish the credit-worthy borrowers from the not-so-credit-worthy borrowers. (2) Banks' post-loan disbursal monitoring and supervision is weak. Thus, they are not able to monitor and ensure productive use of the loans. Moreover, if the loan repayment instalments are not received in time, they are not able to initiate immediate legal action against the borrowers or salvage any part of the loan in the absence of collateral. The transaction costs of administering small loans are also very high. Microcredit addresses most of these problems as it incorporates innovative financial practices. Microcredit implies small loans extended to groups of poor persons who undertake self-employment projects that in turn generate income, enabling them to provide for themselves and their families. The targeted population generally comprises poor women and micro-entrepreneurs of low-income households.

Definitional Issue

Microfinance is defined as "the provision of thrift, credit and other financial services and products of very small amounts to the poor in rural, semi-urban or urban areas so as to enable them to raise their income levels and improve their living standards". Micro-finance institutions are those institutions that provide these services. Microcredit is, thus, the provision of credit to the poor and the very poor, who lack access to credit provided by formal financial institutions. Typical micro-finance clients are low-income borrowers and usually, but not exclusively, women. They are often household-based entrepreneurs who have a steady source of income, however small. Their sole source of credit is the moneylender. They lack secure, convenient and reliable savings services and perforce depend on informal systems as a hedge against emergencies or large lifecycle expenditures.

Microfinance generally refers to small-scale financial services, primarily credit and savings, provided to people who farm or fish or herd or who operate small enterprises or micro-enterprises where goods are produced, repaired, recycled or sold. Services are also offered to people who provide services, work for wages or commissions, gain income from renting out small amounts of land, vehicles, draught animals or machinery and tools to other individuals and groups at the local level of developing countries, both rural and urban. Such households may have multiple sources of income. Savings services allow savers to store excess liquidity for future use as well as to obtain returns on their investment. Credit services enable the use of anticipated income streams for current investment or consumption. Overall, micro-finance services can help low-income borrowers reduce risk, improve management, raise productivity, obtain higher sums as returns on investments, increase their incomes and improve the quality of their lives and those of their dependents.

SHG–Bank Linkage Programme

The provision of microfinance through banks has been experimented with successfully in India. In 1990, the National Bank for Agriculture and Rural Development initiated a pilot project of linkage of 500 SHGs with banks. In 1996, the SHG linkage programme linking the non-formal sector represented by the SHGs and the institutional credit delivery system of commercial banks cooperatives and the RRBs was operationalised throughout the country.

In 1996, the RBI included financing of SHGs as a mainstream activity of banks under priority sector lending. Over the years the SHG–Bank linkage programme gained momentum and as on 31 March 2002, 4.61 lakh SHGs have been credit-linked by various financial institutions. The cumulative amount disbursed stood at Rs 1026.34 crore. Thus, the SHG–Bank linkage programme has emerged as a major microcredit provision model in India. The mission statement on microfinance is to extend financial services to half of India's un-reached and underserved poor, numbering 100 million, through 1 million SHGs, with a focus on women, through various micro-finance interventions by 2008. A series of initiatives to create an enabling environment have been exercised to ensure that complementary and competitive models of micro-finance delivery are encouraged to co-exist and grow.

Studies by various agencies have shown that the self-help savings and credit groups have the potential to bring together the formal banking structure and the poor for mutual benefit. The benefit to the formal credit institutions lies in the externalisation of part of the credit cycle: assessment of credit needs, identification of borrowers, disbursal of loans tailored to borrower needs and requirements, more effective supervision of end use of loans leading to better loan repayment, reduction in the formal paperwork involved and a consequent reduction in transaction costs and perhaps most significant, improved recoveries (the joint-liability group model has shown dramatic recovery rates). The NGOs have a critical role in organising the rural poor into SHGs. These organizations have emerged as critical links between organised credit-disbursing agencies and those who have the need and are able to obtain credit from these institutions. In view of the effectiveness of NGOs in fulfilling this function and the demonstrated need for routing financial assistance to the poor through some intermediate agency, the SHG–Bank linkage model has been adopted as the dominant paradigm.

Microfinance Development Fund

The Microfinance Development Fund has been operationalised by the RBI through the NABARD and with contributions from the RBI and commercial banks. The share of commercial banks has been computed as a percentage of their net working funds in proportion to their capital to risk assets ratio.

The objective of the Fund is to boost the movement of microcredit. The Fund is geared towards the training, capacity building and sensitisation of banks, NGOs, SHGs and government extension agencies as well as to provide start-up funds to micro-finance institutions to meet their initial operating deficits, meet the cost of formation and nurturing of SHGs, design new delivery mechanisms, promote research and dissemination of best practices, study international best practices and their applicability in the Indian context. The Fund is also expected to address institutional and credit delivery issues, issues related to institutional growth and transformation within the existing legal and regulatory frameworks, issues related to business practices, ethics and governance and issues related to access to sources of funding to ensure sustainability of the institutions functioning as financial intermediaries. It aims to catalyze the micro-finance sector by deepening and widening it, building new products, encouraging financial innovation and intermediaries, increasing the economic efficiency of existing institutions to enable them to provide better financial services to the poor and to strengthen the framework through which micro-finance services are provided.

Externalisation of the Credit Cycle

The problem of tracking and screening good borrowers is taken care of as the groups themselves select their members. The group has the responsibility of ensuring that an income-generating project is taken up which will pay for itself and enable the group to repay the bank instalments. Repayment rates are 98%–100% in the case of the loans availed of by micro-borrowers. Hence, it is effective for redressal of poverty. Bank–NGO–SHG partnerships are very useful, as NGOs possess extensive knowledge of local conditions and are able to reach segments of the rural population not targeted by banks. The tripartite partnership of banks, NGOs and SHGs helps to develop innovative approaches. The NGOs are involved in the conceptualisation, design and monitoring of programmes and new approaches to address development problems and issues. These SHG lending programmes also foster social, economic and political empowerment of the poor. They help build local institutions. Interventions are more participatory in nature and help to create and maintain community-based social and economic infrastructure. However, as in any emerging industry, there are some concerns.

A Note of Caution

Microfinance should be viewed as one other approach to supplement not supplant the existing credit delivery system. One of the pitfalls that banks should avoid is the numbers approach. They should not pre-decide that 'x' number of groups have to be formed. This will otherwise lead to the proliferation of non-viable groups. There should be no element of subsidy, otherwise groups may be formed on paper, merely to avail of the subsidy. Before the groups are credit-linked, an adequate gestation period should be allowed to them to enable them to become cohesive groups which will be able to take correct decisions. The costs that are to be incurred in the capacity building of these groups are also quite high, and it is yet to be seen whether the costs of forming, strengthening and holding the hands of groups compare with the administration of direct, small loans. Great care should also be exercised to ensure that loans are not extended to groups to repay part of the earlier loan, i.e., the loans should help the poor overcome poverty and not be a source of trapping them in a cycle of debt. The lending rate should be concessional. Intermediation for removal of poverty needs to be holistic not minimalistic, i.e., credit alone cannot help the poor overcome poverty. An integrated financial services approach is required and this requires continuous monitoring.

Poverty Eradication

Promoting equitable and sustainable development from the bottom up in ways that enable the poor to create income and wealth for themselves is a widely shared ideal. One of every three persons in India is poor, and two of three are undernourished or malnourished. If we include those who are deprived of safe drinking water, adequate clothing or shelter, the number is considerably higher. Finally, if you also include people who are above the officially-defined poverty line but are vulnerable in the sense of not being adequately insured against rising prices, unemployment, illiteracy, declining income, old age and disease, you get a huge majority. Poverty eradication has been on the agenda of public policy for more than 50 years yet the percentage of the population which is below the poverty line continues to be at unacceptably high levels.

Microfinance is one way of reaching the hardcore and asset-less poor which has demonstrated its effectiveness. An important concern of microfinance has been to increase penetrative outreach so that credit can be institutionalized and a larger number of people can benefit through improved access to credit. Microfinance has also shown how greater access can be attained with sustainability of the financial institutions.

Micro-finance programmes are unique in that they foster the participation of the poor in the processes of economic growth by creating employment opportunities, increasing the access of the poor to income generating assets and by raising the productivity of these assets, both physical and human, enabling the poor to manage risk better. In periods of change it also helps to mitigate the transitional costs of the adjustment process for the most vulnerable groups. Subsidised interest rates, administered loan allocations and targeted credit programmes were designed to displace informal sources of financial services. As these did not rest on a base of community empowerment, the programmes met with very limited success. Microfinance presents itself as a viable alternative to the traditional strategies for attacking poverty.

Models of Micro-finance Delivery

The two major approaches to microfinance are the poverty lending approach pioneered by the Grameen Bank of Bangladesh and the commercial finance approach of the Bank Rakyat Indonesia. Grameen Bank extends small loans of less than Rs 4000 to the asset-less and the hardcore poor, who lack physical collateral but may be in a position to offer social collateral. The Grameen Bank extends loans to them on the joint liability of all the group members and uses peer pressure to ensure the recovery of its loans. The Grameen Bank finances the poor owning less than half an acre of land. Loans are for the purpose of household enterprises and are extended to small groups of five or ten members that undertake thrift and credit activities utilising their own resources. These loans are extended for small income-generating projects and farm activity and are extended to individual borrowers within the group. The group provides the guarantee for end use and recovery of loans. If one borrower within the group defaults, the other members of the group bring pressure on the defaulting borrower to make good the loan. The penalty for individual default rebounds collectively on the group who are not able to access fresh loans. This stick has proved to be an effective recovery guarantee mechanism. The members of the group are also given the freedom to self-select borrowers to constitute their groups. Not surprisingly, affinity, activity or association links these groups. The groups meet regularly and recovery instalments are also paid in to the Grameen representative at these meetings.

The loans are small and meant for setting up income-generating projects. The Grameen Bank offers a variety of financial products and has a vast outreach especially among rural women borrowers. Several groups are federated to form centres. Loans can be given to individuals to pursue individual activity within the group or to the group as a whole. Strict credit discipline is maintained.

Sixteen Decisions of the Grameen Bank

A larger social purpose is also sub-served as members take a pledge to implement the sixteen decisions that carry social messages. The frequent meetings lead to a greater follow-up of the end use of loans and also to bonding among the group members. The Grameen Bank has adopted a credit plus approach through its sixteen decisions.

1. We respect the four principles of the Grameen Bank – we are disciplined, united, courageous and hardworking – and we apply them to our lives.
2. We wish to give our families good living standards.
3. We will not live in dilapidated houses. We repair them and work to build new ones.
4. We cultivate vegetables the whole year round and sell the surplus.
5. During the season for planting, we pick out as many seedlings as possible.
6. We intend to have small families. We shall reduce our expenses to a minimum. We take care of our health.
7. We educate our children and see that they can earn enough money to finance their training.
8. We see to it that our children and homes are clean.
9. We build latrines and use them.
10. We only drink water drawn from a well. If not, we boil the water or we use alum.
11. We will not accept a marriage dowry for our son and we do not give one to our daughter at her marriage. Our centre is against this practice.

12. We cause harm to no one and we will not tolerate that anyone should do us harm.
13. To increase our income, we make important investments in common.
14. We are always ready to help each other. When someone is in difficulty, we all give a helping hand.
15. If we learn that discipline is not respected in a centre, we go along to help and restore order.
16. We are introducing physical exercise in all centres. We take part in all social events.

It has transformed into the world's largest bank, serving 2.3 million borrowers, 94% of whom are women, and all of whom were living in abject poverty before they began receiving micro-loans. These small loans have been used to capitalise more than 500 businesses, including food processing, cottage industries and trading. Several replications of the Grameena Bank model have emerged such as the Amanul Ikhtiar in Malaysia. The Centre for Rural and Agricultural Development of the Philippines, The Society for Helping and Awakening the Rural Poor through Education in India and Activists for Social Alternatives are among the other prominent ones.

Bank Rakyat Indonesia Model

The second approach, that of the Bank Rakyat Indonesia (BRI), is characterised as the financial systems approach. In 1983, the micro-banking division of the BRI was cut off from subsidies and granted full management autonomy. Its good practices have included carefully crafted financial products, high interest rates on savings and loans, staff productivity incentives, rewards to borrowers for on time repayment and good governance. The BRI has a special assignment from the government to provide banking services with special reference to agricultural credit to the farmers known as Usaha Tani. The Bank serves all segments of the banking industry including micro-medium and large businesses and both individual and corporate clients. The BRI's unit desa system (the micro-banking division) has made the Bank famous due to the successful provision of financial services to low-income borrowers. In 1984, BRI began its new programme of general-purpose credit called Kupedes. The Kupedes kredit Ummam Pedesan, offered through the penetrative outreach of the unit desa, system broke even in two years. Initially, small loans were extended for productive activities. By 1986, this also included a package of savings services provided throughout the country. The spread between the loan and deposit interest rates was set to cover all estimated costs, financial and non-financial, and to generate a profit. Unit desas have been profitable since their inception, and even in the worst phase of the recent economic crisis continued to provide stable savings deposit and credit services to their members.

A 1996 report of the World Bank Operations Evaluation Department assesses their success on the following basis: "The program succeeded because the banks loaned at market rates, used income to finance their operations, kept operating costs low and devised appropriate savings instruments to attract depositors. By mobilising rural savings, the unit Desa system was not only provided with a stable source of funds, it also kept financial savings in rural areas thus helping growth and development in rural areas. In the countryside, other reasons for success included the simplicity of loan design which enabled the banks to keep costs down, effective management at the unit level backed by close supervision and monitoring by the centre and through the institution of appropriate staff training and incentives for good performance."

BancoSol Model

The BancoSol is a financial institution, which targets low-income micro-entrepreneurs and provides financial services to them at rates that are commercially viable. The Bank for Solidarity (Banco Solidario), Bolivia emerged through solidarity in group lending and was the first bank in Latin America built expressly to provide financial services to micro-entrepreneurs on a national scale. The bank emerged from the Fundación para la Promoción y Desarollo de la Microempresa (PRODEM), an NGO that provides commercial credit to micro-entrepreneurs. PRODEM was founded in 1996 by ACCION International, a US-based NGO operating in Latin America, and by a group of Bolivian business leaders. Funding was provided by USAID, the Bolivian Social Emergency Fund, the Calmeadow Foundation and donations from international and Bolivian foundations and the private sector. PRODEM became highly successful in delivering and recovering microcredit provided at interest rates that provided full cost recovery. However, being an NGO and dependent on donor funding, it remained capital-constrained. PRODEM was legally restrained from collecting savings from the public or borrowing from the Central Bank. To gain access to other sources of funds, increase the volume of lending and provide full financial services to micro-entrepreneurs,

PRODEM's Board of Directors decided to set up a private commercial bank. To meet the needs of micro-entrepreneurs in exchange for an 18% share in the equity of BancoSol, PRODEM's loan portfolio and staff were transferred to the new bank. BancoSol, like the BRI's unit desas, became financially self-sufficient and sustainable in less than two years after it was set up. USAID's study of 11 microfinance programmes lists BancoSol as being profitable and self-sufficient in 1993, calculated on a commercial basis. The overall contribution made by PRODEM and BancoSol reaches far beyond their clients. BancoSol has demonstrated that regulated, financially self-sufficient micro-credit institutions can access international commercial markets, thereby removing funding as a constraint to the development and growth of microfinance.

New Paradigm

The new paradigm lays emphasis on the idea that given enabling economic, political, legal, regulatory and demographic conditions, commercial institutions can be developed to provide financial intermediation for the economically active poor, and can also deliver services at the local level profitably.

The two major approaches, the poverty lending approach and the financial systems approach, are still being refined. One sharp distinction between the two is often drawn. The poverty lending approach focuses on the poorest of the poor through government, donor or subsidised funds. The financial sector approach targets the economically-active, poor micro-entrepreneurs. Building on their existing skills and capacities, seeks to set up viable income generating projects (IGPs). Sustainable IGPs that enable them to build income streams and generate cash flow which would be sufficient to pay back the loans and also plough back funds to expand their micro-enterprises. Thus, Bank Rakyat Indonesia and BancoSol advocate commercial microfinance for the entrepreneurial poor.

The funds needed for micro-finance institutions to expand their reach on a large-scale can come only from the vast resources of the financial system, with self-sufficient institutions emerging as financial intermediaries to facilitate the efficient movement of capital between savers and borrowers. Such commercially viable micro-finance institutions can also eventually access funds from Central Banks and directly from markets. Banks lack the large-scale capacity for retail lending which SHGs possess.

Positive Features

More than 80% of the world's population does not have access to financial services, either for credit or for savings from formal institutions. Worldwide there is a massive demand for micro-finance services. Financial institutions such as banks generally consider the provision of small loans and deposit services an unprofitable activity due to the prohibitive transaction costs of extending small loans, the problems in identification of borrowers and the difficulties faced in recovery of loans. Hence, institutional, commercial microfinance has remained at a low level. From the borrower's point of view, the crucial words in microfinance are access and cost. Though subsidized loan programmes provide cheap credit, they do not provide lower income households with widespread access to credit. Informal moneylenders in aggregate provide wide access but generally at prohibitive cost. On the savings side, the poor need secure, convenient, voluntary savings services which formal financial institutions do not extend to them.

Where available, sustainable institutions providing microfinance help the poor to reduce vulnerability, smoothen consumption and increase incomes. Microfinance can facilitate:

- a direct improvement in the economic activities, political empowerment and the quality of life of the working poor
- increase employment of the poor
- lead to a shift in government orientation from credit subsidies to Poverty alleviation. The productivity, incomes and quality of life of hundreds of millions of people could be substantially increased through access to institutional savings and credit facilities delivered locally.

The success of microfinance lies in that the micro-finance model involves the local communities in the design, implementation and monitoring of the programmes. The affinity groups or SHGs promoted by disinterested organizations have successfully created institutions which can be suited to the existing village environment, and have the autonomy to take quick operational decisions and cater to the individual needs of the poor. Affinity groups held together by traditional social relations and shared needs and interests are self-sustaining institutions. In India, pro-poor interventions recognize the need to ensure that the opportunities for improved livelihood are widely available across the entire spectrum of society, that the security of these livelihoods is promoted and that the constraints that inhibit and exclude people from participating in and sharing the benefits of development are removed. Micro-finance interventions that are community-based, target vulnerable groups like women, scheduled castes and tribes and the landless poor and help to support decentralization and empowerment at the local level.

Need for Many Solutions

The demand for financial services is very diverse among the poor and any sustainable response has to be pluralistic. Only micro-finance institutions (MFIs) are suited to cater to these credit plus demands as formal financial institutions dispense restricted services. However, SHGs lack financial muscle and here a linkage with formal financial institutions works well to meet the demand for financial services. They foster linkages with upstream financial institutions with a much larger capital base. MFIs have a mandate of ensuring sustainable poverty reduction. MFIs strengthen the self-reliance of the people and their Self-help Promoting Institutions (SHPIs). Viable MFIs and viable formal financial institutions are inextricably bound together. The aim of an MFI is to strengthen both individual self-help capacities and institutional viability. Banks provide loanable funds. The SHPIs help to increase the outreach of the banking system by increasing their access to financial services. In order to create an enabling environment for microfinance, several steps have been taken in the recent past. To ensure financial sustainability these institutions are allowed to charge cost covering interest rates. Interest rates applicable to loans given by banks to micro-credit organizations or by the micro-credit organizations to SHGs' member beneficiaries have been left to their discretion, with the exception of the interest rate ceiling applicable to direct small loans by banks. Banks are at liberty to formulate their own models or choose any conduit intermediary for extending microcredit. As a further incentive, bank loans extended for microfinance either directly or through an intermediary are treated as part of banks' priority sector lending. Microcredit is also to be included in branch credit plan, block credit plan, district and state credit plan of each bank. Banks have been advised that they may prescribe their own lending norms, keeping in view the ground realities. They may devise appropriate loan and savings products and related terms and conditions including the size of the loan, the unit size, the maturity period, the grace period, the margins, etc. The intention is to provide maximum flexibility in regard to micro-lending, keeping in view the prevalent local conditions and the need for provision of microfinance. The credit should be for consumption, production loans for various farm and non-farm activities of the poor and also include their other credit needs such as housing and shelter improvements.

Thus, a great deal of necessary flexibility has been imparted so as to ensure that banks are proactive. However, significant progress has still not been registered, and greater efforts are required to ensure that microfinance expands. One way of doing this is by scaling up the existing micro-finance intermediation so that besides financial strengthening they also have access to the managerial and professional expertise of the banks. Another way is to downscale banks to increase their micro-finance intervention efforts. Ideally both strategies should grow in tandem to promote microfinance.

The role of microcredit as the most suitable and feasible alternative in accomplishing the goals of growth and poverty alleviation is now well recognised. Microfinance embodies the basic democratic ethos of self-development through a participatory approach. The experiment of microfinance in India through the conduit of SHGs linked to banks has demonstrated considerable democratic functioning and group dynamism. Their adroitness in assessing and appraising the credit needs of members, their business-like functioning and efficiency in recycling funds, often with repayment rates nearing cent per cent, have proved that this is among the best alternatives in improving credit delivery to the poor. Recognizing their importance, both the RBI and NABARD have been spearheading the promotion and linkage of SHGs to the banking system through refinance support, and initiating other proactive policies and systems. A couple of case studies highlight the role played by the many micro-credit institutions in the rural economy. The programme of microfinance has made rapid strides in India. The programme began in 1992 with a modest pilot project of linking around 500 SHGs with half a dozen banks across the country has grown to cover 31,000 rural outlets of more than 500 banks, with a loan portfolio of more than Rs 2,000 crore on 31 March 2003. The programme has enabled the formal banking system to reach the doorsteps of 116 lakh very poor households through the conduit of 7.17 lakh SHGs. Two of the many case studies of successful microfinance models are of the Swayam Krishi Sangham and the Prathama Bank.

Swayam Krishi Sangham and Prathama Models

The Swayam Krishi Sangam (SKS) and the Prathama Bank are two good illustrations of successful models of SHGs. While the SKS model represents an SHG formed by a formal agency other than the banks but directly financed by banks; the Prathama model, on the other hand, is a specimen of those SHGs formed and financed by the banks. The SKS has emerged as one of the catalytic forces behind the spread of the micro-finance movement in Andhra Pradesh. The Prathama Bank, being the first regional rural bank, commands a long-standing experience in the field in the state of Uttar Pradesh.

The SKS and the Prathama Bank target poor rural women, with the SKS focussing especially on the drought-prone region. The methodology adopted for group formation under the SKS, inter alia, includes (1) selection of villages based on the levels of poverty, main economic activities and type of land, and (2) conducting project meetings to create awareness. A group is formed with five members and a sangam evolves when eight such groups are constituted. The Prathama Bank, on the other hand, relies on the expertise of the Vikas Volunteer Vahinis (VVV) – a club consisting of volunteers who command local acceptability and goodwill and act as informal ambassadors of the bank to the villages. Village meets with the help of VVVs are organized by the bank to impart awareness among the people.

The SKS and Prathama models leverage technology and novelty in the promotion of SHGs. The SKS offers a variety of savings and loan products meant both for consumption and income generating activities and has pioneered smart cards and palm pilots (electronic passbooks). It has developed fully automated and integrated in-house management information systems (MIS) which enable virtual real time access to portfolio, client and staff information in all its branches. It has also developed Microsoft Excel-based financial models for different periodicities to monitor cash management, track financial performance against targets, and project operational growth. These new initiatives have proved helpful in lowering the cost of transactions, increasing the productivity, reducing the scope for error and fraud, and improvement in the accuracy and timeliness of management information systems.

The Prathama Bank has also taken several initiatives such as the setting up of an exclusive Women Development Cell, Micro Credit Innovation Cell, launching of Rural Entrepreneurship Development Programme for training SHG members in various crafts, starting of SHG primary school in each village, launching of novel schemes like Prathama Swachata (Sanitation) Yojana and Gas (LPG) Connection Scheme.

Within a short span, both have posted an improved outreach and coverage. As at the end of June 2003, the outreach and network of SKS has grown to cover eight branches encompassing 524 village centres, serving 17,058 customers. As at the end of the fiscal year 2003, with an outstanding credit portfolio of Rs 4.9 crore and savings portfolio of Rs 36 lakh, it has achieved the annual targets, maintaining a repayment rate of 99%. Over 85% of its clients are marginalised members of society. The total loans outstanding at about Rs 0.02 crore in the year 1999 have grown, within four years to Rs 5.12 crore in 2002–3. In the case of the Prathama Bank, as at the end of March 2003, more than 4,500 SHGs encompassing 65,000 members were credit-linked with an amount of Rs 12.6 crore, disbursed for various income generating activities comprising dairy, retail shops, zari work and other related activities.

A cost-benefit analysis involving the case studies under review reveal divergent trends, though administrative expenses for administering an outstanding loan of Rs 100 witnessed a decline in both cases in the recent years. While interest earning on an outstanding loan of Rs 100 increased in the case of the SKS, it, however, declined for the Prathama Bank. Furthermore, the gap between income and expenditure widened for SKS, while the Prathama Bank recorded a surplus income continuously over the years. While the SKS depends on foreign donations, the dependence of the Prathama Bank on outside agencies in the form of borrowings has been quite minimal.

Table 6.1 SHG–Bank Linkage: Cumulative Progress

(Rupees in crores)

As on 31 March	No. of SHGs Financed	Bank Loan Disbursed
1	2	3
1999	32,995	57.07
2000	1,14,775	192.98
2001	2,63,825	480.87
2002	4,61,478	1,026.34
2003	7,17,360	2,048.67

(Source: NABARD)

The significant increase in the number of SHGs linked during 2003 was possible due to the active involvement of 504 banks, 2800 NGOs and many other agencies including developmental departments of different state governments. The credit linkage programme covered 523 districts in 30 states and union territories. The notable features are the active participation of women in the programme accounting for 90% of the total SHGs and the strong loan repayment performance of SHGs at more than 95%.

Both in terms of promotional grant support to NGOs and developing capacity building outreach of various partners in formation and nurturing of quality SHGs, greater financial allocations and efforts are required. The amount of cumulative grant support sanctioned for promotion and linkage of SHGs, as on 31 March 2003, aggregated to Rs 10.4 crore covering 564 NGOs and 78,011 SHGs. However, release of grants, at Rs 4.5 crore, constituted 43.2% of the sanctioned grant, resulting in the promotion of 51,945 SHGs, of which 26,229 SHGs are with credit linkage.

Emerging Concerns

Thus, the micro-finance programme has made significant progress, both in terms of coverage and outreach. However, there are some issues of concern which deserve attention.

- The coverage of poor families in the SHG movement is yet to gain momentum. Out of 52 million poor families (260 million poor) in the country, only 11.6 million families (58 million poor) or 22.3% of the poor families were covered as on 31 March 2003.
- Another area of major concern is the uneven growth of microfinance. As on 31 March 2003, of the total SHGs credit linked, Andhra Pradesh accounted for 39% followed by Tamil Nadu, Karnataka and Uttar Pradesh. These four states together accounted for 69% of the total SHGs credit-linked and four-fifths of the total amount of bank loans as on 31 March 2003.

Table 6.2 Share of States in the Cumulative Number of SHGs Credit-linked (end of March 2003)

States	Percentage
Andhra Pradesh	39
Tamil Nadu	14
Karnataka	9
Uttar Pradesh	7
Maharashtra	4
Other States	27

(Source: NABARD)

If we consider the major models, design issues and parameters of evaluation, we find that there is no single demonstrable institutional form with optimal utility that works best in providing financial services in rural areas. Government policies that translate to good governance and the overall economic environment are the main determinants of project performance. There is, in sum, no magic seed that works everywhere, at all times and in all climates. In India we have not singled out any one model as superior. Several models have been allowed to co-exist as long as the ultimate objectives of increasing access to credit to the poor with institutional self-sufficiency are served. This also enables financial innovation for designing new delivery mechanisms and promoting research, management information systems and for the dissemination of the best practices in microfinance. Financial products and services on offer can be tailored to meet the needs of poor borrowers. We have seen the emergence of NGOs that have been drawn into financial intermediation as a matter of expediency.

The rural poor are largely dependent on agriculture to sustain their meagre incomes. In urban areas, the poor, especially women who bear the double burden of being poor and being women, are concentrated in the unorganized sector of the informal economy as workers or home-based providers. Developments in the last two decades in the provision of financial services to the poor, both savings and credit, have demonstrated the potential of microfinance. Poverty is an unacceptable human condition. Microfinance is an important means to address the critical challenge of poverty.

To achieve scale with outreach and sustainability, it is essential to move away from the model of microfinance delivered exclusively through government-sponsored programmes and develop a market-based institutional capacity. Regulation by governments and central banks leads to a one-size fits-all uniformity. Good intentions have unintended evil consequences. The programmes do not result in efficiency. Distortions in markets subsidies lead to market imperfections. Though there is no need for regulation, there is definitely a need for an active role for governments and central banks in establishing favourable policies and supportive laws to facilitate the smooth functioning of rural financial markets and for encouraging the entry of new players. They must, however, limit their direct intervention. A greater role has to be assigned to private providers with emphasis on transparency of operations, efficiency and accountability.

References

Hulme, D. and Paul Mosley. 1996. *Finance against Poverty,* vol I. London: Routledge.

Pant Joshi, Deepali. 2002. 'Micro Finance: Need of the Hour'. *Journal of the Agricultural Finance Corporation of India.*

Pitt, M. and Shahidur R. Khandekar. 1996. 'Household and Intrahousehold Impact of the Grameen and Similar Targeted Credit Programmes in Bangladesh'. World Bank Discussion Paper No. 320. Washington DC: The World Bank.

Rhyne, E. and Otero Maria, eds. 1994. *The New World of Micro Enterprise Finance.* London: Intermediate Technology Publications.

Robinson, S. Marguerite. 2002. *The Microfinance Revolution: Lessons from Indonesia,* Vol. II. Washington DC: World Bank Publications.

Yaron, J., P. B. Mc Donald Jr. and Gerda L. Piprek. 1997. 'Rural Finance Issues: Design and Best Practices'. Monograph Series No.14. The World Bank.

SEVEN

Micro-finance Initiatives for Equitable and Sustainable Development

Poverty is defined as the deprivation of basic capabilities. Over the past few years India has focused on efforts at scaling up and mainstreaming microfinance by harnessing the resources of the formal financial sector to expand poor people's access to savings and credit.

The supply-led models of development and credit-delivery are now giving way to models of participatory development focusing on demand-led growth. There is growing evidence that micro-finance programmes have the potential of assuring equitable and sustainable development. The real challenge lies in mainstreaming microfinance through the banks to ensure that outreach and sustainability grow in tandem. Institutional self-sufficiency and economic viability are synonymous. Both can be assured through banks. The focus today is on expanding access to growing numbers of low-income borrowers and savers and harnessing the resources of the formal financial structure to that end.

Challenges of Rural Finance Intermediation

Several challenges still confront rural financial intermediation; challenges of selecting the set of institutional design and policy alternatives that will prove to be most effective in different socio-economic environments. These challenges include:

- refraining from utilising subsidy and concessional interest rate driven models as the only vehicles for service delivery to the poor
- encouraging financial service provision for the poor, through both rural and urban operations, as opposed to an exclusive focus on the delivery of supply-led agricultural credit or subsidy-driven credit for input provision
- providing savings services and not merely credit services

- implementing best practices in microfinance by adopting them and adapting them to specific socioeconomic/socio-cultural contexts.

Strategic Issues

Some of the emerging concerns that are engaging the attention of financial intermediaries, financial institutions and policy makers are:

- The huge unmet demand for micro-finance services, especially among the poorest of the poor. As the economy grows more diversified, credit needs increase. The 1999 census report states that about 70% of Indians live in rural areas and are largely dependent on agriculture. The rural economy is growing more diversified as rural households strive to move into non-farm and non-agricultural activities to ensure additional sources of income. Overall, 35% of India's population is poor and more than 30% of the population still lives below the poverty line. Poverty is both chronic and transient. Across the country more than 470 million people live on less than US$1 a day. There is a great demand for micro-finance services from households and enterprises in the informal sector of the economy. In the informal sector, micro-enterprises provide an income stream for poor entrepreneurs. They recycle and repair goods that would otherwise become waste and provide cheap food, clothing and transportation for poor people including those at the lower levels of the formal sector who would not otherwise be able to live on their small salaries.
- The exclusive focus on credit rather than on both savings and credit. Savings have been termed the forgotten half of microfinance, as most of the models are credit-driven. The contribution of financial markets to development cannot be restricted to providing credit but must offer savings instruments to facilitate transactions. The desire and need to save are great. The poorer the family is, the more desperately it needs to save for protection against emergencies and to meet urgent lifecycle needs such as births, weddings and funerals as well as to cash in on the opportunities that liquid assets ensure. Money at hand has obvious drawbacks, especially for the poor. It can be stolen, borrowed by relatives, readily consumed or lost. It yields no interest and the net present value declines with inflation. Savings instruments, which are highly liquid and divisible, are needed most by the poor to diversify and manage risk. Incomes limit the range of assets poor households can hold, hence the tremendous demand for savings services.

- The lack of sustainability of most of the micro-finance institutions. Most NGOs are characterized by a high level of operational inefficiency and have a very limited capacity to serve an increasing segment of the market on a continuing and sustainable basis. Most of the State-sector institutions that provide micro-finance services have been created within and nurtured by a distorted policy environment and are characterized by various degrees of financial repression. They do not have a business culture.
- The growing number of financial intermediaries across the country with no overall authority for guidance and streamlining procedures.
- No clear guidelines, norms or parameters for evaluation of the micro-finance institutions.
- The need for regulation among these institutions.

State-sponsored Initiatives

Government-sponsored programmes for increasing the flow of credit to the poorest of the poor are strategized through the commercial banks. These programmes were based on the concept of Antyodaya of helping the poorest households first. The Integrated Rural Development Programme implemented throughout the country since the 1980s was the most well known of these programmes. These government-sponsored programmes had a component of credit from banks and a complement of subsidies from the government. The programmes met with limited success. Though well-conceived, they were poorly executed and wrongly targeted, with inadequate follow-up. As a consequence, they were stymied by poor recoveries, leading to waning enthusiasm for banks lending to the sector. The subsidised credit programmes, particularly those meant for the rural poor, were the first attempts at extending credit to the assetless poor. Though crafted with laudable intentions, they were not as successful as envisaged due to the inherent limitations in project design, execution, etc. The subsidised and below-market interest rates charged led to loans being cornered by influential persons. This also led to capital-constrained rural finance providers as the bank's portfolios were characterised by large loan losses and high arrears.

Role of Informal Finance

Micro-finance initiatives build on these strengths of the informal sector. In rural societies, these behavioural relations are utilized to ensure a set of economic entitlements for participants by assuring them access to income streams. These rights are extra-legal, in the sense that they are neither sanctioned nor protected by the legal system and are usually non-tradeable. Micro-finance practitioners recognize the importance of these familial or behavioural relations which are used to reduce risks in poor societies. These behavioural relations are utilized as insurance substitutes and collateral substitutes. The joint liability group builds on this social collateral to effectively extend credit to the assetless poor who are far beyond the formal financial system. Rural development practitioners are of the view that informal lenders who are very efficient are best suited to fulfil the needs of the penny economy. The informal lenders are moneylenders, small traders, relatives, friends and similar non-institutional networks. Widespread use of informal finance suggests that it is well-suited to the needs of most rural communities. This market would not have been thriving, if there had been no takers for it. Thus, though it is recognised that the interest rates charged are high, the need for credit is so compelling that there is no dearth of takers for loans even at high interest rates. Informal lenders provide valuable financial services at a relatively low cost.

The role and strength of informal finance agents in small-scale rural economies and their importance to low-income households should not be underestimated. The informal sector allows low-income borrowers access to services at a relatively low cost. This is possible because the informal sector is the natural environment for rural people though they typically charge high rates of interest. Microfinance has proved that it can replicate the environment that the poor are most comfortable with, and extend outreach to low-income borrowers without fleecing them. Many SHGs have developed successfully through simple operations. In India, the SEWA Bank, which effectively mobilised rag-pickers and beedi workers into small groups has now emerged as a full-fledged urban cooperative bank.

Objectives and Goals

Like many popular mass movements, the micro-finance movement is characterised both by widespread agreement on broad objectives and by multiple rifts on key issues. The movement itself is driven by the shared commitment to provide credit for small enterprise formation and growth. It is also bound together by a common rhetoric of concern for the poor. This unity of commitment and rhetoric, however, masks a variety of philosophical approaches, types of institutions and borrowers, and delivery systems that shelter uneasily together under the big tent called "microfinance".

The movement has come to be divided into two by two broad approaches, or opposing camps, to the best way to help the poor through access to financial services: the institutionist approach and the welfarist approach. Jonathan Morduch (1998) refers to this division as the micro-finance schism. The irony is that while the worldviews of each camp are not inherently incompatible, and in fact there are numerous MFIs that appear in practice to embrace them both, there nonetheless exists a large rift between the two camps that makes communication between them difficult.

The institutionist approach focuses on creating financial institutions to serve clients who are either not served or are underserved by the formal financial system. The emphasis is on achieving financial self-sufficiency; breadth of outreach (meaning numbers of clients) takes precedence over depth of outreach (meaning the levels of poverty reached); and positive client impacts are assumed. The centre of attention is the institution, and institutional success is generally gauged by the institution's progress toward achieving financial self-sufficiency. The best-known examples of the institutionist approach are Bank Rakyat Indonesia (BRI) and Banco Solidario (BancoSol) in Bolivia.

Institutionists argue that a primary objective of microfinance is financial deepening, the creation of a separate system of 'sustainable' financial intermediation for the poor. Theirs is a 'financial systems' approach to microfinance, in which the future of microfinance is dominated by numerous large-scale, profit-seeking financial institutions that provide high quality financial services to large numbers of poor clients. Because of their insistence on financial self-sufficiency, institutionists eschew subsidies of any kind. The institutionist position is articulated in virtually all the literature coming out of the Ohio State University Rural Finance Program, the World Bank and the Consultative Group to Assist the Poorest (CGAP) in the World Bank, and USAID. It is also found in the many writings of Maria Otero (ACCION International) and Elisabeth Rhyne (formerly of USAID) (see, for example, Otero and Rhyne, 1994). Most published literature in the field of microfinance espouse the institutionist approach.

Welfarists, on the other hand, emphasize depth of outreach. Welfarists are quite explicit in their focus on immediately improving the well-being of participants. They are less interested in banking per se than in using financial services as a means to alleviate directly the worst effects of deep poverty among participants and communities, even if some of these services require subsidies. Their objective tends to be self-employment of the poorer of the economically active poor, especially women, whose control of modest increases of income and savings is assumed to empower them to improve the conditions of life for themselves and their children. The centre of attention is the 'family'. Like the institutionists, welfarists have assumed more impact than they actually have been able to document. The most prominent examples of welfarist institutions are the Grameen Bank in Bangladesh and its replications elsewhere, and FINCA-style village banking programmes in Latin America and, more recently, in Africa and Asia.

Much of the scepticism about the financial viability of microfinance-providing institutions rests on the premise that microfinance is donor-driven poverty alleviation. In fact, it is increasingly understood that only the application of commercial principles to microfinance can ensure the sustainability of operations. Sustainability is the key word. This translates to the long lasting capacity of institutions to increase penetrative outreach and reach those previously excluded from financial services. Sustainability makes it attractive for all stakeholders. Commercial microfinance is a potent force. Financial institutions and committed stakeholders will play a crucial role in fusing the small-scale, donor-driven microfinance of today with the formal financial systems of tomorrow, systems that will ensure provision of high-quality financial services on a permanent and ever increasing scale to millions of poor households around the world. Microfinance at commercial rates, that is, cost-covering rates of interest for microfinance providers has achieved tremendous outreach. This approach has the merit of converting latent demand into effective demand, removing the expectation of low interest rates and capital subsidies that have spoilt borrowers over the years, restoring repayment norms and most importantly, ensuring participatory development by including local stake holders and building grassroot financial structures. Microcredit empowers the borrowers – it helps free them from poverty and enables them to take charge of their lives and their destinies.

Major Models

In India, it is expected that by utilising the over 139,000 rural retail outlets of the formal banking sector comprising 33,000 branches of commercial banks, 14,500 branches of RRBs, 92,000 cooperatives servicing a population of 4700 per rural outlet, will considerably expand the outreach of micro-credit providers.

There are four major micro-finance models prevalent throughout the world:

1. institutions that provide microcredit but are not allowed to mobilise savings from the public as they are not regulated or publicly supervised. A large number of micro-credit providers are in this category.
2. banks or financial institutions wholesale funds to NGOs who retail these funds to SHGs.
3. the NGO emerges as a financial intermediary.
4. banks emerge as grassroots-level developmental agencies and lend directly to the SHGs.

There are several issues that impinge directly on the twin objectives of expanding access to microfinance and integrating microcredit as part of the formal financial sector.

India has not restricted itself to any one approach. Innovation, competition and new institutions are needed to widen and deepen the financial markets. This will increase avenues of access to funds for the un-reached poor and soften their vulnerability to external shocks. The poverty lending approach may not be successful across the board. The financial systems approach often ignores the socio-cultural issues that may affect the ability of the poor to become economically active in order to avail themselves of such services. Rather than focus on which approach is better, in line with the focus on multiple institutions. We have encouraged multiple models.

Credit-plus Approach

Microfinance fosters a credit-plus approach where NGOs play a proactive role.

- Microfinance links financial intermediation with social intermediation. It also encourages the technological innovation, infrastructure building, institutional development and human capital formation that directly increase the productivity of resources. Thus, it fosters other growth-inducing processes.
- The Indian model has three variants. In the Bank–SHG linkage model, SHGs are linked to banks and banks lend to groups with the help of NGOs and Self-help Promoting Institutions (SHPIs). In the second variant of this model, banks lend directly to SHGs which they set up. In the third variant banks lend to intermediaries in the non-formal sector for further lending to ground-level groups or individuals. Banks wholesale credit which NGOs retail. This leads to the externalization of part of the credit cycle, of identification of borrowers,

primary processing of their applications, etcetera, it also assures recovery as the intermediary organisation takes on the onus of effecting recovery. The linkage of local intermediaries to the aggregate financial system increases the viability of informationally advantaged enforcement effective agents, NGOs and SHPIs, because they are essentially grassroots agencies with good information about borrowers hence the twin parameters of adverse selection and moral hazard are avoided. As they have an ongoing relationship with the borrower any snags arising in the income generating process can be immediately addressed so that the project generates adequate income enabling repayment of the loan. This helps to overcome covariate systemic risks and increases the opportunities for financial intermediation.

- The non-financial ingredients of growth and development matter. However, a credit plus approach including literacy etcetera can effectively be implemented only by micro-finance agents.
- The poor do not only require loans; savings services are just as important for them. The poorer the family the greater the need to save to meet life cycle needs, emergencies such as ill health, combating disease and for cashing in on opportunities, like purchasing an asset or getting a job. Deposit facilities are just as important for the poor where they can store their savings safely and reliably without fear of theft.

Role of Banks

Banks have a crucial role to play in increasing microfinance as, unlike the NGOs or the foreign financial lending agencies which can only have a limited line of credit, the banks have access to financial resources. Banks, however, need to downstream their projects to meet the financial needs of small borrowers. Down streaming means banks have to reduce minimum loan size and be more flexible on collateral requirements. They need to introduce more cash flow oriented lending techniques and effective loan tracking systems. The lending rate ideally should cover the cost of funds and minimal profit margins. Loan appraisal procedures need to be strengthened. Banks, especially rural banks and commercial banks with their interpenetrative approach through their large network of rural branches, are in a good position to engage in micro-finance activities. As banks are subjected to audit, inspection and control, the chances of misuse of funds can be reduced. Secondly, banks also possess a degree of expertise in loan appraisal and professionalism which an NGO might lack. Hence, the bank-led microfinance model of growth is a more favoured model.

A three-pronged approach has been adopted with mutually complementary and reinforcing strategies. Firstly, financial institutions such as cooperative and commercial banks, RRBs, and LABs are mainstreamed in a supportive policy and institutional environment. Secondly, the larger micro-finance providers are encouraged to expand their services through conversion to local area bank (Basix is one such example). There are also financial linkages available through the SHG–Bank linkage model to enlarge their services. Thirdly, the growth of a range of community development financial institutions owned and managed by the community, SHG clusters and a federation of SHGs are encouraged.

For greater access to the financial system one of two things will have to occur with respect to the MFIs. Either the financial institutions will have to offer micro-finance services downscale or the MFIs will have to become licensed and upscale.

The growth of financial intermediaries that address the needs of small-saving and small-borrowing micro-enterprises is being encouraged, while strengthening and increasing capacities of RRBs, Cooperatives, LABs and commercial banks to mainstream microfinance and bring it to the centre stage.

As an incentive for banks to lend to this sector, microfinance now forms part of banks' priority sector lending portfolio and this is monitored by the RBI, including microcredit as part of their corporate credit plans. Interest rates have been freed and micro-finance providers are free to charge interest rates on a cost-covering basis or as per their reading of the micro-finance market. Banks are also free to design and to price their own products as per their commercial judgement.

Role of Financial Institutions

NABARD and the Small Industries Development Bank of India (SIDBI) are active partners in the SHG–Bank linkage programme. The SIDBI has instituted a micro-finance development fund for training and capacity building of micro-entrepreneurs. In his Budget speech for the current year, the finance minister has also emphasized the importance of small and medium enterprises that have great potential for creating jobs and employment opportunities and for powering economic growth.

Regulatory Concerns

Regulatory issues also impinge on the processes of institutional strengthening. Regulation of microfinance is now taking centre stage as the major issue confronting this nascent industry. NGOs, commercial banks and central banks are all involved in this debate. It is interesting to first review the major arguments advanced for and against regulation and then to view these through the prism of the proponents' underlying objectives.

- NGOs with large micro-credit operations are major proponents of regulation. Seeking to gain access to larger donor funds, i.e., seeking to fund themselves, NGOs desire regulation which would add to their credibility and facilitate access to credit lines from donors, the government, central banks and the public.
- Sometimes NGOs believe that regulation will promote their business and enhance their standing with the public, making it easier for them to garner public deposits.
- Some governments, NGOs and donors want financial licenses to be more easily and widely available to increase the efficiency of financial intermediation access to both savings and the consequent increase in lending operations.
- Governments and central banks are often of the view that setting up a special window for the regulation of microfinance will expedite the emergence of sustainable MFIs who will not be capital constrained.
- The central bank and governments often share the apprehension that with unlicensed micro-finance institutions, the safety of depositor's funds cannot be ensured. The safety of deposits may be jeopardised through the operations of rogues or fly-by-night operators out to make a quick buck by floating Ponzi schemes. The desire to protect the safety of depositor funds, which is the mandate of central banks, prompts the focus on the need to regulate these institutions.
- Many MFIs charge very high rates of interest. Governments and central banks may share the view that interest rate caps should be put in place to ensure that depositors do not have to face exorbitant and usurious rates of interest.
- Central banks/Governments are often concerned by the weakness of MFIs; their fear is that MFIs are too loosely regulated by their own boards and donors, so if an MFI were to fail it could bring down the emerging market in disrepute with negative consequences for future growth and development of the sector.

- Microfinance is also getting a high political profile in several countries, especially since the microfinance summit of 1997. Governments feel that they have to do something about microfinance for reasons that combine concern for the poor with the demands of practical politics.
- Regulation also serves as a mode of tightening controls on the activities of foreign funded NGOs whose activities governments may wish to monitor more closely.

In India, the cautious view is that direct supervision of MFIs would stifle the growth of this sector and the demands of uniformity would put a complete stop to financial innovation.

There are practical problems bank examiners would face in the regulation of MFIs. The costs, both financial and human, are very high. At present, donors have periodic audits to ensure the end use of their funds. Accounts must be submitted to registering agencies such as the Office of the Commissioner of Charities. Banks and NABARD have their own rating agencies.

Keeping in view all of the above, stress has been on loose regulation through a self-regulatory organisation model with the insistence that those organizations, which accept deposits from the public and do not restrict themselves to accepting savings from their own members, must register themselves as non-banking finance companies which come under the regulatory umbrella of the central bank.

Evaluation of Success or Failure

How can the success of MFIs be evaluated? Jacob Yaron, through his seminal work in 1992, has introduced a framework for assessing the performance of rural financial institutions. This has gained wide acceptance among practitioners and academics. The framework posits two primary criteria, outreach and sustainability. It is premised on the assumption that rural financial intermediaries (RFIs) can provide a broad range of services to the target clientele in an efficient manner and have the desired impact of expanding incomes and reducing the impact of poverty. Evaluation on these criteria is a quantifiable proxy for judging the efficiency of RFIs.

Outreach is measured by several indicators such as the number of clients and average loan size as proxy for income level. Sustainability is assessed by calculating an RFI's prevailing average on lending rate and the percentage by which this would need to be increased for it to break even or to make it fully autonomous, that is, subsidy independent. The subsidy dependence index also indicates the cost to society of subsidising an RFI as opposed to the interest earned by the RFI in the marketplace. The main factors that contribute to self-sustainability are adequate interest on lending rates and interest rate spreads, high rates of loan collection, high levels of savings mobilization and low overheads and administrative costs. A growing number of successful RFIs provide adaptable and replicable methodologies.

These successes indicate ways of developing institutional capacity that will ensure the growth of sustainable institutions delivering efficient services to the rural clientele. An understanding of informal financial markets and the nature of informal contracts in a particular community can provide guidance on the range of workable practices within the community and identify market opportunities to better meet the demand for financial services in that community. Accountable, strong management information systems, personnel and effective savings mobilisation characterise the successful institutions.

Policy Choices or Implications of Regulation

Currently the concern is with securing the stability of the entire financial system. The rural credit delivery system has a multi-agency approach, which encompasses the Cooperatives, RRBs, LABs, urban cooperative banks and non-bank finance companies under RBI regulation. The core concern is to ensure that none of these is beset with structural problems.

In trying to manage bank risk, the supervisor has to work in a political minefield, as the owners of banks are seldom under-represented in the political process. The supervisor's legal authority to enforce compliance or manage clean-ups is often inadequate. Monitoring healthy banks and ensuring their continued state of health is challenging enough, though the real difficulties arise in restructuring weak banks. In such a scenario it is daunting to append disparate and diffuse MFIs to the regulatory paradigm.

It would prove difficult to bail out an MFI in the event of it facing difficulties. If a bank is experiencing structural difficulties, the first arrow in the central bank's quiver is a capital call to shore up the bank's capital so as to ensure the bank's continued ability to meet the claims of its depositors. This cannot be done in the case of MFIs. Large micro-finance providers, even those partly owned by donor agencies cannot immediately produce the requisite additional capital, as their request has to be routed through donor agencies, which may or may not decide to bail out the institution. Finansol of Colombia is one such example. An MFI organised as a finance company, Finansol suffered serious loan losses, reducing its cushion of owners' capital. The supervisor issued a capital call that the principal owner, Corposol, was not able to provide. The NGO board members, not being affected by its failure, chose not to bail it out.

The second arrow in the quiver of the central bank is placing a temporary freeze on the advance of fresh loans. Often succeeding, this serves to protect the interests of existing depositors while efforts are made to resolve the problem. In the case of an MFI, the moratorium has potentially very harmful consequences as most clients of MFIs repay loans in the hope of fresh loans and with the expectation of receiving reliable and responsive future services. If the MFI denies prompt follow-up loans to clients who have punctually repaid their loans in the past, it is breaching an implicit contract. The minute the news spreads, many borrowers will stop repaying their existing loans, creating further difficulties for the institution. A related problem lies in that an MFI's principal assets consist of micro-loans that have little value once they are out of the hands of the team that originated them.

In the case of a bank, which is in trouble, the central bank uses the third arrow in its quiver – it encourages acquisition by a stronger bank. Most of the sick bank's loans in case of institutional failure or apprehended weakness are still backed by collateral guarantees, hence the borrowers' incentive to repay is mitigated. The healthy bank taking over the loan portfolio can expect to recover most of it and therefore has an incentive for acquisition. There may be other incentives, for instance, the physical infrastructure of a failed bank in an area which is under-served by the stronger bank. The acquiring bank would also receive an infusion of funds from the central bank and government as part of a bailout package. Hence a sick bank is rarely left to fail. In the case of an MFI, if the loan portfolio comprises micro-loans, the costs of collection would be higher than the actual recoveries. The MFI's loan portfolio would be of little value and a healthy institution would not desire to take over the contaminated portfolio. This would burden the central bank with a problem that it can well afford to avoid.

Costs of Regulation

The non-financial costs of regulation would be to stifle competition and financial innovation as the MFIs would devote their energies to attempts to circumvent existing regulation. This would lead to the institution of caps on interest rates, making sustainable microfinance even more difficult. So far programmes have been left free to price their own products. Interest rate controls would put a stop to this freedom. Prudential formal regulation under the aegis of the central bank carries with it the implicit understanding that it must vouch for and assume responsibility for the soundness of the regulated institutions.

Examples of Non-financial Regulation

Examples of such regulation could include:

- registration/licensing
- disclosure of ownership/control
- publication of financial statements
- reporting to the central bank
- adherence to all controls instituted by the central bank, applicable to all financial institutions regardless of typology
- external examination audits, supervisory examination by central bank auditors and compliance with off-site monitoring norms

Regulatory Straitjackets

Regulation permits no exceptions and is comprehensive. MFIs that do not accept deposits should not be regulated. Credit-only MFIs are allowed to accept small deposits that more often than not are part of the loan contract. Most clients are net-debtors most of the time, hence the risk to them in case of institutional failure is relatively low. Compulsory deposits do not pose a significant risk to the country's financial system because the amounts in question are small and restrictions on withdrawal exist.

Non-prudential Regulation

MFIs can ideally be subjected to a form of non-prudential regulation that would require them to register and identify the partners or parties which control them, give clients transparent interest rate information and produce financial information in a meaningful manner. Regulation must also have some in-built regulatory threshold beyond which there will not be regulation. The cut-off can be determined by asset size or number of members. Some benchmarks would be required as several MFIs are micro-finance intermediaries. The rotating savings and credit associations and the accumulated savings and credit associations lend to and borrow from their own members. They are informal credit suppliers. Their small size, community-based nature and local roots provide for effective supervision by their members. It would be very difficult and prohibitively expensive for the central bank to seek to regulate these institutions. However, they seldom pose any risk to the country's financial system.

Savings: The Forgotten Half of Microfinance

A powerful argument advanced by some experts is that if these small community-based organizations are disallowed or prohibited from accepting deposits a great disservice is done to the poor. The safety of their funds outweighs the risks as the other available savings options for them involve even greater risks. Consider the risks of the other savings options available to them: cash kept at home can be stolen and livestock can perish. Hence the unsupervised, community-based depository may be the least risky option for the saver. If central banks regulate, they accept the onus of:

1. affirmatively vouching for the institutions' soundness
2. standing behind depositors as insurers whether explicitly or implicitly.

The shortage of licensable MFIs and not the absence of prudential regulation is the real constraint to the growth of this sector. A license from the central bank is an assurance that the licensed institution is credible and safe. It should be profitable enough not only to cover its costs today but also to pay the full commercial costs of the money its license will allow it to leverage in addition to generating a surplus to fund growth and perhaps provide a return to attract high-quality investors. Institutions that have not demonstrated their ability to function at this level of sustainability should not be licensed. Non-profitable institutions that eat into their equity will put their depositors at risk.

Supervisor's Narrow Focus

The supervisor focuses as much on profitability as on solvency and on equity as a percentage of assets. When a central bank issues a license, it imparts its certification and signals that the institution is safe and in most countries it assumes the de facto risk of supervision. Regulation by the central banks can also be read as promotion. Being under regulation is like riding a Ferris wheel – once you get on you cannot get off and have to accept regulations which may hinder and cramp growth. The self-regulatory model has been mooted as best in the Indian context. The microfinance industry is in a nascent stage and the self-regulatory organization appears to be the optimum solution. Keeping in view the difficulties of regulation and the costs it entails, it is expected that the self-regulatory organization will promote federations of MFIs which will:

- disseminate the best practices
- encourage innovation
- articulate high and uniformly applicable standards
- set transparent and consistently uniform reporting standards
- assist in the training and capacity building of members
- provide central liquidity management
- develop and encourage the growth of rating agencies

The creation of a separate regulatory window for MFIs in India is also premature as there isn't a critical mass of licensable institutions.

Policy Implications

The present position in India is that of trying to create an enabling environment for the growth of microfinance. The NGO and SHG linkage models and the growth of dynamic, responsive micro-finance intermediaries are being encouraged. Efforts are being made in this direction and the freeing of all interest rate controls on microfinance is a significant step towards this end. Successful NGOs also have the option of conversion to a local area bank or an urban cooperative bank, subject to the fulfilment of all other requirements. Only MFIs are exempt from several provisions of the RBI Act if they are registered as non-profit under section 25 of the Companies Act. The vision is of a strong and capable micro-finance sector emerging as an intermediary of the financial system. While the SHG–Bank linkage model appears to be the dominant one, Grameen and Sewa replications are also doing good work.

Summation

One thing is certain – microfinance is here to stay and is growing as a powerful means of empowering the poor and increasing sustainable credit outreach. In the context of our comprehensive national strategies of poverty eradication, the focus is to integrate policies at all levels. These include economic and fiscal policies, capacity and institution building, so as to empower the people living in poverty by improving their access to skills and training and microcredit schemes, devising ways and means to allow for greater acknowledgement of the role of the informal sector so as to evaluate its share in the national economy and, where appropriate, to improve its productivity by increasing training and access to capital, including microcredit to facilitate its eventual integration with the formal economy. The focus also includes establishing, strengthening and expanding microcredit and other financial instruments adapted to the needs and potentials of marginalized people and vulnerable groups so as to improve their access to productive resources and microfinance.

There is no single optimal level or form of intervention. The most appropriate intervention will depend on the objectives and on such variables as the demographics of the target clientele and the socio-economic environment. In designing interventions, governments can mix and match instruments by supporting pilot programmes or providing seed capital.

New Challenges

However there are still certain challenges to be met.

- Policy reforms are necessary to ensure the development, growth and efficient functioning of rural financial markets.
- Legal and regulatory reforms. Underdeveloped legal and regulatory provisions that require attention are, illustratively, provisions regarding land titling and collateral for typical rural assets relative to urban assets. There is no sequentiality in reforms and legal and regulatory reforms may precede the policy reforms.
- Inadequate financial infrastructure is another challenge to be met. This includes legal, information regulatory and supervisory systems for financial institutions and markets.
- Limited retail-level institutional capacity. Most retail-level institutions do not have adequate capacity to expand the scope and outreach of services on a sustainable basis to most of the potential clients. The poor still have inadequate access to credit, savings and insurance services commensurate with their need for these services. Poverty, low population density, isolated markets, highly covariant risk and seasonality often result in high transaction costs, lack of traditional collateral, high income fluctuations and limited opportunities for

risk diversification. These features differentiate rural financial markets from urban ones and fail to attract traditional for-profit financial intermediaries.

- Inadequate investments in agriculture and rural development. The insufficient investments in physical infrastructure (especially irrigation, roads, electricity and support services for marketing, business development and extension) continue to increase the risk and cost of microfinance and particularly discourage private investments in the provision of micro-finance services on a significant scale.
- Inadequate investments in social intermediation. The low level of social development is a major constraint on the expansion of micro-finance services on a sustainable basis. This is particularly true with respect to the poorest, women in poor households, poor in resource-poor and remote areas and ethnic minorities. The development of sustainable microfinance to reach a large segment of the potential market requires supporting social intermediation on a large scale.

Benefits to the Rural Poor

These challenges serve to underscore the benefits the rural poor would gain from access to efficient consumption-smoothening mechanisms and financial services that would enable them to free themselves from poverty. To this end, well-designed interventions, incorporating special products and operating procedures are necessary. Rapid growth is the only way of combating poverty, creating a favourable policy environment and pursuing reforms in areas where these are most required, so as to put in place policies to upscale and mainstream microfinance. There is definitely a need for proactive action by governments and central banks in establishing the favourable policies and supportive laws that will lead to the smooth functioning of rural financial markets and rapid growth in the rural sector. The legal and regulatory framework should receive the same attention as income expansion. Raising average rural incomes is not sufficient to reduce poverty if equity considerations remain un-addressed. Micro-finance interventions must be encouraged to grow so as to achieve scale and sustainability. Simultaneously, however, the parallel administration of programmes of targeted interventions through government is also justified. Sometimes short-term contingencies dictate immediate redress as flood relief or provision of financial assistance following natural disasters.

The main issues in maintaining a favourable policy environment for rural financial intermediation are maintaining macro-economic stability, removing urban bias in policies so as to promote the growth of integrated and resilient financial markets operating in a virtual macro-economic environment. Microfinance is at a critical juncture – for further growth momentum, it needs a favourable policy, a legal and supportive environment and strong rural financial institutions.

Financial Services

Microfinance is the delivery of financial services to poor people, provided in an efficient, responsive and financially sustainable manner. It should ideally encompass a range of financial services – lending, savings and insurance – that poor people need, and that help poor people to build income and assets, lubricate their household economies, manage and mitigate risk and work their way out of poverty. What distinguishes MFIs is their orientation to fill a gap left by larger conventional commercial or government-sponsored institutions in the provision of financial services to poorer households and smaller enterprises. MFIs seem to promise a means to provide an especially valuable form of assistance directly to disadvantaged sections of society in a relatively cost-effective manner. Microfinance may thus play a significant role in financial sector development, and therefore in overall development. Microfinance is increasingly emerging as a credible alternative to the distribution of credit through the institutional credit delivery system. Microfinance, therefore, needs to be treated as a vital part of the financial system, with the special needs of micro-finance operations and institutions recognised in financial sector policies and regulations.

In order to understand the role that microfinance can play in reducing poverty, it is important to understand conceptually the mechanisms by which financial services can affect poor people's lives. Poor people live in a high risk and changeable environment. They need to be able to take advantage of opportunities that lead to improving income or economic status to protect themselves against the risks of crises or shocks, and to cope with these when they arise. Poverty reduction then is part of a process of increasing income and economic stability which leads to improved fulfilment of basic needs and access to services. The empowerment of women can contribute to facilitating control of resources which allows for improved access. It is also about developing a range of assets that will reduce household vulnerability to physical and economic shocks. Shocks can be combated through the development of financial assets as income-size, regularity and security stemming from stability of income streams which lead to savings and allow access to loans and the development of human skills. Financial services can contribute by helping to stabilise, diversify, smoothen and increase incomes.

Needs of the Poor

The biggest financial need for people (poor or otherwise) is to assemble 'lump sums' of money ("making muckles from mickles" as Stuart Rutherford puts it) to cope with opportunities and demands. Despite their small incomes, the poor are faced, surprisingly often, with expenditure needs which are large in relation to the sums of money that are immediately available to them. These lump sums can be acquired either through credit or savings. Understanding why lump sums are needed by poor people provides an understanding of how financial services may be useful and what impacts (positive and negative) these may have on poor peoples' lives. There are basically four areas where the need for lump sums may create hardship or problems and where a poor person's livelihood may be strengthened by credit savings or financial services.

1. Opportunities: Poor people need lump sums in order to invest in opportunities – economic or social. Money may be invested as working capital or as productive assets for an income generating activity. Other opportunities may not be related to economic returns.
2. Consumption: There is often a difference between people's consumption patterns and their income. Household consumption patterns, for example, may require regular small purchases, or occasional large ones, for example, for clothes, buying food in bulk, or housing; income is never evenly spread through the year; poverty is seasonal and income erratic. In both the eventualities, money may not be available when it is needed and this may lead to inefficient management of household finances.
3. Life cycle needs: All people have major predictable occurrences throughout their lives, such as birth, marriage, death etcetera; these require relatively large outlays of funds.
4. Crises and emergencies: Unpredictable events such as illness, death, accident, and fire are common occurrences, but affect the very poor more deeply as they are more vulnerable to their negative impacts.

Micro-finance impacts directly and significantly on income/poverty. Credit invested in an income-generating enterprise such as working capital or in productive assets, leads to establishment of a new enterprise or the growth of an existing one. Profit from the enterprise provides increased income, and a general strengthening of income sources. Financial services access has a large part to play in reducing vulnerability. Microfinance is an important enabling input; it has the potential to impact on poverty in a holistic way supporting client livelihoods, reducing vulnerability, fostering social and economic empowerment and thus releasing people's potential to achieve their goals.

Microfinance has been prevalent in poorer regions of Asia and Africa in different forms for as long as the formal financial institutions have existed. The most common form is an example from north India, the Dhobis Beesi – a system of pooling and sequential loaning of funds by internal lottery or bidding by its members. Farmers, shopkeepers, transporters, hawkers, barbers, tailors and carpenters all had their own variation of the beesi, which functioned simply as a saving-cum-loaning group. They saved, they withdrew the savings and the groups disbanded. They are also known as merry-go-rounds because everyone gets a chance to obtain a loan from them. These indigenous groups operate as an informal shadow capital market in the small villages and towns of rural India; they serve that one important function which banks and formal financial institutions are unequal to – they provide cheap and timely credit to those who have little to offer by way of collateral.

Critical Role of MFIs

Though almost all pervasive, these indigenous groups excluded women and the very poor, small peasants, landless, wage-dependent labourers and small artisans; these sections were targeted by NGOs and they form the core of the SHG movement. The provision of cheap and timely credit is the greatest achievement of the SHG movement. It has taken a cue from indigenous groups. Savings mobilisation and loan repayments within homogenous groups are remarkably high since default is low and the enforcement of contract high. Under the joint liability group model, SHGs report very high recovery rates, further, poor individual savers and borrowers are able to disperse their risks to the group as a whole thus becoming to that extent more eligible as credible borrowers for loans from formal financial sector sources. With the easy availability of credit the poor are first able to meet their immediate needs of consumption and then commence utilisation of credit for productive endeavour.

For most people microfinance means providing very poor families with very small loans to help them enhance productive activities or develop their tiny businesses. Even when there are no net gains in income, significant impact in terms of reduced vulnerability can be achieved through the establishment of more regular, reliable, resilient and diversified income streams. Insurance can provide lump sums that can be used to pay for unexpected needs. Increased investment in food, health, housing, education etcetera, leads to healthier, more-skilled people living in better environments, better-equipped to cope with problems. Microfinance helps clients to accumulate or retain physical assets. Assets are increased either through direct loan use, as a benefit of a rise in income or through the use of profits generated by investment in a loan. Clients can also protect existing assets through investment in vaccinations for livestock, or by using savings or credit to cope with shocks when they occur. Poor households invest in physical assets for three main reasons.

Collateral Substitutes

Household assets are those that primarily contribute to the quality of life and may also provide security and possible income in case of future need. They are primarily held as savings in kind such as livestock. Productive assets are used to generate income such as land/houses for rent or equipment for a business. The social capital developed through group-based interactions may mean there is an increased network of people to assist in case of a crisis. These changes in risk and vulnerability are central to the achievement of poverty reduction. Over time microfinance has come to include a broader range of services: credit, savings and insurance services. Although early experiments date back 30 years, microcredit came into prominence in the 1980s in Bangladesh, Brazil and a few other countries. What makes microcredit different is that it avoids the pitfalls of an earlier generation of targeted lending by insisting on repayment, charging interest rates that could cover the costs of credit delivery and focussing on client groups whose alternate source of credit is the informal sector. Consequently, the emphasis of microcredit has shifted from rapid disbursement of subsidised loans to prop up targeted sectors towards the building of local sustainable institutions to serve the poor. Microcredit has been a private non-governmental initiative, and in this lies the success which has allowed it to outperform virtually all models of development.

Concept of SHGs: Inbuilt Strengths

The basic concept of an SHG is simple: it is an informal affinity group of members facing similar socio-economic situations and analogous problems. It is generally a small homogenous group of 15–20 members. Savings are necessary, but the contribution to the group corpus is generally indexed to the members' ability to pay. Generally the group, in consultation with its members, decides a particular amount that each member may contribute. SHGs, through the group corpus built up through their own savings, begin their activities by making small interest-bearing loans to themselves both for consumption and for productive use. After a sufficient period of internal lending, members develop the confidence to access credit for larger needs, and to seek working capital and larger loans from formal financial sector institutions for setting up income-generating activities. Each SHG operates as an autonomous institution with its own set of norms and style of functioning. This is in line with what suits the group most to function and sustain itself effectively. Peer pressure works as an effective collateral-substitute, and ensures proper repayment and end use of funds. One of the most remarkable features of the SHGs is that they keep their own accounts for money and internalise financial discipline. There is utmost transparency in the functioning of the SHGs; members make their own decisions and working in a small group allows SHG members to appreciate the needs of others and prioritise their own needs. The group also allows for a platform for the articulation of problems with a view to their resolution and promotes a larger consciousness and awareness of the world. This is the first step to political empowerment, which, as a natural corollary, succeeds economic empowerment. The formation of SHGs facilitates interaction with the larger external environment; it leads to the development of increased self-esteem and social empowerment for the members of the group.

Feminisation of Credit

The SHGs have enjoyed remarkable success with women members. The economic position of women is weak, both within the family and outside; through participation in the SHGs women gain economic strength, and both visibility and a voice in the home, the workplace and the community. This helps to create sound local financial institutions managed by women at the hamlet, cluster and block levels which link with mainstream financial institutions. The primary purpose of these institutions is to provide a separate line of credit for consumption and emergencies through their own savings to prevent investment credit from liquidation, move out of the exploitative informal financial system – primarily from moneylenders – and help to establish a sound mechanism to regulate household cash-flow for managing the seasonality of income and to internalise the practice of treating external loans as their own funds – not funds received through loan melas or subject to the concessionality/remission of loan waivers or amnesty schemes.

The SHG model, in a sense, formalises the indigenous savings and credit systems, which women are already familiar with, to provide a continuity to people's initiatives and grant due recognition to the potential of the local system. It localises the financial institutions managed by people, 100% repayment reduces the lending and borrowing cost by linking with mainstream financial institutions. The basic strategy of these community banking programmes comprises the following key activities: mobilising women and giving them an opportunity to experience their own economic position and the nature and causes of exploitation; regular interactions, exchanges and exposures which increase their mobility and provide an opportunity for them to express their ideas; providing collective learning; reinforcing confidence and building a positive self-image; mobilising of own resources and management of the same for their own benefit through regular savings management and extension of credit which, in turn, teaches them financial skills; linking women's groups with formal financial institutions where credit management is by the groups and transacting with banks as their clients and not beneficiaries, in order to enhance their access to external resources and to create control over them by women; training and building leadership qualities by transferring the roles and responsibilities of managing their own groups and activities; skill-building and training in specialised business activities and financial management; the promotion of women-managed business activities for providing ongoing support and linkages to make the economic activities viable and ensure their further growth and expansion. Whilst the motivation for many MFIs to target women is often instrumental, based on women being more compliant, reliable and easier to access, there are also important motivations based on the need to impact on poverty. It has been conclusively established that women are more disadvantaged, marginalised and poorer than men. There is a large body of literature examining the building of women's social assets or capital and their empowerment through microfinance, ensuring empowerment. This process also ensures higher repayment rates, financial viability, self-management and sustainability. The support for income generation includes credit for either supporting an existing activity or initiating a new activity, as part of the support. Loans are provided for both working capital and asset creation, as their own savings are not sufficient to meet their needs. These loans are provided either through linking with local banks or through cluster associations and federations. The period of loan and terms of repayment vary with the type of activity and the capacity of the members. Interest rates can range from 24% to 36% and the repayment period can vary from six months to three years. Larger loans to upgrade housing/shelter are mobilised through federations by linking with apex financial institutions. The interest rates are considerably lower for such loans and vary from 15% to 18% per annum and the repayment period is also normally spread over seven to twelve years. The SHGs also successfully establish linkages. These generally take the form of linkages between primary groups and commercial banks, which considerably facilitates the access to assured lines of credit. As part of the linkage with commercial banks, the primary savings and credit groups are provided with bulk loans, the group acts as a financial intermediary and retails these loans to their members and linkages between federations of groups and apex lending organisations as SIDBI, NABARD, HDFC, HUDCO and RMK where the line of credit support is provided to the federations. Federations act as financial intermediaries and lend to member groups.

Uniqueness of Microfinance

Microfinance is unique in that it addresses the key questions of collateral and risk in unusual ways. When a commercial bank lends money, the borrower is normally required to put up collateral. The poor have no collateral of significant value which shuts them out of the commercial credit market. MFIs lend against alternate forms of collateral which have proven around the world to be extremely effective credit guarantees. Various forms of alternate collateral are used by MFIs.

Social collateral is the most common alternative and is used in two main types of lending schemes, village banking and solidarity group lending, both of which offer small, short-term working capital loans. Prompt repayment is rewarded by access to higher loan amounts. Many programmes also require participation in a structured savings programme which requires a percentage of the borrowed amount to be kept in savings as an additional guarantee. Village banking is the second alternative form through which microfinance is extended. According to FINCA

International, one of the most active MFIs in Africa, "A village Banking group is a group of twenty-five to thirty people who guarantee each other's loans and run a democratic organisation, meetings are highly participatory. Members select their own members, elect their own leaders, design their own bylaws, keep the books, manage the accounts/funds and are fully responsible for loan supervision including enforcing penalties for non compliance". Another way of lending is on the solidarity group or JLG pattern. Solidarity group lending is less formalised, involving groups of typically three to ten people who guarantee each other's loans. Each group member's performance affects the others in the group – if one member is late or doesn't pay, the whole group is penalised according to the standard loans and policies established and enforced by the MFI. Some micro-lending programmes lend relatively higher amounts of investment capital to individuals for starting a business. Most of these do not use social collateral, but require chattel items to be put up against the loan. A chattel item is something which may not have a high value in terms of money but has a high personal value to the individual in the context of his/her economic activity. Examples range from a tailor's sewing machine, a restaurant's table and chairs, an atta chakki machine etc. To manage risks inherent in any loaning, MFIs use a combination of the following risk management techniques to mitigate the risks of unsecured lending.

Small loan sizes, typically starting at Rs.100–2000 a month, practice short-term lending by keeping the loan cycles small usually for periods ranging from three to twelve months. Rewards for on-time repayment are readily extended in the form of future access to higher amounts; savings are to be made proportionate to the amount borrowed. There are regular group meetings where payments are made, in the presence of the group. Penalties such as fees, denial of higher loan amounts or waiting periods, are levied for late payment. Training in financial and business management techniques is provided to borrowers. The interest rates have a higher risk factor built into them. The administration of small loans, including the processing and tracking of frequent payments, is a costly exercise. To cover their costs and risks, MFIs charge relatively higher rates of interest than the commercial banks.

Microfinance: Emerging Threats

However, several factors still inhibit the growth and development of microfinance. Most countries have interest rate controls and State interventions to address perceived market failures. Though we have not instituted interest rate controls on the micro-finance sector, we have encouraged subsidised credit programmes as the Swarnjayanti Gram Swarozgar Yojana, the Swarn Jayanti Shahri Rozgar Yojana, the differential rate of interest scheme and State-sponsored programmes. Even under the SHG–Bank linkage programme the banks continue to have a say in the determination of activities which the groups can take up and the fixation of frequency of repayment instalments. The institutional credit delivery system also has a limited retail capacity. Banks do not have the adequate capacity or will to enable micro-finance providers to grow or to provide a wide variety of services on a sustainable basis. Credit is of a piece with social intermediation; a minimalist approach cannot be successful as a poverty intervention effort. Institutional diversity coupled with a strong commitment to outreach and sustainability, is also essential to meet the diverse demands. The financial infrastructure should be in a position to encourage innovations, growth and divergence. Over 500 million of the world's economically active poor people run profitable micro- and small businesses. Micro-entrepreneurs have shown that they repay market-based loans and use the proceeds to increase their assets, their living standards and their roles in shaping societies. NGOs, other specialised financial institutions and some banks have shown that microlending works on the ground. Financial services to low income entrepreneurs may be the single most effective way to reduce poverty and achieve broad-based economic growth. Yet fewer than 2% of low-income entrepreneurs and producers have access to financial services from sources other than moneylenders. To fill this gap, policy makers need to move beyond the pendulum swings between structural adjustment and social expenditure. Economic participation of the bottom 50% needs to be brought to the centre of the development agenda. Perhaps, governments, financial intermediaries and other sources of funds need to adopt new paradigms and take on new roles in building financial systems that work for the majority. Those living below the poverty line rely almost entirely on informal sources of finance (moneylenders, traders, commission agents, relatives, etc.) to meet their consumption credit needs, at annual rates of interest which may be as high as 36% to 76%. Formal intermediaries, through their commercial lending programmes, meet only 2.5% of the credit needs of the unorganised sector. An important obstacle in accessing formal sources of credit is the inability of poor people to provide collateral security.

In the last decade, the SHG–Bank linkage programme has become India's fastest growing model of microfinance (SHGs formed by NGOs/formal agencies but directly financed by banks, SHGs formed and financed by banks and SHGs financed by banks using NGOs and other agencies as financial intermediaries). An array of specialised MFIs has also emerged. Despite this the demand for financial services far outstrips the supply and the MFIs remain heavily dependent on subsidies. The SHG–Bank linkage programme has been embraced by banks largely due to the refinance and subsidies received from NABARD and only partly due to the political mileage it nets them (figures for March 2002 are: loans 10 million, refinance 8 million). Expanding outreach is a sought-after goal; the need to attain financial viability and sustainability is still a secondary objective. It is possible for MFIs to free themselves from subsidy dependence only when they have access to alternate sources of finance. At the present juncture MFIs in India have not reached this level of maturity. Alternate sources of finance can be capital markets, as in Bolivia and Brazil, or private sector partnership where adequate return on investment is assured. There has to be a progression to this level of ability to access wholesale financing and for this necessary preconditions and rating benchmarking parameters have also to be met. In the initial years all MFIs have negative cash flows and are in need of government subsidy, by charging cost covering rates of return, they can cover transaction costs and reach break-even levels. Whether they are able to cross the threshold to financial profitability remains an open-ended question. Programmes which target the poorest of the poor should not charge cost covering interest rates; to do so would be to burden the poor.

Unorganised Sector: Compelling Needs

Alternative sources of small equity, efficiently administered are necessary to provide support to the unorganised sector. It is doubtful whether microfinance can ever fully meet the growing needs of the unorganised sector. The poorest of the poor need credit to meet their life cycle needs. As poverty is also seasonal, in the lean season, credit is required to fulfil consumption needs, and for production and investment in housing, microenterprise, agriculture, life insurance, health, crop and livestock. On any approximation, there are over 110 fragmented but nevertheless operational landholdings and over 40 million non-farm microenterprises; all are in need of working capital and investment credit usage. In the case of asset-holding groups below the poverty line, the credit need is roughly $15 million while in the case of 50 million landless households, this would be approximately $20 billion, of which at least $5 billion would be consumption credit.

A large percentage of the need for credit is met by the informal sector. To meet the needs of this sector, it is important to step up outlays for the establishment of small cohesive affinity groups of SHGs to whom it is easier, cheaper and more practical for formal institutional agencies like banks to extend credit. The SHG mode is designed to reduce informational asymmetries to help mainstream the delivery of credit, insurance and financial services to the unorganised sector. While smaller MFIs need support in streamlining their operations the needs of larger MFIs are frequently more specialised. There appears to be a need for apex institutions, banks and other lenders to evolve complementary approaches for lending and formulating demand-driven training programmes. The number of SHGs is increasing, and they require ongoing nurturing, handholding and umbrella support. Training and capacity-building support is critical in the long-term horizon. It is necessary to build skills for the optimisation of future growth and development. Building tiers of capacity-builders to better meet the needs of different tiers and sizes of institutions assumes importance. An integrated approach as opposed to a minimalist approach seems to work better for the poorest of the poor. Empowered SHGs are the key to ensuring sustainability. Success has a ripple effect and acts as an incentive for others.

Micro-finance sustainability takes time, and is a slow and often painful process. Scaling up, sustainability and capacity building are all ongoing processes. Microfinance is extended by formal institutions as banks, semiformal sources as the NGOs and informal sources: relatives/associates. It has been defined in the Indian context as the provision of thrift, credit and other financial services and products of very small amount to the poor in rural, semi-urban and urban areas to enable them to raise their income levels and improve their living standards. MFIs are quite simply those institutions which provide these facilities. The RBI had set up a microcredit special cell in 1999 and the NABARD had appointed a taskforce on supportive policy and regulatory framework for microfinance. The RBI has been striving to create an enabling environment for the growth of microfinance. Interest rates on loans given by banks to micro-credit institutions or by the micro credit organisations to SHGs/member beneficiaries have been left to their discretion. The banks have been given complete freedom to formulate their own models or choose any conduit intermediary for extending microcredit. No criteria have been prescribed for the selection of micro-credit intermediaries. Banks have merely been encouraged to adopt a cluster approach to development, concentrate on extension of microcredit in a defined pocket, and then focus on replicating it. Size of loan, unit size, maturity period, grace period, repayment schedule etcetera, all the nitty-gritty have been left free and have not been prescribed. There is no regulation, and a loose frame has been put in place within which banks, NGOs and SHGs are free to operate, either singly, jointly or all three in concert. Thus, a large measure of flexibility has been assured through this dispensation. As a measure of incentive for banks microfinance advanced either directly by the banks or through the NGOs qualifies for reckoning under the dispensation of the priority sector loans. Further for judicious credit planning banks have been advised to incorporate microfinance as part of their corporate plan and forms part of their annual credit plan. The disbursal of microcredit advances is also to be subject to close supervision and monitoring.

Adaptation of Banks to Microfinance

Banks have been encouraged to put in place marketing infrastructure and also encourage the growth and development of effective extension of services and the introduction of design and development services and efforts to meet their training, capacity building and development needs. The members of the SHG prioritise loan requests on the basis of needs, appraise borrowers and set their own terms and conditions. (Is it any surprise that repayments are 95%?) Members of the group soon use their pooled savings to negotiate/leverage loans at market rates as multiples of savings to build up the pool. An impact evaluation study commissioned by NABARD threw up encouraging results. It was found that 58% of the households in the sample surveyed reported an increase in their assets – average value of assets per household increased by 72% from Rs.68,439 (US$140) to Rs 11,7939 (US$240), almost all the group members developed savings habits as against only 23%. Earlier 70% of the loans were utilised for micro-enterprise building and consumption loans also showed a significant decline.

While microfinance addresses a number of important issues that have long stood in the way of the alleviation of poverty, microfinance is not a panacea. Microfinance does not improve roads and communications; it does not provide electricity and water supply infrastructure; it does not improve the quality of education. Several MFIs are finding ways to play a role in the financing of health care services but microfinance alone cannot ensure the quality of health care services accessible to very poor people. The eradication/alleviation of poverty is a very complex struggle which requires cooperation and cohesion between governments, development institutions and the poor themselves. Perhaps the greatest contribution of microfinance is that it empowers the poor, giving them both the increased confidence and the financial means to play a larger role in controlling their own destinies. Instead of waiting for governments and development institutions to improve their lives for them, the beneficiaries of microfinance can start to improve their lives themselves.

So far, given the constraints, some banks have ventured into micro-finance activity on their own, untrammelled by the NABARD–SHG–Bank linkage programme. The Oriental Bank of Commerce, a public sector bank has launched a micro-finance initiative in two districts of Uttaranchal and one at Hanumangarh, Rajasthan with a view to enabling rural poor to have easy access to bank credit at their doorsteps, to provide them alternative sources of income and to empower them to take independent decisions, manage their own affairs and secure a dignified place in society. Banking at the doorsteps, frequent and regular contact with the people, hassle free and transparent transactions, close monitoring and building-up of trust under OBGP has removed the information asymmetry between the banker and the borrowers, resulting in zero NPAs. While the decision-making rests with the individual and the Group, the OBC performed its dual role as a Self Help Promoting Institution (SHPI) and a bank through its key personnel in charge of the project, viz, the development manager. The Cauvery Grameen Bank and the Sanchayeeta Deposit Scheme of Cuttack and cooperative banks offer other examples of institutional financial agencies opting for microfinance.

Regulation: A Vexed Issue

Should microfinance be regulated? One argument in favour of this regulation of microfinance is that the savings of the poor need to be protected especially from fly-by-night operators. No hedges in the form of insurance are available to protect their savings.

When savings are used for lending, or MFIs provide only loan services, suitable lending norms may not be in place. There is frequently no supervision of the activities of MFIs and no prudential norms are applicable to them. At present RBI has issued a circular to banks for refinance. The RBI has exempted Section 25 companies engaged in MFI and not taking public deposits from RBI registration and regulation norms. Other than SHGs a large number of NGOs provide savings and loan services to the rural poor. There is no systematic NGO mapping or a mode of regular and systematic collection of information on NGOs–MFIs through nationwide surveys on MFIs.

There are a variety of MFIs and societies registered under the Societies Registration Act of 1860 or similar Acts; NBFCs registered as Section 25 companies, mutual benefit MFIs, state/national credit cooperatives. For profit MFIs are functioning as non-bank financial companies where they accept deposits they are subject to regulation. Legally, savers are clients of NGO–MFIs and not their members. Such NGO–MFIs violate section 45S of the RBI Act. The Vasudev Committee on NBFCs has argued that deposit collection by unincorporated bodies is a cognisable offence. The Task Force had recommended the exemption for such NGO–MFIs from Section 45S and their gradual conversion to NBFCs. The conditions for NBFCs floated by NGOs could be achieved through the registration, regulation and supervision of MFIs.

The registration of MFIs is difficult as they are registered under State/Central Cooperative Acts. Microfinance companies are registered with the Registrar of Companies and RBI (NBFCs). Both are registered and regulated. NGO-MFIs are registered only as charitable societies or trusts and not as financial intermediaries. The audit of these concerns is not governed by the canons of the audit of financial institutions, because they are not, as per their statute, engaged in financial intermediation. A draft Bill on the regulation of financial institutions has been piloted, however, this deals only with those financial institutions (FIs) which will be registered as companies. Should NGO–MFIs be included in this Bill? This has not been envisaged due to the lack of critical mass of these institutions. They are small and widely dispersed, and hence the costs of regulation are high. Financial Institutions coming under the Companies Act (for e.g., NBFCs) are regulated by the RBI, however a larger number of MFIs are non-NBFC types. The Vasudev Committee recognised the need for the decentralisation of regulatory functions for supervision of smaller NBFCs.

Self-regulatory Organisations (SROs) also have an important role to play. One SRO could, functioning as a base-level regulator, register a minimum of 50 MFIs, set performance standards, evolve accounting standards for them, conduct their audits and inspections and devise a regular reporting format. The task force on regulatory policy had suggested a lower net-owned fund of Rs 25 lakh as most NGOs cannot mobilise large funds. They cannot transfer their assets to NBFCs and therefore will rarely be pure MFIs. The Vasudev Committee recommended a higher net-owned fund for all NBFCs. The draft bill on regulation of FIs indicates a lower NOF of Rs 25 lakh for commencing business without accessing public deposits. In order to upscale the purveyal or increase the influence of micro-finance institutions, in India it has been suggested that an enabling environment should be created to facilitate the registration of NGO-MFIs and to set up SROs to regulate them. Such SHG federations and NGO-MFIs taking small thrift from their clients are exempt from the purview of Section 45S of the RBI Act.

Self-regulation as a value demands belief systems and high internal capacity building with adequate institutional practice. Self-regulation as a 'tool' results in managerial competence and as a 'core value' of the organisation results in organisational integrity. Though self-regulation can imbue the organisation with an ethical work culture and thus has several positive effects, it also has sharp limitations. When there is too much flexibility it can also lead to an abdication of responsibility and accountability. The evolution and acceptance of a sense of shared purposes and values may take time. Too much internal control may lead to 'inbreeding' and may be 'closed' to external views, and waste energy and lead to frustration if internal capacity to address many open issues is limited. High quality people with commitment are required to ensure self-regulation as a core value of the organisation. This works better in small organisations; sophisticated capacity is required to design self-regulation as a value in very large institutions. Microfinance needs to be treated as a vital part of the financial system, with the special needs and features of micro-finance operations and institutions recognised in financial sector policies and regulations.

Microfinance Should be Regulated

There appear to be basically three views on why microfinance should be regulated: to safeguard the poor depositors, to ensure protection of borrower funds, and to ensure that no financial activity which involves the taking of deposits from the public is left unregulated. Similarly, there are two basic reasons adduced for not regulating microfinance. Firstly, it would only serve to stifle innovation, as energies would be spent merely in attempts to circumvent the regulation and find ways round it.

One suggestion is that despite its advantages, the formal institutional structure is not suited to the task of providing micro-finance services in a committed and sustainable way and that the major policy initiative should be to take the NGO-specialised micro-finance institution route by creating a favourable policy environment. An extended version of this argument is that if at all formal sector institutions wish to get into the risky and costly business of microfinance, they should do so by identifying SHGs, nurturing NGOs and routing wholesale funds for micro-finance activities through them. This broadly represents India's linkage model.

A diametrically opposite view is that the growth of the NGOs and specialised MFIs should not be supported by institutions or the State. The example of State support extended to Cooperatives in the early 1960s through 1970s and their subsequent politicisation and bureaucratisation are examples of the results of state patronage. It is reiterated that if the formal sector were to form groups or extend patronage to SHGs, it would lead to all sorts of distortions.

A third view is that the NGOs lack muscle and 'scale' in terms of infrastructural outreach and financial strength, and such muscle is possible only through the restructuring, recapitalisation and re-energisation of the formal system. It is argued that while NGOs and specialised MFIs are invaluable for demonstrative effect and should be encouraged wherever possible, the real sector to be addressed for scaling up micro-finance delivery is the commercial banking system. This view takes its stand with the BRI model.

Advantages of Informal over Formal Institutes

There is enough documentation on the advantages that MFIs enjoy over formal sector institutions. Formal sector institutions, especially commercial banks, RRBs and Cooperatives, do have certain advantages over other players. Firstly they are regulated institutions fulfilling conditions of ownership, financial disclosure and capital adequacy. This helps ensure prudential management. They have the required physical infrastructure including a network of branches from which they can expand and reach out to a number of micro-finance clients. They have well-established controls and internal administrative and accounting systems. This helps them to keep track of a large number of transactions. They do not have to depend on the government or donor sources because they have their own sources of funds. The financial services offered by them can, with suitable redesigning, be made attractive to the micro-finance clientele.

Having looked at the comparative advantages, it is pertinent to flag the issues relevant for a major thrust to be made by banks as formal sector financial institutions for extending microcredit in accordance with international best practices. The policy and regulatory environment in India has improved substantially since the initiation of the reforms of 1991. Prior to the restructuring undertaken as a consequence of the financial sector reforms, the argument was that banks in India were subject to a repressed financial environment characterised by the mandatory prescription of high reserve requirements, interest rate ceilings and targeted credit policies. This environment has altered substantially, interest rates have been freed, reserve requirements have been lowered and banks are pretty much free to design their own products. The commercialisation of microfinance has been prompted on the basis that MFIs should rely on savings and commercial borrowings rather than donor grants. Institutions that mobilise savings from the public should be subject to prudential regulation. Regulated structures would provide more assurances to commercial lenders and investors.

Social Objectives

Microfinance NGOs have no owners, and NGO boards can be dominated by social objectives, resulting in structures that have limited accountability or focus on efficiency and profitability. However, most countries do not have the legal structures or regulatory regimes in place that would make such conversions feasible or desirable. Many microfinance NGOs are not yet of the size, efficiency and/or profitability to make incurring the costs of legal conversion and regulation feasible or desirable. In countries where the performance thresholds for becoming a regulated MFI have been low, weak NGOs have become weak regulated MFIs with little of the anticipated benefits in performance improvements or mobilisation of commercial deposits. Financial Institutions are generally subject to two forms of regulation; prudential regulation which seeks to reinforce their financial soundness and non-prudential regulation. There are three good reasons for introducing supervision and three equally valid ones for guarding against this imposition. Protection of depositors is the first plea in favour of regulation, keeping in view the clientele of microfinance – poor and at times even dispossessed people. They would definitely not be market-savvy and can easily be taken for a ride and be subjected to usurious interest rates which would push them even deeper into poverty. They are also highly unlikely to have diversified portfolios so any loss from the failure of an MFI would naturally affect them gravely.

Secondly, there is a need to protect borrowers from monopolistic lending practices of MFIs. An MFI may enjoy considerable local market power, especially if it operates in a remote area and has high operating costs. At times it can lose its mission and focus more on recovery targeting and less on enabling its clients to set up income generating projects. Thus, there would be valid grounds for regulating its activities, especially its pricing policies.

Promotion of the MFI Sector

Under certain circumstances, regulation and supervision may promote the development of the sector as an institution known to be well-regulated and closely supervised; it may be able to mobilise deposits from the public and obtain financing at a lower cost more easily. The promise of official sanction in the form of licensing and greater operational freedom may prompt the management to accelerate development of the MFI by offering newer products and acquiring the necessary expertise. The development of the MFI sector could be seriously imperilled if there are fraudulent MFIs. Though the effect of the failure of an MFI might not leave a ripple on the surface of the larger financial system as the institutions involved are always much smaller than the conventional banking system, the failure of a fraudulent MFI can affect the public's trust in all financial institutions. Hence this is adduced as a reason for introducing regulation and supervision of financial institutions. Weighed, however, against the costs of regulation, both tangible and intangible, the argument is specious.

The principal costs are:

Costs to Supervisors: Just as the operating costs of MFIs are often high relative to the size of their portfolio, the cost of supervision may also be disproportionate to their financial importance or the underlying interests that supervision is meant to serve. MFIs are often small, numerous and located in remote regions, and suffer from poor record-keeping. Hence, the supervisors may have to devote considerable resources to monitor what are, for the financial institution as a whole, relatively insignificant institutions. The supervisor's direct costs will have to be borne, either by the MFIs, which may already have high costs, or the formal financial sector, which will have to pass the costs on to their clients. Furthermore, in many developing countries, skilled supervisory capacity may be in short supply. Employing individuals with these scarce skills to supervise MFIs could endanger effective supervision of institutions that are more central to the financial system.

Costs to Supervised Institutions: The compliance with regulations will necessitate fulfilling a maze of regulations. Satisfying both on-site and off-site supervision can be administratively burdensome and expensive for an MFI. These costs are ultimately passed on to the clients of the MFI in the form of higher fees and interest rate spreads, leading naturally to slower growth in the provision of financial services to disadvantaged groups. Regulatory prescriptions and the costs of complying with regulations may discourage new MFIs from entering the sector, thus encouraging oligopolistic behaviour of the existing MFIs. The strength of MFIs lies in their ability to innovate and thereby allow their clients greater access to financial services. Regulations may make it onerous to introduce such innovations, for instance, an insistence on higher provisioning for loans not backed by conventional collateral but nevertheless secured by social capital. The one-size-fits-all approach will be intensely frustrating and could seriously damage this nascent industry.

Stifling of Innovation and Competition: Regulation and supervision restrict the ability of MFIs to experiment with new forms of loan agreements as well as systems to attract deposits; this may happen as a result of discouraging or prohibiting innovations that are not foreseen in the regulatory framework.

The international experience so far has been mixed; among the banks studied, four administrative structures were used to carry out micro-finance operations. These were fully independent retail centres, affiliated to the bank but with their own lending policies, staff and information systems that report to the larger bank. A few such centres are the unit desa of Bank Rakyat Indonesia, Banco del Desarollos the micro-finance subsidiary in Chile and the Social Enterprise Program of the Bank of Nova Scotia in Guyana.

Lending through NGOs who in turn lend to microenterprise clients: Banco Wiese in Peru.

Semi-independent micro-finance units, lending directly and/or through specialised windows in each branch of the bank, are staffed with a micro-finance credit officer. Administrative and financial functions are integrated into the larger bank. A few such units are Banco Agricola Comercial, El Salvador; Banco del Pacifico, Ecuador and Financiera Familiar, Paraguay.

In fully integrated operations, wherein small business credit officers also handle micro-enterprise clients, all administrative, personnel and financial systems are integrated. A few such integrated operations are Centenary Bank, Uganda; Multi-credit Bank, Panama; Caja de Ahorro y Credito; Los Andes and Banco Sol, Bolivia. During the 1990s, polarising debates seethed between advocates of the 'commercial' approach and those that saw their mission as serving the 'poorest of the poor'. From the mid-1990s, leading MFIs have worked together to build performance indicators and standards for the micro-finance industry.

Public Policy

These initiatives have been motivated by the recognition that microfinance must demonstrate very high performance on portfolio quality, efficiency and sustainability if MFIs are to be recognised as integral members of the financial system, capable of mobilising commercial bank borrowings. Effective ways of looking at efficiency, risk and profitability need to differ for micro-finance portfolios relative to traditional banking activities and for micro-finance practitioners well-placed to determine the appropriate performance indicators and standards for the industry. MFIs that do not mobilise savings are also the financially sustainable. It is also recognised that microfinance is not the answer for all of the world's poorest families; some will need support other than microfinance if they are to move out of poverty before they can graduate to microfinance. Experience demonstrates that the financial needs of poor people are best served by encouraging a broad range of institutional types in order to provide efficient and responsive lending–savings insurance and other financial services that these people need to build their businesses, increase income and assets and reduce risks. Poor people need sustained access to an evolving set of financial products and services which can be provided only by financially sustainable institutions dealing with diverse segments and products, each in a position to increase outreach and grow with the needs of the clients. The public are not likely to warrant regulation by traditional bank supervisors. For non-regulated MFIs some other means have to be put in place for ensuring transparency and accountability. Consensus now exists among most major micro-finance providers and actors that microfinance must work for the poor and must be sustainable.

References

Agabin, Meliza and Jorge Daly. 'An Alternative Approach to Rural Financial Intermediation: The Philippine Experience'. Occasional Paper.

Barenbach, Shari and Craig Churchill. 1997. 'Regulation and Supervision of Microfinance Institutions: Experiences from Latin America, Asia and Africa'. CGAP Occassional Paper No. 1.

Blumberg, Rae, et al, eds 1995. *Engendering Wealth and Well-being: Empowering for Global Change.* West View Press: Boulder.

Granovetter, Mark. 1985. 'Economic Action and Social Structure: The Problem of Embededness'. *American Journal of Sociology*, vol. 91.

Grindle, Merilee. 1998. *Searching for Rural Development: Labour Migration and Employment in Mexico.* New York: Cornell University Press.

Ledgerwood, Joanna. 2000. *Microfinance Handbook: An Institutional and Financial Perspective.* Washington DC: The World Bank.

Lim, E. R., M. Uy and J. Toureille. 1999. *Microfinance in India.*

Longhurst, Richard, Robert Chambers and J. Swift. 'Seasonality and Poverty: Implications for Policy and Research'. IDS Bulletin.

Meyer, John. W. and Brian Rowan. 1977. 'Institutional Organisations: Formal Structure as Myth and Ceremony'. *American Journal of Sociology*, vol. 83, no. 2. The University of Chicago Press.

MicroSave-Africa. *Savings in Africa: A Collection of Studies.*

Murdoch, Jonathan. 1999. 'The Role of Subsidies in Microfinance'. Journal of Development Economics.

Mutesasira, Leonard K. 2000. 'Savings and Needs in East Africa: an Infinite Variety'. MicroSave-Africa.

Peck, C. R., Christen and Richard Rosenberg. 2000. 'The Rush to Regulate Legal Frameworks for Microfinance'. CGAP Occasional Paper.

Pischke, Von J. D., Dale W. Adams and Gordon Donald. 1983. *Rural Financial Markets in Developing Countries: Their Use and Abuse.* Baltimore: Johns Hopkins University Press.

Powell, Walter W. and Paul J. Di Maggio, ed. 1991. *The New Institutionalism and Organisational Analysis.* The University of Chicago Press.

Rutherford, Stuart. 2000. 'Raising the Curtain on Microfinancial Services Era'. CGAP Focus Note.

Rhyne, Elisabeth. 2001. *Mainstreaming Microfinance.* Kumarian Press.

Scheiner, Mark. Development Finance Institutions: Measuring Subsidy.

Sen, Amartya. 1993. 'The Economics of Life and Death'. *Scientific American*, May.

Stuart, Guy. 2002. 'A Commercial Bank Does Microfinance: The Case of Sogesol, Haiti'. Kennedy School of Government Case Study. Harvard University.

Wilbur, Robert H., ed. 2000. *The Complete Guide to Non-Profit Management.* Smith, Bucklin and Associates, Inc.

Wright, Graham A. N. 2001. 'Market Research and Client Responsive Product Development'. MicroSave-Africa.

——. 'Principles and Practice: Myths of Regulation and Supervision'. 2000. MicroSave-Africa.

Wright, Graham A. N., Robert Christen and Imran Matin. 2001. 'Introducing Savings in a Microcredit Institution'. MicroSave Briefing Note.

Yaron, J., B. McDonald Jr. and Gerda L. Piprek. 1997. 'Rural Finance: Issues, Design and Best Practice'. The World Bank.

United Nations Capital Development Fund. 'Increasing Access and Benefits for Women: Practices and Innovations among MFIs'. Survey Results.

——. 2001. Supporting Womens' Livelihoods: Microfinance that Works for the Majority, A Guide to Best Practices.

——. 'Innovating from Experience: Gender Initiatives in Microfinance'. Roundtable Proceedings.